SHE WHO RIDES A PEACOCK

INDIAN STUDENTS AND SOCIAL CHANGE

SHE WHO RIDES A PEACOCK
INDIAN STUDENTS AND SOCIAL CHANGE

MARGARET L. CORMACK

FREDERICK A. PRAEGER, *Publisher*

NEW YORK

BOOKS THAT MATTER

Published in the United States of America in 1961
by Frederick A. Praeger, Inc., Publisher
64 University Place, New York 3, N.Y.

Library of Congress Catalog Card Number: 62-7957

PRINTED IN INDIA
BY Z. T. BANDUKWALA AT
LEADERS PRESS PRIVATE LIMITED, BOMBAY

To

MY SONS

PETER and ROBIN

who like me and my parents were born in India,
and
who have kept me interested in youth and the world they face.

... in a country where one finds only a wild desire
for freedom without any respect for it, and even
without the will to achieve it.

NIRAD C. CHAUDHURI, in *Autobiography
of an Unknown Indian*

Preface

SHE WHO RIDES A PEACOCK, the Goddess of Learning, has had innumerable devotees through the ages, but perhaps never before has anyone dared to tender advice to her, especially in the shape of a suggestion to dismount her peacock of academic tradition, look to India's needs in higher education, and help India's future leaders understand and construct a new way of life. This is precisely what Dr Margaret Cormack has set out to do in this somewhat unusual book on a fairly common topic, viz., the state of higher education in India. But, then, Dr Cormack has a very special title to the role of a gentle censor. She was born in India, spent the early years of her life in the country, and had already 21 years of experience in India prior to returning to it as a Fulbright professor attached to the Annamalai University.

The author is an eminent educationist, with a social scientist's equipment, in addition to an academic background, for investigating the facts of the situation and drawing conclusions. Her aim was to determine Indian college and university students' conscious awareness of and attitude toward the social change related to 'traditional' India becoming 'modern'. The method she adopted was that of securing voluntary responses to a questionnaire, and although she is aware of the inadequacy of this method by reason of the lack of access to the subconscious, she has used the material she has gathered with a trained social scientist's skill and the understanding of a sympathetic mind.

A glance at the list of the contents will reveal the wide scope of Dr Cormack's well-conceived and wisely executed plan of enquiries, against the broad perspective of India's independence and renaissance and in the setting of her series of Five Year Plans of Economic and Social Development. The results are set out in brief, with her own interpretation of the students' responses, so that the conclusions can be tested by the reader against the statistical premises.

In the concluding chapters of the book the author proceeds to a broader interpretation of the ascertained opinion and it is here that, in my opinion, she has given evidence of a sensitive understanding of the current situation in India in regard to topics like student indiscipline, the growth of India's nascent democracy and the progress and pitfalls of India's internal social revolution, and, lastly, the critical problems that the youth of today in India, as elsewhere in the world, is facing in this modern environment of rapid cosmic change. Her overall conclusion, with which few will disagree, I imagine, is that India's real problem is not 'student indiscipline', 'corruption' or 'party-politics', but the deeper phenomenon of social change, the pace and direction of which can in a community like India's be influenced significantly by culture consciously moulded by democracy and education, so that organized discontent can be directed into social dynamism.

She ends on a message of hope, that with improved conditions of teaching and learning Indian universities will succeed to a greater degree than at present in preparing their students for the morrow.

SHE WHO RIDES A PEACOCK is an eminently objective, wise and readable book, and will stimulate thinking in Indian educational circles on the fundamentals of the problems in the field of higher education.

C. D. DESHMUKH

Former Chairman,
University Grants Commission, India.
NEW DELHI
May 10, 1961.

Foreword

INDIAN educators and more specially the training colleges will welcome this book, so foundational to the understanding of Cultural Transmission in India.

"Corruption" has entered the University portals. Teachers and students are part of the "Party Politics". "Youth has suddenly started defying elders." The problem of student indiscipline, the current talk of educators and journalists today in India, is both acute and urgent.

Dr Margaret Cormack, Professor of Social Science and Education, Brooklyn University, New York, U.S.A., has undertaken in this book the onerous task of giving scientific bases for this puzzling phenomenon. Many reports and articles are daily appearing in the newspapers on this recognized problem. But few have attempted a scientific analysis. The present psycho-cultural analysis, though exploratory, has undoubtedly generated several hypotheses for the much needed thorough and specific researches in the area.

Having spent the most impressionable years of her life in India —a period of 20 years—Dr Cormack is uniquely sensitive to the Indian background and has not missed anything that requires a sympathetic and masterly touch in dealing with this intricate material of Indian Social Change. With an intuitive grasp of the problems that face the "Indian Mind", she has attempted an honest, frank—though pleasantly bitter at times—and fair analysis of "Indian Students and Social Change".

The book is of special value to the Colleges of Education in India. The only scientific discipline offered by training institutions in India is Educational Psychology, and even this is inadequately treated in many of our institutions. It is only recently that comparable attention to social sciences is balancing the over emphasis on Educational Psychology. Educational Sociology is slowly finding its place in our Training Programmes, though it is still regarded as of subordinate importance. But the new field of Educational Anthropology is still an unborn child in our country. And yet, ironically, the key concept of Anthropology—Culture—is perhaps the most overworked term in our educational literature. Dr Cormack's present book, I hope, will prepare the ground for greater attention to 'Social Foundation courses' in our teacher training programmes.

"India's problem is not student indiscipline, 'corruption', or 'party politics'—it is the deeper problem of Social Change".

How rapid is the present change in the Indian Social Structure? How deep-rooted are the traditional values? What is the pattern of emergent values? How are the emotional structures in depth and at intermediate personality levels such as attitudes to authority, being affected? What changes are taking place in the 'social character', verbalized idea-systems and world-view of Indian students? Is there, and if so, what is the nature of the unique typology of social sanctions that is operating amongst the youth of the country? These and many other questions are raised in this book for the educators and the social scientists to research and seek answers.

The problem of student indiscipline in India is a problem of cultural transmission. Should the educator be a 'transmitter'or an 'innovator' in this rapidly changing culture? Or should he be both these? Let each educator redefine his role in the context of the present, rapid social change in India. In times of relative cultural stability, institutions and educators could rely upon 'traditional' values to serve as cultural compressions on the youth and maintain their 'discipline'. But when cultures change rapidly owing to deliberate planning and other forces of 'culture-contact', how can the pattern of 'emergent' values be utilized for effective transmission and compression? Answers to these questions are imperative and a proper valuational orientation of educators and teachers is a prerequisite to the solution of 'student indiscipline in India'.

An analysis of any society reveals a close connection between its institutions and values and the method of satisfying the material needs and drives of its members. As these methods change, the societal structure and the social relationships also change; and these in turn, will affect the cultural habits of men.

The above relationship among the various aspects of culture may be likened to a pyramid—at the risk of an over simplified analogy —divided into a number of horizontal cross sections. At the base of the pyramid may be placed the material needs and drives of man. Above this base is the cross section representing the techniques and tools of winning the physical environment in a way as to lead to the utmost satisfaction of the members of the culture. Resting solidly upon these two cross sections is the section representing the economic, social, political and educational institutions which help in systematizing life in the culture. The capstone apex of this cultural pyramid represents the value-system, the worldview and the philosophy of life. This capstone once established cements the entire cultural pyramid and gives meaning to the whole range of human experience in the culture.

The central idea in the above analogy is that value-system is not independent of the social institutions existing within a culture; no social institution emerges except in relation to the existing techniques and tools of production aimed at satisfying man's needs. This concept of culture-integration is basic to the researches in the field so well explored by Dr Cormack in this book. She refers to this integration in her unique way, the 'Cosmic Dance'. "Does culture make the man, or man make the culture"? Let each reader and each educator answer this question for himself.

Unless the psychologist is studying the differences in personality and development in different subcultures in a society, he is likely to regard the cultural milieu and particularly the values represented as goals within it, as constant and as end products. And since the psychologist's interests are in the areas of individual differences and in the variability of emotional states, he is led to examine child training, particularly that occurring in the earlier years for antecedent-consequent relationships of personality patterns. But the social scientist working with the dramatic variations in the patterns of cultural foci—viz, ethos, values, attitudes etc.—from society to society is largely led to examine the sources of uniformity in 'social character', which is as much or more a direct function of what happens to children in later years of development and to adolescents and young adults, than what happens to them in early years of childhood days. 'Social character' is functional within the whole social, economic and political structure of a culture.

A problem like student indiscipline is embedded in the field of 'social character'. Therefore any attempt to isolate the antecedent variables of student indiscipline must fit into a psychocultural *gestalt* or a sequence of life experiences extending to "socio-economic changes". "family changes", "marriage problems", "religion and ritual", and "politics and parties".

Dr Margaret Cormack symbolizes these changes that are taking place in India as the 'struggle between Lakshmi and Saraswati'. I have no doubt whatsoever, that Dr Cormack's analysis of 'Saraswati dismounting from her peacock' will not merely stimulate extensive social science research, but also will give scientific bases for the "puzzling phenomenon of youth suddenly defying its elders" in India.

VYAS THIRTHA

College of Education,
Osmania University,
Hyderabad, A.P.

Contents

Contents

SHE WHO RIDES A PEACOCK

Introduction

Return to India, 1959

MY 21 years of experience in India prior to this Fulbright year spanned the two world wars—a period of ferment, tension, and interest. It was the era of the growing Independence Movement and of the dying British colonial Empire. It was the end of the "supremacy of the white man", the beginning of Asian renaissance. It was also the period when science began its impact on methods frozen in time. I remember the thrilling speed of the model-T Ford, the miracle of electricity, the magic of refrigeration. I also recall the independence riots of the first world war, and our childlike disappointment in not having the chance to eat the food stored in the British mills against our possible imprisonment. With more mature years and attitude, during World War II I felt the impact of the anti-white "Quit India" movement, and with others hoped India was ready for the independence that was imminent.

This year, "back home" in the land of my birth after 14 years' absence, I have found progress beyond any optimist's dreams— and problems greater than any pessimist's forebodings. Most roads are paved, much plumbing is "flush", most consumer goods are made in India, and the telephone has become both necessity and nuisance ! Kwality, Happy Boy and Tek Hom ice cream are peddled in the streets to children who "demand" this luxury. More importantly, schools, colleges, universities, hospitals and welfare agencies dot the cities and the countryside. Indians know they are dealing with themselves and their own future, and they are building with pride and determination, if not always with cooperation and skill. Industry has changed the face of the large cities—buses and trams

1

busily transport the workers and shoppers. The small cities, bazaars, villages, and paddy fields look much the same as before, but beneath the surface they, too, are changing. "Progress" has become India's "most important product", though few can define "progress" or direct its course. In many ways the problems attendant to progress seem universal—certainly Americans recognize much that is related to industrial urbanization—but much is uniquely Indian. Time is telescoped in a nation's urgency to come of age, and though much is adopted from the West more has to be adapted to Indian conditions and values.

Perhaps my own life has helped me to appreciate the human tensions caused by rapid change. It is difficult in one life-time to move from leisurely living in an "out-station" compound composed of four families to the hectic pace of New York City. It is a big change to go from an educational institution of 180 to one of 25,000. As a child I rode in a bullock cart, and the three-mile trip from Pasumalai to Madura was an event, the annual 75-mile trip to the hills (via train, bullock cart, and dooly) a major adventure. Today I frequently drive more than 75 miles in the course of a normal professional day, and long distances are jet-propelled, "the body arriving before the mind is ready". As a child I was nurtured to Puritan precepts that seemed immutable in time. But as a mother and professor I prod youth to look, feel, think, question, build. No rationalization of action is less acceptable than "that's the way it always has been done". But it is difficult to move so fast, to seek for fruits before strengthening roots. It takes knowledge, confidence, and *energy*. One must occasionally "touch home base", as it were, and I have discovered anew this year that I am more at home in bazaars than on Fifth Avenue, that I am happier on a bicycle than in a subway. "Change" is worthless in itself, and if it brings an inhuman kind of existence it is a worse tyrant than tradition. We must accept change in these days of science, but if we are to retain our humanity we shall have to guide and direct it along humane paths.

In a former research study, *The Hindu Woman*,[1] I sought to discover how Indian girls interiorized the *traditional* feminine role. It was clear when I made the study in 1950, however, that fundamental changes were beginning to take place in society and

[1] Margaret Cormack, *The Hindu Woman*, New York City, Teachers College Publications, 1953.

in psyche, and I determined to make a study of these changes. But on this return to India in 1959 it did not seem urgent to study the changing Indian woman—she is doing all right ! It seemed more useful to study university students in relation to social change. Quantitatively they are largely a "new group", and qualitatively they constitute India's future leaders and specialists. This first post-Independence generation probably holds India's future in its hands, for decisions made and patterns set in these formative years will affect the centuries to follow. How, then, are these students being educated for modern adult life ? What are they thinking ? Do they understand the future that is taking shape in democratic, scientific, and secular terms ? Do they think about this future analytically, constructively, creatively ? Are their mentors helping them to do so ? Is the future of India safe in their hands ?

My research project, then, had as definite aim: determination of college and university students' conscious awareness of and attitude toward the social change related to "traditional" India becoming "modern". To what extent do the students' ideas differ from those of their elders ? How do they feel about the differences ? Do they have problems and conflicts ? In what do they feel security ? In what do they find happiness ? Are they concerned only with self and family, or are their horizons widening to nation and world ? What is their attitude toward authority ? In what do they see prestige? What are their ideas about changing India? In short, how are they building the bridge from "traditional" to "modern" India?

During the course of my project I deliberately refrained from defining "traditional" or "modern", seeking to discover respondents' own views. My own definitions, however, must be made clear in relation to my socio-psychological interpretations of data. I understand "tradition" as consisting of "the ways things always have been done", virtue lying in time-sanctified patterns. In this case the "way of life" is the Hindu culture, which involves a hierarchical conception of individual and social life. Roles are inherited and prescribed, are clear and attainable. How one performs his roles—forming his destiny—is his own business. The Wheel of Life toward Nirvana can be finite or infinite depending on virtue or vice in role performance. Thus men in their total existences are equal; in any cross section of time they are unequal. Social mobility relates to progress on the Wheel, not to life during any one chapter —where society is frozen into interdependent layers. A "modern" view of life involves finding new ways of doing things via scientific principles and methods (this does not negate all traditional customs and values), and virtue lies in man's use of his rational powers for the control and modification of his physical and social environment. It involves rejecting inherited roles and making new ones —and might be called "making one's destiny". Certainly this view of life tends to give individuals a more temporal view of existence, with emphasis on a "better life here and now". As for "modern" society, it is democratic and secular, in opposition to authoritarian and aristocratic systems in which power has been vested in a few.

I started my research project in Annamalai University in South India, to which institution I was officially attached, and where I fortunately had a "head start" with some knowledge of Tamil and of South India. After many hours of interviews with many students, chiefly in the social sciences, I acceded to the advice of Indian colleagues and formulated a questionnaire for further use in Annamalai and other university centres in India—though I planned also to continue using the interview method. It will be noted in this questionnaire[2] that many possible responses are supplied—in most cases I got them from students—but that considerable scope for write-ins was allowed. A few of the questions proved of little use, but most have brought interesting and illuminating response. A few students objected to questions on politics, justifiably wondering what their political views had to do with social change. I submit that specific views do not apply, but it was necessary to ask specific questions in order to determine interest in "the larger and newer problems of India". Certainly I shall interpret them only in that context. For the most part there was lively interest in the questionnaires. I never administered them without taking time to explain what I was doing, why, and how— finally soliciting *voluntary* help on my research. With those who volunteered (I rarely had enough questionnaires for all the eager volunteers) I held a discussion on the difficulty of giving "honest answers", a procedure that may have helped to minimize this problem in verbal response.

With all due regard for the limitations of the questionnaire method, there is no doubt the credits outweigh the debits in this study. For one thing, Indian students are dealing with a foreign language—of those I met, only the students at St Xavier's College

[2] See questionnaire in Appendix

in Calcutta demonstrated easy fluency in English. Most can respond more usefully if they can read slowly, write their answers slowly. Furthermore, their training has been in written expression, almost not at all in oral. And, in some contrast to my experience with American students, I found most oral responses more "careful and reserved" than the written. Apparently the anonymity of an unsigned paper going to a complete stranger invited frank opinions. Finally, the questionnaire method enabled me to reach a great many students and retain their responses in writing. Many students could spare 15-20 minutes of class or study time for the presentation of the questionnaire, but could not have spared hours for an extended interview during the day. The questionnaires could be taken home and returned another day. An amazingly high percentage were returned—about 85 per cent—which says much for students who had to spend one to three hours on their questionnaires. Needless to say, I could not have used such a long questionnaire in the U.S., nor would I have had such a high return. The students' response to my project and to my appeal for assistance was clearly a *personal* response to a *person*—to an American, a professor, one who was born in India, and a mother of sons their age. I am deeply appreciative of this gift of time and thought.

With the help of the U.S. Educational Foundation in India, suitable channels to appropriate institutions were determined. Taking my 500 questionnaires and interview pads I travelled for some months, staying about a week at each of various educational centres. My data represents student response at Annamalai University, Madras (the Madras School of Social Work and miscellaneous University of Madras students), Calcutta (Bethune College for Women, St Xavier's College for Men, Scottish Church College, Jadavpur University), Santiniketan (Visva-Bharati University), Banares (the College of Education at Banares Hindu University), Lucknow (Department of Anthropology in the University of Lucknow, Kanja Kubja College), Delhi (Lady Irwin College, Miranda House College of the University of Delhi, miscellaneous students in the University of Delhi), Chandigarh (College of Engineering in the Punjab University), Baroda (Departments of Education-Psychology and Home Science, Baroda University), Bombay (Elphinstone College, miscellaneous students from the University of Bombay), Hyderabad (the Colleges of Education, Science, Engineering and Medicine in Osmania University, the Women's

College). Some of the above students are represented only by interviews, others by questionnaires. I shall never forget this intimate experience in India, as I travelled by trains, as I shared meals with families in my compartment, as I lived in university guest rooms or private homes, as I visited schools, villages, and various projects. Whenever possible I reciprocated by sharing my thoughts in speeches and seminars. The problems of education and of helping youth to mature are relatively similar the world over.

It will be clear to social scientists that my study is limited, and I offer it only in terms of its limitations. It is, at best, partial and tentative, and its greatest value ought to lie in questions raised. I did not have complete coverage of India, though Madras, Andhra Pradesh, West Bengal, Uttar Pradesh, the Punjab, Delhi, Gujerat, and Bombay are represented by institutions, and there are some respondents from Madhya Pradesh and Kerala. I made no attempt to get a scientific sampling in each area or institution, for to have done so would have entailed at least a year of sample-determination. Calcutta alone has 148 institutions of higher education, with 1,40,000 enrolled students. Sampling would have been desirable but not essential for the purposes of my study. I hope deeper and more exact inquiries will be made, leading to specific information as regards various institutions or types of students. I was seeking a general response, and my data represents information received from students of differing sex, age, family background, religious practices, areas of study, intended careers, types of colleges, and geographical areas. Most of the students were urban—the urban pattern is beginning to dominate—but some were from rural areas. I had only one request beyond that of access to students specializing in different subjects, and that was for students who spoke English reasonably well. For this reason, except for the students of Scottish Church and St Xavier's Colleges in Calcutta, I generally saw the older students—those in the final B.A. year or in post-graduate studies. The older students in most institutions, in any case, proved more able to understand and discuss matters pertinent to my inquiry. I also discussed some topics with administration and faculty members. They were able to tell me much about the institution, its problems and trends, its student composition, and also their own views on terms such as "discipline", "indiscipline", "freedom", "authority", and "maturity".

I shall not attempt to generalize about any one group—my data is insufficient for that purpose—though occasionally I shall point out some interesting feature of group response. It does seem valid to make some generalizations about differing male and female response.

Perhaps my greatest frustration was lack of access to the sub-conscious, though I constantly reminded myself that my aim was determination of the *conscious* attitude toward change. I shall point out some of the areas needing research in sub-conscious feelings, for it is my conviction that no accurate appraisal of attitude can be made without this information.

In addition to the questionnaires I had many interviews, usually with students not given the questionnaires, though in some cases with students who had completed their response and who requested further discussion. Many came again and again. For one thing I had invited questions about the West, and no doubt a flesh-and-blood American professor seemed a legitimate spokesman. Then, too, many commented that they could "understand" me, as they could not most Americans. They referred in part to ideas but chiefly to enunciation. In fact, I often came to feel that this was my unwitting and unplanned "best contribution !"

India has long been known as a "traditional" country, social change having been so suppressed that a "static society" prevailed. But the external impact of the West and the internal struggle for self-determination culminated in Independence and a stage set for change. Chapter 1 attempts to place this moment of India's development into historical context, giving special emphasis to under-the-surface changes. Chapter 2 briefly describes the Plans and the system of education, higher education in particular. Chapters 3-11 report data obtained from questionnaires and interviews, and contain some generalizations and interpretations. Generalizations are useful but dangerous ! So far as possible in these chapters I am making them only in descriptive and summary fashion. But if social science is to serve its function, it must deal with generalizations—hopefully including generalizations about differences—and I hope I shall not be criticized for my attempts. Generalizations do not, of course, give the total picture, for India is rich in its variety and its exceptions. It is the place of the arts to deal with particularizations, with the individuals that are unique and thus more "human".

Descriptive generalizations, however, are themselves of little value without attendant interpretation, and perhaps the chief value of my study lies in Chapters 12-14, in which I attempt socio-psychological analysis. Chapter 12 addresses itself to the critical problem of student indiscipline and is my general critique of higher education in India, Chapter 13 to that of developing social responsibility for democracy, and Chapter 14 to general problems of a changing society. This analysis is offered with all the professional integrity at my command, but also with much personal humility. Any society is complex, and Indian society seems more complex than most others. My intention is to be scientifically critical—I confess, in unscientific concern over a country I respect and love. If the picture seems at times too brutal or adversely critical, I should like to point out that analysis of any current system of higher education would receive harsh judgment. The problems of universities, of professors, and of students in India are much like those I know in America, differing sharply only in timing and degree. Further, the views of my Indian colleagues are no less kind. It is abundantly clear that this transition phase of Indian history contains much confusion, but it is my conviction that constructive changes come out of confusion. My concern lies in the belief that progress can never be taken for granted, that changes will not be improvements unless they are understood and intelligently directed. At the moment Saraswati is finding it difficult to dismount from the peacock of educational tradition. What she does in these critical and formative years of New India is exciting to watch, exciting to share.

It has been my great privilege this year to meet many of India's leaders. They will probably not remember me—one Fulbrighter among many—but I shall not forget them and their devotion to the nation. President Rajendra Prasad, Vice-President Radhakrishnan, Prime Minister Nehru, Defence Minister V. K. Krishna Menon, Minister of Education Dr Shrimali, Executive Secretary Dr Saiyidain, Minister of Science and Culture Dr Humayun Kabir, former Vice-Chancellor of Baroda University Hansa Mehta, All-India Women's Congress leader Lady Rama Rau, Sir C. P. Ramaswami Aiyar, various vice-chancellors, distinguished journalists, and a number of important academicians. I hope before I leave to meet C. D. Deshmukh, chairman of the University Grants Commission, whose statements and efforts I much admire. It was not to these leaders I went for data on my study, however. They control India's present destiny, but it is the students who represent future leadership.

This study could never have been made without the help of countless friends and colleagues. I want to thank Dr Reddick, Mrs Bose, Dr Bina Ray, and other members of the U.S. Educational Foundation in India, who have given generously of advice and assistance. I am also grateful to John Lund, Frank Dorey, Ruby Dube, and other officers of the U.S. Information Service, who have encouraged and aided me throughout. Ed Whiting, sculptor and architect, a fellow Fulbrighter, is responsible for both the title of this book and the cover design of Saraswati. He and Sally Whiting shared my most exciting and confusing days of creativity. Many other Fulbrighters aided me professionally and personally. I am especially grateful to "Danny" and Pamela Daniels, Eloise Hay, Tony Potter, Dick Schermerhorn, and Eugene Link. Here in Kodaikanal, Agnes Liddle and Betty Hilty have sustained me with daily recreation and refreshment, not to mention serving as readers of my uncompleted manuscript. And Virginia Jesudason gave valuable aid in compiling data—I much appreciate her patient help. Further help on data presentation was skilfully and generously given by my friend, Dr Lynn Vendien.

But I am particularly grateful to my Indian friends and colleagues. Annamalai University transcended official host duty in taking me into its community. Mr Narayanaswami Pillai, the vice-chancellor, and Mr Meenakshi-Sundaram, the registrar, have told me their university is always my home. I respect and appreciate this invitation and hope to return many times to my home. I thank Dr Mercy Cornelius, chairman of the social science department at Annamalai, who helped me start my study. Thanks go, too, to many other administrators and professors throughout India. They are too numerous to mention, but I think warmly of Drs Padma and Meenakshi in Annamalai, Mr George and Miss Kuruvilla in Madras, Mrs Emerson and Dr Taylor in Calcutta, Mrs Ray in Santiniketan, Miss Varshney in Banares, Dr Majumdar in Lucknow, Dr Deulkar in Delhi, Professor T. K. M. Menon and Smt Renuka Mukerji in Baroda, Dr and Mrs Bannerjee in Bombay, and Dr and Mrs Vyas Thirtha in Hyderabad.

My deepest thanks go to the hundreds of students who aided me. Their cooperation, patience, kindness, and candour has been professionally helpful and personally heartwarming. Whenever I am inclined towards pessimism as regards India's problems, I think of the students I have come to know this year. They are like students of any country—living from day to day as best they can in terms of their heritage, but who must also turn troubled eyes towards an uncertain and unknown future. It is their task to summon intelligence and energy toward making it more *known* and *certain*. They are not going to remain passive, as the students of Korea, Japan, and Turkey have not. If world brotherhood ever obtains on this planet it will come through global cooperation toward the conditions of integrity that the youth of the world is demanding.

MARGARET CORMACK

Kodaikanal, South India
April 15, 1960

1 | *Independence and Renaissance*

THE "Golden Age" of India may have been the Vedic Age, the era of epic wars, the Mogul Age, or the British Raj—it has been so variously described—but history may judge this present age as that of greatest "gold". An ancient and rich civilization, long quiescent, submissive, and degenerative, is awakening to its own strength and purposes. India is being re-born as she synthesises past and present into a new civilization. Shape and substance are being fashioned *now*. Vinoba Bhave recently said, "Politics and religion are giving way to science and spiritualism". If India can understand and use science spiritually, she will loom large in this world of rationalized power.

Colonialism

"The roots of the present lie in the past." What in India's past explains her pattern of resurgence, her areas of reluctance, her blend of copy and creativity ? We cannot here trace her moments of glory and defeat, her leaders famous and infamous, her contributions and her absorptions. The "modern" period begins, perhaps, with the Islamic invasions from 1000 A.D., when the Persian influence on India was not unlike the Norman influence on England. It was the period when India lost herself, but in so doing began to find herself anew. The Persian language, dress, manners, architecture, art, music, and poetry made their temporarily unwelcome but permanently enriching imprint. What had been "foreign" became "Indian", and yet "foreign-ness" continued to rankle, continued to act as an abrasive catalyst toward self-determination.

As the Mogul Empire decayed and crumbled, the British East

11

India Company took over, successfully staking its claim against the rival French, Dutch, and Portuguese adventurers. At first this new Western "god" was welcomed, for Hindu India was at low ebb. Sanskrit was decried as obsolete, degenerate Hinduism was considered superstition. India seemed unable to rise out of disorganized chaos and looked to new winds. Perhaps the Western winds would blow India clean. It was soon evident, however, that these new gods had feet of gross clay, that they wanted only to milk India of her human and material riches. Great Britain, like all colonial powers of that period, wanted cheap raw materials and labour for her expanding industries, a market for her goods, an area of expansion for surplus population, and a vital link in her global Empire. Well before the Great Mutiny of 1857 and subsequent imposition of the Raj, reaction had moved against the West and toward indigenous Indian patterns. Once again the "foreign" was hated, but this time the experience of opposition slowly led to the growth of effective Indian leadership and nationalism.

Many historians have described and evaluated the British colonial period. We point out here only that harsh conditions of subjection, if not too brutal (as seems to be the case in South Africa), do force individuals and nations to evaluate their condition, to decide what they want, and to work for freedom. Political, economic, intellectual, and social subjection in India was the foundation of her renaissance. This is not to condone colonialism, but to see in it the goad to growth. Even the period of greatest "benevolence", the Curzon period of the late 19th century—a period in which the Raj "gave" much in terms of transportation and communication, medicine, education, and welfare, and in which much was gratefully received—led to increased Indian determination to assume the direction of Indian destiny. Patrimony is fine for children, unacceptable to adults. Further, patrimony shapes laws and institutions designed to perpetuate childhood. Not until Indian self-government was definitely planned did Great Britain belatedly train Indians for responsibility and leadership.

Nirad Chaudhuri beautifully describes the end of one period and the troubled beginning of another. "The many-sided world which lay around us was, in one of its aspects, a world of murder, assault, robbery, arson, rape, abduction; and, in another, a world of disputed inheritance, contested possession, misappropriation of money, betrayal of widows and minors, forged wills, and purloined title-deeds. But there was consolation and security in the clear feeling which all of us had that these terrifying aspects of the world constituted only a thin layer between two more solid ones. The layer of simmering greed and violence which preyed on our peace of mind seemed to rest on a rock-like foundation of quite different composition never permeated or corrupted by it. We called this lower stratum religion and morality, things in which everybody believed and things to which in the last resort everybody returned. Overhead there appeared to be, coinciding with the sky, an immutable sphere of justice and order, brooding sleeplessly over what was happening below, and swooping down on it when certain limits were passed. Its arm seemed to be long and all-powerful, and it passed by different names among us. The common people still called it the Company, others Queen Victoria, and the educated the Government. The feeling, thus ever present, of there being a watching and protecting Government above us vanished at one stroke with the coming of the nationalist agitation in 1905. Afterwards we thought of the Government, in so far as we thought of it in the abstract, as an agency of oppression and usurpation. None the less, although deprived of its subjective halo, the protective power survived for many more decades. Today everything is giving way. The thing overhead, once believed to be immutable, has blown up and the primordial foundation of rock below, on which we thought we had our feet firmly planted, is rotting into dust."[1]

The early 20th century saw rising tension and trouble. Many Indians studied in the West, saw scientific and industrial progress, witnessed democracy in practice. Ram Mohan Roy and other early reformers were followed by others—Rabindranath Tagore, Gandhi, and Nehru among them—who led their people in a cry for self-determination, for integrity, for an India that could recapture its lost heritage and also find a new self. That they succeeded in the Independence Movement is due in large measure to principles and methods that commanded sympathetic response in much of the West, including a changing England. The reforms of 1919, the Simon Commission, the Round Table Conferences, the Gandhi-Irwin Pact of 1931, the Government of India Act of 1935, and provincial autonomy in 1937 were definite moves in the direction

[1] Nirad C. Chaudhuri, *The Autobiography of An Unknown Indian*, Macmillan, 1951, p. 48.

of self-government. But it was World War II, a turning point for England and Empire, that forced official promise of full independence. India made it clear that she intended to rule herself. "Quit India" meant just that, and the white man knew it.

Independence

Thus India turned in 1947 from opposition to construction, though Partition—so unforeseen and traumatic—demanded all immediate energies in stanching the flow of blood and in giving relief to millions of stunned refugees. It was 1949 before the constitution was formed, 1950 when the Republic was born, and 1954 when the major reorganization of States took place. India had settled down and could turn to building. The infant democratic Republic had to bring democracy to the people, had to start the long and difficult task of changing a people used to paternalism to one understanding and practising citizen-participation. It was consciously recognized by top leadership that India would have to become a *new nation* based on a *new psychology*. The *personalities* of people would have to change before India could truly become secular, scientific, and democratic.

The Constitution guaranteed full adult suffrage, separation of Church and State, an end to untouchability and some other social inequalities, and education for all. But undergirding this ideology lay the need for food and a more human standard of living. The fabric of society had to be woven of structures "guaranteeing and delivering the goods". Individual rights, state autonomy, and national unity were all essential—yet sometimes in conflict, at least in priority. What is more important for a hungry person, food for his own stomach, or long-term and nation-wide schemes that could eventually end the tyranny of economic scarcity ? How does a nation best develop its citizens' social consciousness—by permitting political power to all, accepting their immature use of it, or by tutelage toward civic responsibility ? How does one educate a people long denied adequate learning—by providing schools for all, whether good or bad, or by educational expansion that is only as rapid as quality obtains ? What does a nation do about multiple languages—permit each person his own heritage, or insist he learn and use a national medium ? As we of the West know well, when decisions are made politically, issues are often handled in an atmosphere of emotional politics. Democratic power is often as corruptible as autocratic power, and democracy demands more maturity than any whole people has yet demonstrated.

The ruling Congress Party is often accused of retaining its power through Independence slogans and symbols. Many feel it should have disbanded after achieving Independence, as suggested by Gandhi, permitting new parties to form around platforms of construction. But it cannot be said that the Congress Party has had no post-Independence principles and programmes. Firmly wedded to democratic socialism, it has launched the famous Five Year Plans in the determined effort to bring scientific agriculture and industry to an underdeveloped nation. Criticism of the Party grows, but opposition from parties to the right or left has been too weak and divided for effective challenge. It seems clear that India will continue to support those who won her independence as long as Nehru and "the prison clique" are here to lead her.

Transition

What are some of the under-the-surface changes and conditions that could explain the current mixture of national progress and personal corruption, that could explain the blend of national stature and personal insecurity ? The nation is free, but human tension is rising.

1. *It is, clearly, the second stage of Independence*, the dynamic of the Movement gone. There is less defensiveness and scape-goating, though many still rely on the rationalization of "colonial subjection". But there is also less "purpose", the social cement of the Independence Movement dissolved. There is a lack of national unity, though the Chinese border incident has aroused some sense of national danger. Regionalism, usually language-based, is strong, and in some ways "caste community" is important—especially in the South. People seem to identify more easily with a cultural sub-group than with the political entity of nation. On the other hand, caste practices are weakening, and "caste" is becoming a bad word, especially among the educated.

Poverty and hunger still stalk the land, but new political and economic opportunities are opening up daily. When there are mushrooming opportunities, *opportunists* flourish—and, indeed, seem to stifle the spirit of freedom that released them. It takes a long time to control those who use freedom at the cost of others; it takes a long time to know there will be no control unless citizens forge it.

The past, then, is receding—but there are only vague and unformulated glimpses into the future. There are no plans, there is no shape. "After Nehru what ?" symbolizes the general question, with responses invariably relating to the certain rise of other leaders rather than to clarification of national aims. In other words, it is a *transition period* that is predictable, but which needs soon to move constructively to evaluation and a more realistic look *forward*. Patchwork on the frame of the Independence Party is clearly not good enough, and the people are beginning to be restive over this procedure. India needs an effective opposition party and a bolder and more independent press. Many people probably also need more social legislation—as minimum wages and pensions—as the kind of security needed to undergird moves to new and unknown patterns. It is difficult to judge whether people will move to something better because they *must*, because they are so insecure they demand something better, or whether they do so through orderly and guaranteed growth.

2. *Industrialization and urbanization* are bringing changes. The per capita income in 1948-49 was Rs. 246.9; the 1956-57 estimate is Rs. 294.3.[2] The general standard of living is higher—witness, for instance, the enormous new use of bakery bread, biscuits, sweets, soft drinks, and ice-cream—but the social dislocations of the industrial pattern mount, too. Unemployment, especially of the educated, is severe and apparently increasing. The Labour Movement is gaining power, but its programmes are questionable, its leaders naive. Security is precarious, and hence the family is still the chief institution of social security.

The joint family is breaking up, however, especially in the cities. "Separate" families are becoming common, each unit responsible for education, employment, standard of living, and decisions. Even where joint financial responsibility still obtains the strains are growing. A Calcutta medical student perhaps voices the feelings of many in saying, "I worked extremely hard to pass my examinations and get my M.B.B.S. Why should I support my younger

[2] *India*, 1959, Government of India, p. 187.

brother and his family? He is a lazy fellow, a playboy, who wouldn't study. I worked for my status—let him work for his."

Family changes and tensions are seen in other ways, too. There is a rising number of working women, especially in the growing middle class—it is often an economic necessity. At the same time domestic servants are becoming scarce and expensive, for they earn more in fewer hours in industry and have more permanent security. This increases the burden on women, as housework is still time-consuming in traditional diets and methods of preparation. When there is only one woman in the household, and when she has outside work as well as domestic work, she cannot be the kind of wife and mother the traditional family has known and honoured.

Men are having to take increasing individual responsibility for career and family welfare, in many cases without the background training and experience for such responsibility. And "all children must be educated now". Boys have become economic liabilities (except among the lowest working class) and generally cannot contribute financially until they are adult.

Delinquency and crime are rising in the cities. The reasons are familiar to any social scientist—the vast impersonality of society results in "anomie" or "alienation", in the sense of being alone and unrelated to others in an inhuman world. Mental illness is a natural consequence, and suicide is often the "solution".

But the city grows in importance—in its economic opportunities, in its cultural and recreational advantages, in its *power*. Few who experience urban life want to return to the "backward" villages. Figures vary and are no doubt inaccurate, but the percentage of India's population in rural areas is decreasing rapidly. Officially, in 1921 88.6 per cent of the population was rural, in 1951 82.7 per cent.[3] Unofficial estimates drop the current rural percentage still further—Humayun Kabir says to 60 per cent. The locus of power is clearly shifting from rural to urban India—it is the city that is now setting values for the nation.

3. *The village is changing, too,* and many research studies, current and planned, attest to this revolution. The Community Development Programme, which varies in its effectiveness from area to area, has yet to make its biggest impact. Increased production is not yet marked (there is a difference of opinion among planners

[3] *India*, 1959, Government of India, p. 45.

whether production or changed attitude has primacy), but change of attitude is definite. The shift of policy from national direction (welfare) to the leadership of local panchayats[4] (self-help) ought to result in more local initiative and a more permanent benefit. The panchayats and councils themselves have changed, and though traditional and hereditary power figures still dominate in decision-making, lower castes and women are represented. It is not unknown for Harijans to use their new power, and the distance from caste street to cheri[5] is narrowing. Economic power is beginning to take the lead over hereditary, religious dominance.

Better roads and more bicycles and buses increase two-way communication between villages and cities. Radio and newspapers link the discussions under the village banyan tree with those in the Lok Sabha.[6] Schools, hospitals, and welfare agencies are widely available and increasingly used. Perhaps the most profound influences are those of the cinema and of politics. Village women are following urban feminine fashions; village men are arguing cooperative farming and chemical fertilizers. It is also significant that the returning college boys are the current heroes of the village lads—as returning soldiers were after the war. Their clothes, their crop hair-cuts, their slang, their ideas are copied. This identification can only lead to a greater number going to college. In many villages it is the expectation—if not always the realization —that boys will go to secondary school, that girls go to elementary school. Even this expectation is "revolution". Many boys and an increasing number of girls are attending colleges, sometimes on scholarships, sometimes supported entirely by a family that is willing to sacrifice for this new opportunity.

4. *A revolution of expectations* sweeps the land. People at all levels *want* material goods and comforts, education, better jobs, holidays, medical care. The traditional attitude of *resignation* to conditions, which in excess becomes *apathy*, is changing both to *hope* and to attendant *tension and anxiety*. The psychological results are not

---

[4] The "panchayat" is the group of five elders that governs the village. It is now elected.

[5] The "cheri" is the Harijan, or outcaste, section of the village, physically separated from the caste section.

[6] The "Lok Sabha" is the "House of People" in the central legislature in New Delhi. The "Rajya Sabha" is the upper house.

always benign, but improvements can arise only from discontent, only from tension and a conscious effort to change the course of apparent destiny. This change in expectations is resulting in some frustration and bitterness, but also in some creativity. Much depends on the attainability of objectives, and, as some have put it, "the price of rice". But, most importantly, successful change depends on the farmers' understanding of new methods and on their willingness to try them. The majority are understandably conservative, but many are placing their hopes in new ploughs, new seeds, manure, gas generators, electric pumps, insecticides, etc. With the help of the National Agriculture Exhibition, they are beginning to think in terms of the tools of science and the aid of Extension officers in contrast to the whims of nature.

5. *A desire for social mobility* "here and now" is new in a country that has seen status-rise in terms of eons of existence, in terms of a personal *karma* fashioned from untold chapters of faithfully performed *dharmas*. Many parents want their children to have chances they were denied, want them to be in new occupations, want them to be *different.* It is a fundamental change from wanting sons to be like their fathers, daughters to be like their mothers. It involves moving from adaptation to hereditary, prescribed roles to finding and creating new roles. The opportunities are greater, but some securities weaken. A prescribed niche in society may be restricting, but it is certain.

It is not surprising that this aspect of progress is leading to tensions. Children get much of their education—their induction to adult roles—outside the home, with all this means in addition and subtraction as regards their knowledge and experience. They are consequently much less wise about many matters, but in formal learning they often know more than their parents. They understand more about science, and they may get "new ideas" in the areas of politics, religion, and social custom. Parents who wanted their children to be different often decry the difference—for difference brings distance. Many parents no longer understand their children, and vice versa. Further, social mobility frequently results in geographical mobility, and families become scattered. Those who educate their children most highly are the least likely to have their grandchildren grow up around them.

It is education, then, that is chief promise and chief threat.

Even the children of illiterate parents have the opportunity to become engineers, scientists, doctors, government officials. Many of them retain their love and respect of parents, but an increasing number find themselves living in a different world—a world of ideas and actions their parents cannot enter.

6. *Education is increasingly available to all.* Primary education is free in many areas and soon will be in all. Secondary and higher education are expanding rapidly, with scholarships given to many and admission guaranteed for Harijans. It is estimated that 60 per cent of the students now in colleges and universities are "new students". The approach is chiefly quantitative, with prime emphasis on greater numbers served by more schools. We shall criticize this approach in its results in later chapters, but no one could fail to understand the popular demand for education. Unfortunately many do not understand education as "learning", for they come from backgrounds devoid of books, intellectual conversation, or the search for new ideas. There is, instead, a search for *status*, and status obtains through the certificate or degree. It is undeniable that this current compulsion for degrees is far from wholesome, but individual students cannot be blamed for this emphasis when society has decreed certificates and degrees as essential qualifications for desirable jobs. When, tragically, many do not obtain jobs, their frustration is partially soothed by the social prestige attached to the academic degree itself. One status factor that leads to much unemployment among the educated is the attitude that those with degrees should not demean themselves or jeopardize their families' reputations by accepting jobs with inferior title or salary. There is little feeling that "any work experience is useful", and too many educated persons remain idle.

In any society where a person's status is rather largely in terms of his relationship to others, "prestige" is vital to self-respect as well as to family reputation. Prestige-consciousness is nothing short of pathetic in India. Once derived from hereditary position, prestige depends increasingly on educational qualifications. Every resident of India is familiar with degree-laden letter-heads, even including "B.A. failed", for to have sat for the examination is indication of some distinction. We recently heard a poignant conversation regarding what should be printed on a girl's stationery —B.A. (Hons.), or M.A. The decision was cast for both degrees, though it was pointed out that the "B.A. (Hons.)" was the more important. It is our hypothesis that this compulsion for public prestige is a vestige of concepts functional to a hierarchical society —and indication that the much-vaunted "equality" is more a political slogan than a social ideal.

7. *Social change is taking place more rapidly than most realize.* Traditional India is trying to become "modern", many Indians frankly equating "modern" with "Western". Others react emotionally against Westernization. Whatever the point of view, modern science and technology, modern democratic government, and modern customs are making their impact via Western culture. Youth is much readier to accept the medium than the generation that fought against the West for freedom, and their passion for coca-colas and rock-and-roll music is symbolic of the desire of most to join the world fellowship of youth.

Few object to the new political concepts and structure, though some criticize the regime. Most Indians see the urgent necessity of industrialization, with attendant emphasis on science and on education for a scientific age. But many do not understand the resultant changes in family, caste community, religion, and social customs. No item shows more change and strain than the system of marriage. More is involved than "who makes the decision", parents or couple. An entire social system is at stake. India is perforce changing from a *closed society*, in which young people have no opportunity to meet others or to make decisions, to an *open society*, in which social interaction outside the family is both desirable and necessary. Marriage in the former system is the joining of two families within the caste community ; in the latter it is the mating of two individuals who have chosen each other. Strain is resulting in Indian acceptance of an opening society with insistence on retention of the marriage system functional to a closed society. Conditions, be they Western or modern, are moving toward increased social interaction and toward consideration of individual freedom and rights—including the right to make decisions about oneself. *It is inconsistent to encourage new political and economic patterns in the name of "progress" but insist on traditional social mores in the name of "morality".*

The current acceptable compromise in the system of marriage is "arranged marriage with the consent of the couple". But some young people are beginning to realize that this "consent" is a mere token of independence. "What can we tell about the person except his looks ?" Traditional acceptance of parent-arranged marriage will be increasingly impossible as young people move to more ideas and experiences outside the family context. Arranged marriage, to be acceptable, presupposes young people's faith that their parents "completely know and understand them". Many feel this is still true, but a few are resembling Western youth in their feeling that they are not understood—and their confidence in the old system is crumbling. They love and respect their parents, but they look to their own lives in terms of their own decisions. We predict the numbers of youth in this category will increase.

Few adults are attempting to analyse this area of growing strain. There is a general naive feeling that India can become modern in some ways, remain traditional in others. But society is a somewhat coherent organism, and movement in some areas always brings movement in others. Morality that is functional to one time may cease to be morality in another. Morality is not a philosophical abstraction—it consists of concepts that work.

8. *India has not yet had a social revolution* in the minds and emotions of most of its citizens. Political independence ushered in a democratic political structure, and the plans of the Congress Party were accepted because the Party won independence. Further, a democracy is the modern and anti-authoritarian form of government. Few objected to it, but few really understand or accept it. It is against "inequalities"—yes—but what else does it mean ? There has not yet been time, or indeed reason, for a social revolution in India—for a nation of "paternalistic personalities" to become "democratic personalities". Self-government seen only as national self-determination is yet to be understood as a government into which one puts the self.

Many are asking, "Can democracy work in India now ?" and some are dogmatically stating, "We should have a benevolent dictatorship—as Pakistan does, or as Turkey did under Ataturk." They are seeing that democracy can be a tyrant, and one more difficult to depose than a monarch.

It is tempting to judge democracy as a static system, to adopt or reject. Actually it is a *process* based upon a *principle*. It is a concept that develops in growth, that comes out of the experience of self-government. It does not and cannot arrive full-blown. India is no different from other nations in the failure to understand the deep complexities of democracy or in impatience over its slow maturation. But India differs from the West in the *urgency of immediate results*. The system is being judged by what it is *now* rather than by what it might become in the fullness of time.

9. *The present leadership of India is inadequate* to needed far-reaching plans. As many people know, a democracy needs even more leadership than an autocracy, and leadership in a time of rapid change is critical. Much of India's leadership is excellent, especially in high places. But much intermediate leadership is inadequate. Many people of mediocre training and limited experience are in positions of importance. Some are sincere but ineffective or fearful; others are clever in more ways than one. A few are both competent and dedicated, but they are often frustrated and discouraged. Some become "resigned", others talk openly of leaving India. This is especially true of many in the fields of science or higher education—individuals desperately needed by a nation that seems to reject them. *It may be that friendly foreign assistance in the training and sustaining of effective leaders and specialists is more important than assistance in capital investment.*

10. *Overpopulation absorbs most of India's new efforts and achievements.* This fact is so well known we need not emphasize it here. It is known that the population approaches 400 million, that this represents a 52 per cent increase in five decades, that the rate of growth relative to such a large base is alarming, that the average density of people per square mile is 287 (907 in Kerala and 776 in Bengal), that the falling death rate is increasing life-expectancy.[7] Economists have pointed out that even if the targets of the Third Five Year Plan are met there will be more unemployment then than now. They also know that the rising cost of food relates to the present losing battle between agricultural and human production.

India has officially recognized this problem with the Family Planning Scheme. Upsetting the balance of nature by death control necessitates counteracting with birth control—if nature is not to punish the entire society. Many efforts, short of legal coercion,

[7] *India*, 1959, pp. 14, 44.

are going into this scheme. During the First Five Year Plan there was reluctant endorsement of the rhythm method, and less than half of the allotted 65 lakhs[8] rupees was spent in establishing 600 clinics in rural areas. The current Second Five Year Plan has opened 2,000 clinics in rural areas and 500 in urban, spending 5 crores of rupees and recommending various forms of contraception and sterilization. The proposed plan, under the direction of the Union Ministry of Health, anticipates spending 74 crores of rupees, shifting the emphasis from Family Planning clinics to advice and facilities offered at all medical and health centres. According to a recent report from New Delhi, more than 76,600 persons throughout India were voluntarily sterilized up to March, 1960, from the time the Union Government began popularizing sterilization as a method of family planning in 1956.[9] Of this number 48,000 are women, but the sterilization of men is gaining popularity. It is not surprising that birth control by complete sterilization should be resisted, and aside from fears over surgery and its possible side-effects (however denied medically), there are fears over increased immorality. We have been told that many men are now undergoing sterilization themselves "because they could not trust their wives if sterile". This sentiment undoubtedly does injustice to the many others who have more responsible motives. There are prophets both of doom and hope on this subject. Pessimists predict failure of the scheme in the rural areas—where it is needed most; optimists point to changed attitudes and frank discussion, and predict only problems of "providing medical facilities for all who will soon demand sterilization".

It is probably correct to say that results are so far discouraging, but that there has scarcely been time for solution of this difficult human problem. A genuine desire to have smaller families is common, and as alternatives to hunger are offered they will be increasingly chosen. We of the West, where the subject is officially taboo, can scarcely criticize the bold efforts of India.

11. *Responsibility and trust, essential ingredients in a democracy, are generally lacking.* A sense of responsibility toward others and mutual trust in each other are fundamental to the effectiveness of democracy. This is not to say that all people can or will be respon-

---

[8] 1 lakh = 1,00,000; 1 crore = 1,00,00,000; $1.00 = Rs. 4.75.
[9] *Madras Mail*, May 25, 1960.

sible and trusting, nor that a saccharine kind of "brotherhood" should prevail. It is to point out that democracy is founded on human relationships more than power, depends more on cooperation than competition. If people cannot *generally* trust their co-workers and co-citizens, or if they do not generally feel responsible for them, they probably cannot make democracy work. It is a system founded on *mutuality*. One can view this concept of mutuality in several ways. "We are all in this together", say the realists. "We must love one another", say the spiritualists. And those who lean towards science might say, "If we want to live in a healthy society —one in which we find justice and generosity—we must practise what we want". However one states it, no expression has been better than the Golden Rule, fundamental to all major religions.

Indians daily demonstrate a sense of responsibility toward and trust in members of their family—the in-group—and indifference toward and lack of faith in members of out-groups. Unquestionably centuries of experience in society have shaped their attitudes. Society has been hierarchical, and *separateness*, or *social distance*, has characterized social relationships. It has been region against region, caste against caste, family against family. This means today that institutions like government, business and industry, labour unions, banks, schools, etc. are pasted together by intricate rules, checks, and counter-checks. It is bureaucracy at its worst; competence is corrupted at the source. India is a country of padlocks and watchmen—not because it is a criminal society, but because the padlock symbolizes the petty pilfering people expect of one another—and usually get.

Responsibility and trust are not sentimental abstractions. They are working relationships that make relationships work. They are essential ingredients in a mature democracy and also to its chances of maturing. We shall discuss these concepts in a later chapter, merely recording here that corruption is a symptom of their relative absence. General Indian opinion is that corruption is increasing—the suggestions of C. D. Deshmukh for a tribunal and the shrill exhortations of party leaders indicate cause for alarm. The corruption goes from the postage-stamp level to the lakhs of rupees level, embracing the area of university admissions and examinations on the way. We are told that "getting admission to a government institution—higher or technical—is impossible without heavy bribes paid to the three local officials whose signatures are required for application. Other bribes are often essential for the application to get consideration." Many Christians complain they are losing their faith in pastors—so many are involved in bribery and slander. Income tax evasion is so widespread we hope the tax-payers of those nations aiding India do not discover its extent. It is not serious that corruption exists—it is always with us, in every age, in every nation—but it is serious when most citizens of a land feel there is nothing that can be done about it. It will wane only when people take responsibility for one another's motives and actions, when trust becomes more useful than the padlock.

12. *Social change requires social creativity*, if the change is to be constructive. Judging with a bird's-eye view, it would seem that the most creative area of India is business and industry, at least in the private sector. Rewards and punishments are "built-in", and initiative pays off; obsolescence or inefficiency loses sales and the family fortune.

Government and politics can muddle much longer without correction—and will when there is no strong opposition party. But when there is a democratic constitution, the people will in time demand new patterns if the old are unsatisfactory. There is also a "built-in", if slow, check.

But education, because it is "socialized" and outside the profit-and-loss and vote-mandate patterns, can muddle forever. It can, indeed, deteriorate in vicious circle form, for it has no built-in rewards and punishment device. Its standards depend entirely on the profession; it is mediocre or excellent as the profession shapes it. Political and public pressures can do little but nurture a good profession with liberal rewards or foster an inferior one with second-rate status.

If India is to progress constructively and creatively, then, it is imperative that its system of mass education receive the keenest scrutiny and the most active assistance. *People cannot be creative adults unless their education has stimulated and developed creativity.* To date the system in India is largely "a deteriorated copy of an obsolete model". That it is non-functional to India's needs is rarely disputed, but the proposed patchwork of the system seems inadequate. This may not be an area where "time will solve the problem". *If one does not copy one creates.*

2 | *Planning for the New India*

The Five Year Plans

THE Five Year Plans are India's bold challenge to passive and perpetual poverty. Their three chief aims are: (1) to start building up, by democratic means, a *new pattern of society* which would create a richer and fuller life for the people through higher standards of living, increased employment, production, and a larger measure of justice; (2) to develop agriculture and both large-and small-scale industry; and (3) to give especial emphasis on long-range programmes and development—such as irrigation, power, and conservation—and to build the necessary administration for them.[1] We see thus that production and a changed society are the inter-related aims. It is clear in the statements of the Planners and also from observation of India in 1960 that "a changed society" means chiefly "the reduction of inequalities". As we stated before, democracy is understood readily in relation to increasing Indian objection to the caste system, is rarely couched in terms of responsible citizen participation. As economic power is encouraged and rewarded, it usurps traditional caste power, and class strata develop (blunted, to be sure, by the tax system). The utopia of equality seems as distant as ever, to the delight of some, the consternation of others.

The First Plan was launched in 1952, the more ambitious Second Plan is nearing completion, and the Third Plan—now under discussion—promises to be massive in scope. There is no question that these Plans are immensely significant in India's progress, that most Indians are justifiably proud of them. They are raising India's standards and expectations, are turning a subjected people

[1] *Hindustan Yearbook*, 1960, p. 494.

27

into a constructive nation. But the greatest strength of the Plans —their demonstration of a government that undertakes the welfare of the people—may also be their greatest weakness. Paternalistic personalities expect "the" government to care for them, welcome welfare, bless a benevolent "father". But unless India turns paternalistic welfare into citizen participation the people will continue to see government as "father", not as a cooperative society of "brothers". The Planners understand this danger, and especially in the Community Development Programme—that amazing scheme that has already brought "help to those who help themselves" to more than half the villages—there is now official insistence that further progress stem from local initiative. It is too early to judge the results of this new policy, but these results will gauge the true progress of India.

In the accomplishment of the above aims, early priorities suggested for the first three plans were (1) agriculture, to raise the nutritional base of a malnourished people; (2) industrialization, to raise the general standard of living and to provide full employment for a growing middle class; and (3) education and social welfare, to give equal opportunities in knowledge and health to all. Little semblance of these early objectives remains. Food targets for the First Plan were officially met, but hunger has not been routed, partly because estimates of population growth were grossly inadequate. Industry, despite an almost unlimited market and labour pool, has not been able to develop more rapidly than available capital investment and skilled know-how. Unemployment has not abated; inflation damps desired standards of living; depletion of foreign credit has brought financial crisis, stringent regulations as regards imports, and greater dependence on foreign aid. Further, the people will not wait for education and welfare, and the nation cannot afford to have them do so. Planning has had to work on all fronts simultaneously.

Financial allocations of the First and Second Plans can be seen in Table 1 (p. 29), the figures in crores of rupees representing First Plan actual outlay and Second Plan revised allocations.[2]

Objectives of the Second Plan are summed up in "a socialistic pattern of society", with emphasis on minimizing inequalities. The proposed Third Plan is said to involve 10,000 crores—if Prime Minister Nehru can obtain guarantees of 500 crores foreign exchange

[2] *Hindustan Yearbook*, pp. 495, 498.

TABLE 1
PLAN OUTLAY AND ALLOCATION

		I crores	I %	II crores	II %
1.	Agriculture & Industry	299	14.8	510	11.3
2.	Irrigation & Power	585	29.1	820	18.2
3.	Village & Small Industries			160	3.6
4.	Industry & Mining	100	5.0	790	17.5
5.	Transport & Communication	532	26.4	1,340	29.8
6.	Social Services	423	21.0	810	18.0
	(Education)	(164)		(307)	
7.	Miscellaneous	74	3.7	70	1.6
	TOTAL	2,013	100	4,500	100

annually. Many Indians are concerned about this deficit financing and dependence on foreign credits, but the scope of the Plan depends on it. Planners have had to consider the unforeseen Chinese border situation and its defence implications, and have also had to return to a greater emphasis on agriculture. The target of food grains production has been placed at 110 million tons, as recommended by the Ford Foundation Committee. Whether the controversial Cooperative Farming and Land Ceiling schemes are acceptable or helpful in this increased production aim is hotly argued. Under consideration also is an industrial target of 10 million tons of crude steel, a target that can be met only with greatly increased foreign aid.

The 74 crores tentatively allocated to Family Planning is part of growing attention to social factors. Priority is planned for control of communicable diseases, adequate water supplies, more effective family planning, and further education development.

The main foci continue to be an increased food supply, fuller employment, and the achievement of a self-generating growth. Few disagree with these aims, but there is growing discussion of methods. Should fuller employment come through public works ?

Should the public sector be extended, or should more encouragement be given the private sector ?[3] Can, in fact, the public sector demonstrate industrial initiative or produce quality that is competitive in the world market ? Should imports be so severely restricted ? A serious challenge to the nationalization and welfare principles of the Congress Party has recently developed in the Swatantra (Freedom) Party under the direction of C. Rajagopalachari. Whether this party succeeds in becoming an effective opposition party or not, its free enterprise principles have stimulated thought and discussion.

Whatever criticism may be levelled at these Plans, they are India's most impressive gain. They have already resulted in material progress, have brought objectives that are *specific* and *attainable*, and—most importantly—have turned a people toward handling their own purposes and methods. Whatever "new spirit" obtains today owes as much to the Plans as to the fact of independence. As one example of this self-direction, we include the "Ten Commandments for the Police", an official act of 1951 in West Bengal.[4] We first saw the large bulletin containing these "commandments" in English, Hindi, and Bengali in a tiny police outpost beyond Kalimpong and near the border of India. It hangs, we are told, in every police office in West Bengal.

TEN COMMANDMENTS FOR THE POLICE

1. Work in a missionary spirit to help your fellow human beings.
2. Treat your subordinates as you would like your superiors to treat you. Be fair and just to them. Have no favourites.
3. Smart and clean dress is the first step to discipline. Wear and respect your uniform if you want others to do so.
4. Discipline your habits, movements and thoughts.
5. Keep yourself fit by drill and physical training.
6. Behave politely and courteously but firmly with the public.
7. Never be a bully, do not display bad temper or use abusive language.

---

[3] Much industry is nationalized in the "public sector", and the official policy is extension in this direction. Private industry, the "private sector", is heavily restricted in imports of materials, production, and distribution.

[4] Quoted by permission of the District Superintendent of Police, Darjeeling, West Bengal—who courteously gave us a copy of the bulletin.

8. Live plainly, cleanly and within your means.
9. Be straightforward in dealing with the people and people will love you. Do not seek cheap popularity.
10. Example is better than precept. Do what you want others to do.

Education

Education, thus, is planned and developed in the total context of the Five Year Plans. No area of progress is more noticeable. Not all children are in school (probably less than 50 per cent are), not all parents want them in school (they need their labour, cannot afford their schooling), but most parents today see their children's future security in terms of their education. Tens of thousands of children and older youth are busy and happy in schools and colleges today—whether in classrooms or on the playgrounds. A decade ago few would have had this opportunity—and this generation appreciates its good fortune.

Politicians cannot ignore the growing popular demand for schools, so that in spite of the distressing number of "educated unemployed" there is a quantitative approach to education. Unfortunately the development has been largely in "academic" directions, educational leadership having been too wedded to the pre-war European "classical tradition". The principles and structure of the educational system have been more a product of the past than of Planning. Recent moves towards expansion of technical education and towards emphasis on science in all schools bespeak a needed departure from early aims. The Plans are beginning to use education functionally.

The British Raj had developed the elementary and secondary educational system in India chiefly to produce the large numbers of clerks and minor bureaucrats needed by the regime—though it was stated with pride that secondary leaving examinations were "just like those in England". Many young men and a few women went on in relatively excellent institutions of higher education—especially in the arts, law, and medicine. The Universities of Calcutta, Madras, and Bombay were established in 1857, and by Independence there were 21 universities in operation. Further, the Raj encouraged *British* foreign higher education, and many students, including Gandhi and Nehru, drank at the founts of Oxford and Cambridge.

The newly independent nation in 1947, thus, had the advantage of having many well educated men and women and the disadvantage of experience with and allegiance to a system prior to its recent changes and modification. Even many patriots who were openly fighting England as a colonial power were devoted to her educational principles, and the prestige attached to British education remained firm.

A counter movement, at lower levels, lay in Gandhi's Wardha Scheme, which emphasized "union of mind and hand" and learning that is functional to life in rural India. This philosophy of education moves from "the bottom up", starting with primary education as the base, whereas English education moves from "the top down", standards set in the universities, and all other institutions of education designed to bring superior children up to these standards. And always in the background of memory has been "ancient Indian education", a system in which boys lived and studied for years with their gurus, their mentors in a total way of life. Content of learning was less important than personal identification with a chosen master.

Independent India's educational system, thus, reflects various influences. Gandhi's ideas have had more effect on elementary and social (adult) education, the European classical on secondary and higher education, and the guru has been discarded if not forgotten. The latest influence is American, for thousands of Indian students and professors are studying and lecturing in the U.S., hundreds of American students and professors come to India. At present the English tradition dominates in positions of power, but the ideological struggle sharpens, and it seems logical to predict that the American influence will grow under developing leadership. It is unfortunate that the issues are so often couched in "British" or "American" terms rather than those of sound education for an emergent society. The wisest heads in India, indeed, are looking to neither model in national terms and are turning their minds to Indian needs.

"Education in India is the responsibility of State Governments, the Union Government confining its activities to the coordination of facilities and determination of standards in respect of higher education (through the University Grants Commission), research, and scientific and technical education. Coordination in regard to elementary and secondary education is secured through All-India

Councils. The Union Government is also responsible for the running of four universities (Aligarh, Banares, Delhi, and Visva-Bharati) and such other institutions of national importance as Parliament may by law declare. It also administers the award of scholarships and fellowships in pursuance of the policy of promoting cultural relations with other countries and cooperating with international organizations like UNESCO."[5] All aspects of education, thus—elementary, basic, secondary, technical, higher, rural higher, social (adult), education for the handicapped, physical education and sports, the National Cadet Corps, and youth welfare—are planned and administered by State and Central governments. Theoretically de-centralized, India gives enormous responsibility to the Union Ministry of Education, and until States are better able to exercise their own plans and leadership this central coordination and guidance will be necessary. Indeed, much current criticism suggests too-weak educational leadership in Delhi.

Under the Directive Principles of State policy in the Federal Constitution of 1949, it has been provided that "the State shall endeavour to provide, within a period of ten years from the commencement of the Constitution, for free and compulsory education for all children until they complete the age of fourteen years."[6] Now that the ten-year period is drawing to a close, a study of progress has indicated that revision is necessary. Education cannot be made compulsory until it is first made free. The Scheme has been re-phased to bring all children from 6–11 under instruction by the end of the Third Plan, all children to the age of 14 by the end of the Fifth Plan.

Literacy has mounted rapidly, the official 1951 Census figures showing nearly 25 per cent of the men and 8 per cent of the women as literate (this represents an enormous gain since Independence), and current figures may be double those of 1951. In 1956-57 there were a total of 3,77,718 institutions of education, 357.75 lakhs of students.[7]

The above figures attest to the enormity of both achievement and further needs. The original targets were unrealistic in view of the problems of finance, buildings, teacher training, and family economics. On the other hand, many feel that education has developed too rapidly, that quality has suffered, and that more young people

---

[5] *India*, 1959, p. 108.   [6] *Ibid.*   [7] *Ibid.* p. 110.

have been frustrated by education's promise than have been rewarded by its fruits.

TABLE 2

TYPES OF INSTITUTIONS, 1956-57 [8]

Pre-primary Schools	773	Arts & Sciences Colleges	771
Primary Schools	2,87,318	Professional Colleges	404
Secondary Schools	35,828	Special Educational Colleges	127
Vocational Schools	3,283	Research Institutes	41
Special Educational Schools	49,127	Universities	37

TABLE 3

TARGETS OF SECOND FIVE YEAR PLAN, 1960-61 [9]

Percentage children	6-11	under instruction		62.7
„	„	11-14	„ „	22.5
„	„	14-17	„ „	11.7
„	„	17-23	„ „	2.0

Elementary Education

"Basic education" is the officially preferred form of elementary
education, and systems are being required to shift gradually to the
"Basic" pattern—to the approval of those who understand and
welcome its principles, to the disapproval of those who dislike this
"political imposition". The principles are essentially "progressive"
and Gandhian, involving an "activity curriculum" which emphasizes
learning-by-doing and learning-what-is-functional-in-India. Literacy is a tool rather than an aim, and children learn about health,
nutrition, sanitation, agriculture, and crafts—"the social and
physical environment through productive activities". The results in
India are excellent to distressing, depending on the convictions and
skill of the administrators and teachers involved. Unfortunately the
issue has become increasingly political (Basic Education is the
official policy of the Congress Party, some say in order to capitalize

[8] *Ibid.*   [9] *Ibid.*

on Gandhian loyalties), and the Basic Teacher Training Centres are usually directly under the government—institutions thus separated from the established universities and colleges. What should have been treated as "sound education" has become too much a Gandhian cult, with Gandhi's principle of functionality largely misunderstood. Curriculum tends to freeze at the "hand-spinning level", charts on flies decorate the walls as live flies swarm on children's sores, staff proudly demonstrate their cooperative work system but go home to let their mothers wait on them "as is our tradition". The details that were pertinent to the past may be obsolete in a decade, but reverence for the Mahatma has so sanctified the charkha[10] that its symbolism may already be lost. However, it is encouraging to see the growth of the activity curriculum, and anything that gets the children off their static benches and away from passive learning is commendable. After all, not many can have the advantage of attendance in excellent schools as, for instance, the demonstration nursery school and kindergarten connected to the Department of Home Science in Baroda University.

Secondary Education

Secondary education is experiencing the same difficulties and controversies confronting secondary education all over the world. Is secondary education merely a channel to higher education, available to a privileged few—or is it largely terminal education for the masses ? The first recommendation of the 1953 Secondary Education Commission was "substitution of the present system in which the secondary stage is entirely subservient to university education by a diversified system through conversion of existing schools into multi-purpose types". Multi-purpose schools theoretically offer instruction in languages, social studies, general science, a compulsory craft, and courses in sciences, technology, commerce, agriculture, fine arts, home economics, or the humanities. Actually many schools assuming the title scarcely deserve it, for they may offer only one course—as home economics or manual training—in addition to the "traditional classical". The need for "practical education" is great, but the prestige of academic knowledge remains—and is likely to continue unless and until Indian society uses and handsomely rewards those technically trained.

[10] The spinning wheel, central motif in the Congress Party flag.

Some educators say that jobs for those technically trained are not yet available in large quantity, but many businessmen state they are seeking *now* good typists, good mechanics, good electricians, etc., usually without success.

Secondary education, except for a few progressive and somewhat experimental schools, most of which are privately owned and run,[11] are generally traditional in content and methods. Learning is "passive", most work is memorized for the government examinations. That this kind of education is "functional" training for those who continue the same procedure in higher education is scarcely good rationale !

Indian educational leaders, in clarifying aims after Independence, were far-sighted in seeing secondary education as "essential to democracy" because it

1. gives a great many students experience in democratic participation,
2. trains thousands for positions of intermediate leadership,
3. provides the educational base for teacher training, and
4. is a channel to higher education.

These aims are scarcely visible today—they have been drowned in the ocean of quantitative demands for certificates. But there are some significant experiments and plans, not the least of which is university extension work in the secondary schools.

Critics of educational theory and practice at both the elementary and secondary levels are usually sobered by the reality of financial problems. Few nations can or do pay for educational excellence. Whereas salaries for teachers in India are above the 1950-59 national per capita income of Rs. 290.7,[12] and whereas new raises are going into effect this year, many teachers receive below Rs. 100 per month. A decent standard of living is not possible at this level. Both hardship and low status prevail. India resembles her neighbours in the world in this condition, but differences in degree are so

[11] Among the excellent schools we have seen are The New Era School in Bombay, with Dr M. T. Vyas as principal, and the Sardar Patel Vidyalaya in Delhi, with Dr Raghubhai Nayak as principal. Both happen to be coeducational, Gujerati-supported schools. The former school is especially exciting in its meaningful activities, its spirit of self-reliance.

[12] *Hindustan Yearbook*, 1960, p. 375.

great—at least in comparison to the West—that results are qualitatively distressing. It should be no comfort to India to reflect that teachers are underpaid in most nations, and the profession would do well to focus on its principles and personnel.

There are education associations in India, and they do hold meetings—for instance, the annual All-India Education Conference. But, to quote an Indian educator who has travelled in the U.S. and Europe, "We really have nothing that counts. We need strong associations at each level of education, and one that ties us all together. But it should be quite separate from the Central and State governments !" When the "New Education Fellowship", an international organization, held its international conference in New Delhi this year, over 500 Indian delegates attending, it was clear that both the content (modern education) and the method of the conference (group dynamics) was exciting and helpful to Indian delegates. Delegates from the West (including Australia) felt the organization should shift aims to "international content", leaving the discussion of most educational principles and problems to national organizations. "But we don't have the organizations !" some Indian delegates pointed out. This professional need is acute in India—not only for the clarification of educational principles but also for the stimulation of research and for the support of professional journals.

Higher Education

Elementary education is supposed to fit India's children for "survival in the modern world", secondary education to prepare them for democracy, and higher education to train the intellectually superior for leadership and the top professions. The 38 universities currently operating in India have 763 affiliated arts and science colleges, for which they prescribe the curricula, give the examinations, and confer the degrees. The University of Calcutta alone has 148 attached colleges, serving 1,13,751 students. These universities vary considerably, but most are either *Teaching and Affiliating*, with research and instruction at the post-graduate level and supervision of under-graduate instruction in the affiliating colleges, or *Residential and Teaching*, with instruction at under-graduate and post-graduate levels given in departments. In the latter type of institution many students live on campus in university hostels—

in contrast to residence in colleges.[13] Among the institutions involved in our study, Annamalai, Banares, Baroda, Jadavpur, and Visva-Bharati are the residential type, and Miranda House College (University of Delhi) and Kanja Kubja College (University of Lucknow) are examples of affiliated colleges. There are other types of institutions, too. The Madras School of Social Work, for instance, is not affiliated to the University of Madras, though this is a relationship being considered. The School has its own Executive Board and operates as an independent institution.

Universities derive their powers and functions from various acts of the Central and State legislatures, and are usually governed by Executive Councils or Syndicates which include representatives and nominees of the Central or State governments. There is currently much criticism of the power wielded by these governments. Some universities have politically-controlled Executive Councils, "rationalized" because the universities are state institutions. On the other hand, "independent" institutions are often controlled by a Founder and "his" Board. University Chancellors, titular heads, are usually State governors or other noted political figures (Nehru is Chancellor of Visva-Bharati University). Vice-Chancellors, the actual executive heads, are usually elected by Executive Councils—but often represent political more than professional needs. Several distinguished academicians in different universities have commented to us, "We have no professional autonomy", and "Education has been taken over by politics". The political *nature* of the institutions is obvious, though a few institutions—as the Universities of Bombay and Madras—have had some success in resisting political *control*.[14] We are not suggesting that "control", political or otherwise, is always contrary to educational principles, but we do think that the professional autonomy of most universities is unclear and in grave jeopardy. Especially distressing is the growing number of court cases, in which students, parents, or faculty members go directly

[13] The words "university" and "college" are confusing, as they are used in different ways. "University" sometimes refers to a post-graduate institution, sometimes to an institution combining undergraduate and post-graduate work. "College" usually refers to an under-graduate affiliated college in terms of its *academic* aspect, but it may also describe a *residential* unit.

[14] There is a bitter struggle going on in Madras now, between the State Government, which wants the Tamil medium to replace English in higher education, and the Vice-Chancellor of the University of Madras, who resists both the idea and the political pressure.

to the courts on matters of admission, appointment, or operation. This seems a dangerous precedent, and legal clarification and professional protection of the universities' nature and function is urgent.

State universities are financed by the State and by federal aid. This aid is controlled by the University Grants Commission, a body set up by the Union Ministry of Education in 1953 to aid development schemes and to raise standards. The "UGC", the dispenser of funds, is thus immensely powerful. So far as we are able to judge, this power has been handled with remarkable responsibility in the interests of better education under the educational leadership of the current chairman, Mr C. D. Deshmukh. Under his guidance the UGC has furthered higher and more uniform faculty salaries, better libraries, more hostels, more buildings, new departments, new research, new ideas. In fact, many universities seem to feel nothing is possible without the aid and leadership of the UGC, and higher education has become more centralized than was planned. The Ministry of Education and the UGC, we observe, are not always in harmony, a situation that sometimes makes for delayed or compromised decisions, but which also makes for healthy and needed controversy.

At the request of the UGC and in reference to the Third Five Year Plan, all universities are currently studying their future needs and submitting their requests for new posts, buildings, and departments. It is significant that directions of expansion include much in the social sciences (so needed and inadequate in changing India), the introduction of American Studies, General Education, Technological Education, and research at all levels.

In opposition to these qualitative developments, however, persists the question of quantitative service to a nation of young people that insist on degrees. The official position taken by the Congress Party is "quality" in higher education, but popular pressures on politicians and legislatures have resulted in a mushroom growth that negates quality. University students have been increasing at the rate of 50,000 a year, and the increase now approaches the million mark. Those long denied opportunities, including girls and members of the "scheduled or backward classes", are among the most eager. There is much opposition to the guaranteed admissions, numbers of scholarships, and "easy" degrees given the scheduled classes, and it may be their "guaranteed percentages" will be dropped. Prime Minister Nehru recently said, "Specialized and higher education should be meant only for meritorious candidates. . . . Percentages drown quality."[15] C. D. Deshmukh, one of many deploring the results of mass higher education, wrote in his recent book, *In the Portals of Indian Universities*,[16] "that classrooms are grossly overcrowded, too many politician-teachers have emerged, student indiscipline has grown, and standards have rapidly deteriorated." He blames a paucity of funds, a shortage of trained personnel, and an inherited and lopsided system based on the humanities—and states that standards and courses in India should relate to the Plans and their aims. Nehru is also concerned over the lack of relationship between degrees and Indian needs. "Our system of education can progress only if we have a clear picture of the society we are going to have."[17]

Nothing has highlighted the picture of higher education more than "student indiscipline", and scarcely a week passes without newspaper comment on the subject. It is, in fact, a popular subject of exhortation. Most speakers and writers content themselves with deploring the morals of the younger generation, but a few dig into the underlying causes—unearthing critical questions embracing all aspects of higher education. It is probable that the current inquiry into educational aims, methods, and standards has stemmed from the rash of major and minor student demonstrations, some of which have resulted in university closure, others in the resignation of vice-chancellors. Probably no college or university authorities have rested easy of late, for even in the institutions officially experiencing "no trouble" there is evidence of increasing student expression. "I don't know what will happen now that students are reading about student uprisings in Korea, Japan, and Turkey", a professor mused. "I'm afraid they will become even more intoxicated with a sense of power." Student indiscipline, thus, has become a political as well as a professional matter of concern. We shall discuss this problem at some length in a later chapter, for it is clearly symptomatic of deeper problems.

"Unless the present policy of drift in education policy at the university level is halted, a state of chaos will soon prevail," wrote

[15] In a speech at Patna, as reported in the *Madras Mail*, April 15, 1960.
[16] C. D. Deshmukh, *In the Portals of Indian Universities*, New Delhi, University Grants Commission, 1959.
[17] *Madras Mail*, April 13, 1960.

K. Santhanam, *Madras Mail* commentator.[18] He is one of many concerned over the deterioration of standards in higher education, and gives the causes as rapid increase of numbers, depreciation of standards, indiscipline among students, and confusion due to language changes in the universities. This last item is receiving much current attention. It is undeniable that the medium of instruction is basic to learning, and that any foreign medium is difficult for most students. Those in favour of retaining English as the medium point to its international value, to Indian dependence on English-language texts, and to the lack of scientific vocabulary in Indian languages. Their logical arguments are considerably dimmed by the fact that English has rapidly deteriorated in recent years. Those in favour of adopting Hindi (the "official" language of India) prefer an *Indian* language and point to the programmes of supplying Hindi texts and scientific vocabulary. Many institutions in the North are making this change. But in the South, where Dravidian languages have no resemblance to Hindi, where much more English is spoken than in the North, and where there is militant opposition to the "dominance of Delhi", some agitate for the retention of English, others for the adoption of the regional language. Madras State is officially endorsing Tamil, but there is much opposition from the University of Madras and also from many citizens. So this difficult professional question, too, has entered the realm of politics. Eight universities have already switched from English to Hindi or the regional language, and 14 more propose to do so in the near future. The Minister of Education reiterated in the Rajya Sabha that the Government wanted the regional languages to become the media of instruction in the universities "as quickly as possible".[19] But many politicians who publicly espouse use of regional languages themselves educate their children in English-medium schools, for, like others, they recognize the limiting effect of a regional language, the advantages of a national and international medium. And though Hindi has enjoyed government support for the introduction of Hindi scientific terms and for texts published in Hindi, the majority of professors state "virtual dependence on English texts for many years". "This difficult matter should not be handled by the politicians", a disgruntled professor complained. "It should be handled by the

[18] *Ibid.*
[19] *Madras Mail*, April 20, 1960.

profession. But the trouble is we have no profession—we are at the mercy of the politicians."

These issues and others point to needed examination of the *entire* system of higher education in India, rather than to piece-meal attention. We have described education in India as "a deteriorated copy of an obsolete model". The brightest students in the best institutions stand very well in the intellectual competition of the world, but the majority of students are being cheated. Most tragically, both faculty and students are denied creativity—in a moment of India's history when creativity is most needed. If India is to change constructively, her leaders must be constructively creative. The Five Year Plans put a premium on economic progress, but social and psychological progress beyond the equalization of some inequalities is neglected. A "new society" cannot develop unless Saraswati dismounts her peacock of academic tradition, looks to India's needs in higher education, and helps India's future leaders understand and construct a new way of life.

3 | *The Study and Student Respondents*

THE purpose of our study is to discover Indian students' conscious attitudes toward the social change taking place in India today. Specific information about education and social problems in India should illuminate general world problems of higher education in relation to changing societies. It is our observation that institutions and "the older generations in power" tend to operate on values increasingly non-functional and inacceptable to youth, unless they analyse changes and reformulate principles in the light of new conditions.

This study focusses on *conscious* and subjective responses. They are important in the understanding of youth, but so, too, are sub-conscious attitudes, not contained in this study. Interpretations of the data, thus, must take this limitation into account. Nor does the data warrant descriptive information about any one institution or group—though we shall point out some interesting differences of response. The data does lend itself to "male" and "female" differentiated response and will so be offered.

The 100-statement, multiple-choice and/or write-in questionnaire[1] was prepared after many hours of interview and trial runs with students at Annamalai University. Most of the printed "choices" are theirs. This questionnaire proved applicable to other areas in most respects, though we could now improve it considerably. Some questions brought too-vague responses, a few were misunderstood. Muslim students justifiably found the material on religion "too Hindu", even when they were told to ignore items that did not apply to them. And more responses, as the Jan Sangh

[1] See Appendix

43

political party, should have been included.

Four hundred and four of the 500 questionnaires were returned (not always completely filled out), and the following data relates to them. Our comments and interpretations, however, will include information gained through some 200 interviews, some of them with groups of students in single sessions, others with one or more students in multiple sessions. For the interviews the students generally preferred to come in small groups, and unless scheduled singly by authorities they would not come alone. Those who were forced to come alone tended to remain reserved and cautious. Most were curious as to "what an American lady professor wants with us". But they relaxed and loosened rapidly and became amazingly frank. Many were eager to continue the interview to the point of missing classes, or to come a second and third time. They showed a genuine hunger for discussions as we had, but when urged to talk to their own professors immediately said, "We could *never* talk this way to our professors. They are too aloof; they wouldn't be interested."

Some groups were "mixed", but most preferred sex segregation. Those few groups that were mixed, as in Jadavpur University or Osmania Medical College—where they are used to being together —seemed quite at ease in the situation.

There was curiosity as regards the requested interview, and interest in matters discussed, but little evidence of thought or query. Almost every subject had to be offered, though several—as sex matters or job insecurity—obviously struck prime interest. There was rarely any response to such questions as "Have you any problems, in home or on campus, related to having ideas different from those of your elders ?" Many "problems" did emerge from further questions, but at first few students knew what was meant by "having a problem" or thought they had any. Many said, "There are no problems—we have to adjust to the situation". We suspect the more sophisticated students, however, saw no reason to air their lives with a total stranger !

Students were urged to ask us questions. This brought a pleased attitude, but there was limited response in most cases. Their queries usually related to "life in America", and tended to be on dating, courtship, marriage, divorce, a typical family day in America,. teen-agers, rock-and-roll music, juvenile delinquency, student indiscipline in America, cinema stars, university life, university examinations, and how one gets jobs in America. There were a few questions on the treatment of Negroes, a few on foreign policy (Dulles' remark on Goa has not been forgotten), a few on U.S. military aid to Pakistan. As regards questions we put to the students, highest interest was evinced on contact with the opposite sex, arranged *vs.* love marriages, individual rights, decision making, types of examinations, and student indiscipline.

The Groups Visited

We have responses from three groups in Madras State: Annamalai University, the Madras School of Social Work, and two miscellaneous friendship groups connected with the University of Madras. Annamalia University is a residential-teaching university situated in the rural heart of Tamilnad, south of Madras. Many students come from the villages, and are a relatively conservative and traditional group. Many are militantly "Tamil", and interest in politics is high. The girls are greatly outnumbered, and at least to outward appearances are much more "traditionally submissive" than the urban girls of the North. The students at the Madras School of Social Work, a post-graduate professional institution, are older, more experienced, and more urban. Like all students of social science, they demonstrated a keen awareness of social problems. The miscellaneous, relatively self-confident young men and women in the third group represent an urban, progressive middle class. They are by no means "typical" of the total population, but they are certainly destined to wield much power later. Madras is the largest urban area of "the conservative South". As such it is worldly by mofussil standards, "backward" by some Northern standards. Certainly the students reflect the strain set up between Hindu orthodoxy and "modern business" customs and values. In no city is there more cinema influence, for Madras is one of the chief centres of cinema production and distribution. Cinema "morals" are therefore also in opposition to conservative custom. "Accepted social custom" is considered "very strict", but there is much "illicit behaviour"—behaviour that would attract less attention in the major cities of the North.

Moving to West Bengal, students from Scottish Church College and St Xavier's College in Calcutta were distinctly sophisticated, urban, progressive. St Xavier's students seemed especially highly selected and brilliant. On the other hand, the girls at Bethune College, a Government college for women, were far from sophisticated and seemed naive and sheltered in their experience. Jadavpur University (where we interviewed but did not give questionnaires) is sometimes called the "Sarah Lawrence of India" (though it is coeducational). It is new, has small classes, is boldly trying experimental methods. As in all Calcutta groups visited we noticed a high degree of political interest. All these students of Calcutta differed from those of Visva-Bharati in Santiniketan—Tagore's rural university—who seemed dreamy and relaxed in comparison. But wherever we were in Bengal we found a passionate pride in being Bengali, and we heard "Bengali" much more than "Indian". Bengalis described themselves to us as "the most intellectual and artistic people in India", and certainly the legitimate theatre, Coffee House discussion groups, and radical societies of Calcutta attest to this fact. But, as some rather ruefully admitted, "We rarely carry through with our ideas. The Punjabis' discipline and devotion to work is something we should emulate. But what dull fellows they are !" Many seemed to care little whether they remained traditional or became modern, provided they remained Bengalis, argumentative and artistic. (They reminded us many times of Brooklyn College students.) "We are the best people in India. Do you know any others who enjoy life so much ?"

It is more difficult from our limited experience to characterize the students of Uttar Pradesh—in the College of Education in Hindu University of Banares, a residential-teaching university; the anthropology department of the University of Lucknow, a teaching and degree-granting university; and the science department of Kanja Kubja College, a degree college. Some of the Banares education students were militantly "Hindu" and "anti-white"; the anthropology students of the University of Lucknow demonstrated the excellent influence of the late Dr Majumdar, who knew each of his students well and who stimulated reflective discussion; the Kanja Kubja College students were naive in comparison, but they had a kind of fresh eagerness that was more innocence than ignorance. They were outside the excitement and controversy in which the University students were then embroiled—in connection with the November strikes and university closure. "We don't become easily aroused," one student said, "but when we are nothing will stop us." When asked to describe unique characteristics of people in the U.P., several explained their "home-loving qualities". "We don't like to move even 10 miles from our homes—even for good jobs. That is why it is so important to get rid of corruption here."

Partition severely affected the Punjab, however, and many were forced to take up life in a new area. The hard-working, skilful Punjabis have always been good farmers, and many made arid land become fruitful. Others moved with ease to mechanical trades or engineering. Methodical and disciplined, they seem content with slow but sure ways to get ahead, whether in an old way or new. The engineering students interviewed at Chandigarh were among the best groomed, quietly assured young men we observed. Many had come from homes of disruption or poverty but were confidently moving ahead to mend family fortunes through their own competence.

The urban Delhi students were among the more sophisticated, and revealed the anxieties and problems attendant to relative liberty in a cosmopolitan city. Lady Irwin College girls in Home Science felt they were "modern", but some complained that society would force them back into the traditional mould at marriage. Miranda House College of the University of Delhi, sometimes called "the Bryn Mawr of India", is known to have "the most fashionable and modern girls of India". Most were quietly assured of a reasonably good life at the top stratum of Indian society and were already enjoying "being themselves", though some expressed their frustration over the disparity of their current freedom and future restrictions.

The young men in the miscellaneous friendship group were even more frustrated, especially as regards "mixing with the girls" as they desired. Frequent visitors of the coffee houses and restaurants, they sat around in all-male groups, shifting back and forth from the subject of jobs to that of girls. "Isn't it the same in the U.S.?" one young man asked. We assured him that it was, except that young men could easily meet and associate with girls. "Then that's the country for me !" Social life, more than political or economic systems, seemed the most popular Western attraction.

Baroda, in Gujerat, reflects the advantages of one of the more fortunate areas of India—"in natural resources and in our long-established business-connected wealth". Gujeratis claim to be the best businessmen in India, "better than the Sindhis who are pushing their way in here (as the result of Partition), better even than the Marwaris". They seem to be a strange but congenial mixture of "orthodox" and "modern". Gujerati women are often quite extraordinary in their accomplishments, and lead in important ventures. Baroda University, where we visited the Departments of Education-Psychology and Home Science, justly deserves its reputation of being "a bright spot in Indian higher education". Under excellent leadership it believes in experiment and change in the interests of sound education.

Few Bombay residents "would live anywhere else", so great is their appreciation of urban amenities and opportunities. As in other large cities, class lines are supplanting caste, and economic power is in the ascendancy. The students we saw were among the upper middle class, scornful of "student indiscipline that just makes trouble", keenly conscious of the increasing competitiveness of successful life. "None of us feels secure now. It's unsettling, but perhaps we have to go through this stage. I'd really rather depend on my own ability than on my family's influence—but the trouble is that ability doesn't always count yet. So—we worry—".

Hyderabad, like other interior areas, is on the conservative side of the social spectrum. Osmania University, where we visited students in the Women's College (a separate campus), the College of Education (interviews only), the College of Medicine (interviews only), and the Colleges of Science and Engineering, reflects the recent history of this troubled area. Partition, the Police Action (when India took over the Native State), and the formation of Andhra Pradesh brought radical power and prestige changes. The Muslims, once in virtual control, now suffer discrimination, and at present the Harijans are said to have the favoured position— partly because the Chief Minister is a Harijan. English, Telegu, Kanada, Marathi, Urdu, Hindi, Tamil, and Malayali are all spoken, and schools in various language media are necessary. Despite the varied composition of the populace, however, there seems to be an over-riding love of Hyderabad as a cultural centre. We found little interest in other areas of India or the world.

Generalizing about types of institutions, we conclude the largest are the more impersonal and, in human terms, less satisfying. The smaller institutions, especially the residential type, have higher morale and loyalty. Those that select students with the highest academic ability reflect the highest morale. Their students look to the future with some confidence and find little need to indulge in "adolescent nonsense". Those institutions, as the Universities of Bombay and Madras, that have resisted political control seem freer from intrigue and indiscipline-connected difficulties, though all reflect the background power struggle—in Madras there is a strong anti-Brahmin movement, in Hyderabad it is the Muslim that is challenged. In some universities there is active obstruction to intellectual improvement, in most "there is no obstruction but intellectual achievement is difficult". Very few have the intellectual leadership of Baroda University or the University of Madras.

Most girls seem happier in girls' colleges than in coeducational institutions ("this isn't really coeducational here—it is a man's college but they permit us to attend"). They feel freer and have more opportunities for extra-curricular activities and leadership. The students in medicine and engineering, in contrast to most others, seem content with their curriculum and studies—what they are doing makes sense to them in terms of the future, and jobs are certain. But most Indian university students are frustrated and cynical. They know they *must* get a degree, however disagreeable the method. "One must have an education nowadays. And, anyway, what else is there to do ?"

Altogether, Indian students are like all students in their varied response to university life. Some hate it and are contemptuous of both the institution and its methods. But the majority are grateful and appreciative, and seem fully conscious of the fact that they are enjoying privileges new to the society. A few of the more perceptive, their degrees won, ask whether this education really constitutes progress. "My generation," a modern young married woman reflected, "with all its degrees hasn't half the common sense, the *wisdom*, of our grandparents' generation. They really understood life and people—but we stuff our minds with useless facts."

With respect to following data, we call attention to several items. The youngest students were in Scottish Church and St Xavier's Colleges of Calcutta, the oldest in the post-graduate Madras School of Social Work and the College of Education at Banares. 10/28 students at Banares were married, 6/12 at Visva-Bharati, very few at other institutions. Joint families outnumbered separate families at Annamalai (21-14), the Science College at Hyderabad, and the U.P.—Banares (25-3), Lucknow (12-2), and Kanja Kubja (13-7). But at other institutions the respondents

TABLE 4

DATA ON RESPONDENTS

Number of respondents

	Madras			Delhi			Baroda		Bombay				West Bengal		U.P.			Hyderabad			Total
	Ann.	MSSW	Misc.	Mir.	L.I.	Misc.	Ed-Ps	H.S.	Sc. Ch.	St. X.	Elph.	Misc.	V-Bh.	Beth.	Ban.	Luck.	K.K.	Wom.	Sc.	Eng.	Total
Men	25	10	19			19	4		22	22	4	21	10		21	14	18		12	13	234
Women	10	3	6	26	24		15	19	5		13		2	21	7	..	2	16		1	170
Total	35	13	25	26	24	19	19	19	27	22	17	21	12	21	28	14	20	16	12	14	404

Age		Marital status		Type family		Geography²	
Range : 15-34		Single	360	Joint	142	Large city	162
Average : 20.5		Married	23	Separate	261	Small city	133
						Town	54
						Village	55

² Very loosely applied. Large cities: Madras, Calcutta, Delhi, Bombay.

Religion		Caste[3]		Father's occupation[4]		Mother's occupation[5]
Hindu	338	Brahmin	127	Business & Indus.	113	3
Christian	22	Kshatriya	31	IAS, Govt. Serv.	80	1
Sikh	17	Kayasta	26	Farming	45	..
Muslim	14	Vaisya	24	Engineering	27	..
Zoroastrian	4			Medicine	27	7
Jew	2			Law	21	..
Brahmo Samaj	2			Educ. Lower	21	16
Arya Samaj	2			Educ. Higher	20	6
Jain	1			Armed Forces	16	
				Miscellaneous: scientist, craftsman, clerk, banker, pastor, policeman, journalist.		

Parent's education[6]	M	F	Subject specialization	M	F	Total
Post-graduate	103	9	Science & Math.	82	35	117
B.A. or equiv.	134	47	Social Sciences	62	31	93
Inter	42	21	Humanities, Arts	35	35	70
Normal	2	3	Education	25	24	49
Secondary	69	95	Home Science		43	43
Elementary	24	77	Engineering	21	2	23
Primary	14	57	Medicine	5	..	5
Private	2	15				
None	8	74				

Anticipated career	M	F	Total	
Education[7]	40	49	89	
Engineering	56	4	60	
IAS, Govt. Services	40	4	44	
Medicine	19	15	34	
Social work	7	17	25	
Household	..	14	14	
Business & Industry	13	..	13	
Journalism	6	4	10	Miscellaneous: Indian Foreign
Law	6	3	9	Service, science, writing, architec-
Politics	5	..	5	ture, Armed Forces, further study.

[3] Few responded. Data applies to recognizable responses.

[4] It was impossible to separate "Indian Administrative Services" and "Government Services".

[5] In addition to household work.

[6] Very loosely applied. Much data was difficult to interpret.

[7] Both "higher" and "lower". Some definitely indicated "higher".

represented more separate families, as, for instance, the Madras
School of Social Work (1-12), Lady Irwin College (1-23), Miranda
House (5-21), and Elphinstone College (2-15). The rural interior
areas are naturally the more traditional.

Data on the number of siblings in the family could not be used
because of differing responses. It was obvious that some counted
all the siblings in the *joint* family. We can only conclude that the
average number of children per family in the rural areas is high—
perhaps around 5 or 6—and that the average number in urban
families is lower.

All the women students reported wearing saris or salwars—the
latter fashion is gaining ground in the North. Most of the men
students wear "European shirts and trousers", though some in
Annamalai, Calcutta, and Banares wear the dhoti all or part of
the time.

Data on pocket money is uncertain, for some students reported
allowances including fee and board money. It is clear that in most
residential institutions students need from Rs. 75-150 per month,
and Rs. 1,000 was frequently quoted as an annual sum. Personal
pocket money varies from "nil" to Rs. 60 per month, Rs. 10-15 a
common figure. It is interesting to note that there is a trend toward
a definite weekly or monthly allowance, and students reported that
only a few go by the old system of asking for what they need—and do
not like it. In some institutions pocket money is directly translated
into cinema tickets, and much theft is related to the underprivileged
students' desire to see as many cinemas as their friends. In other
institutions pocket money relates more to new clothes and acces-
sories. This is true not only of the girls—boys want smart blazers,
cigarettes, and cigarette lighters. Very little is spent for food and
drink, though campus coffee houses are becoming more popular.

The majority of students are urban and have educated parents.
In these families higher education is a status and career necessity.
In the less privileged families education is seen as a new opportunity.
23/35 students at Annamalai, for instance, come from villages, and
in this group only a few fathers and no mothers had higher education,
whereas several fathers and 13 mothers had no education. Kanja
Kubja College and Osmania University students also had a low
percentage of parents with higher education. On the other hand,
parents of students at Scottish Church College, St Xavier's College,
Lady Irwin, and Miranda House had a high percentage.

The highest number of farmer fathers is at Annamalai (24/35) and Banares (9/25); the highest number in business and industry is in institutions at Bombay and Calcutta; the highest number in the Indian Administrative Services is in Delhi. We were told at Banares that the son of a sweeper was in Education honours, a peon's son in Engineering.

The great majority of student respondents are Hindu, the largest group of Christians recorded in Madras (where there are many Syrian Christians from Kerala), the largest number of Sikhs in Delhi, the largest number of Muslims in Hyderabad. We hesitated to ask about caste, knowing it is an offensive question to many— and many did refuse to respond. We recorded the castes we could categorize, but were told firmly by several Indian colleagues not to trust the responses—"especially if it is 'Brahmin'."

It is interesting to see the ranking of fathers' occupations in contrast to anticipated careers of students. Despite the fact that some students are unrealistic in their hopes (several plan to be doctors without the training), and despite the fact that many young men will ultimately join their fathers in business, the departure from "hereditary occupations" is marked, the shift toward the professions clear. Few mothers are reported to have careers outside of their home duties, but the number of working middle class women is rising, and many women students anticipate outside work.

Students' Contact with the Larger World

We include in the data some indication of the students contact with other cultures—and the resultant influence as they feel it.

With respect to following data, it is not surprising that few have been outside India (the largest number refers to pre-Partition Pakistan), but the number that have travelled extensively in India is significant. This is a growing trend, and most students expressed their desire to "see India and the world".

The U.S. outranks the U.K. in "felt influence", and West Germany just noses out the U.S.S.R.

No one observing India today will be surprised to see the place of the cinema, with other mass media outranking people. Western influence has been greatest in "dress" and "reading" for the men, "reading" and "ideas on marriage" for the women.

TABLE 5

TRAVEL

Travel	Rank	Total %
Outside India:		
Pakistan	1	5
Ceylon	2	3
Africa	3	2
Europe	5	1
Malaya	5	1
U.S., Canada	5	1
Misc.: Burma, Nepal		
Much in India	32%	
Some in India	30%	
Very little	12%	

TABLE 6

GREATEST NFLUENCING NATION

Nations greatest in their influence on me (Open-ended)	Rank	Total %
U.S.A.	1	74
U.K.	2	67
West Germany	3	19
U.S.S.R.	4	18
France	5	12
Switzerland	6.5	3
Japan	6.5	3
China	8.5	2
Italy	8.5	2
None		8

TABLE 7

CONTACT WITH WESTERN CULTURE

My contact with Western Culture has come through[8]	Rank	Total %	Comparison	
			Male %	Female %
Cinemas	1	84	94	69
Books, magazines	2	67	100	20
Radio	3	66	68	62
Western professors	4	39	40	38
Western friends	5	34	30	38
U.S. Information Service	6	28	34	18
Correspondence	7	18	18	17
Travel	8	7	5	9

Misc. write-ins: friends and relatives abroad, visitors, British Information Service, U.S.S.R. Information Service, missionaries.

TABLE 8

INFLUENCE OF WESTERN CULTURE

en influenced by Western Culture in my	Rank	Total %	Comparison	
			Male %	Female %
Reading	1	76	80	69
Dress	2	55	80	18
Social customs	3	44	45	42
Ideas on marriage	4	38	31	46
Political ideas	5	34	45	18
Music preferences	6	29	27	31
Food and drink	7	27	22	34
Religious ideas	8	15	16	13

[8] Unless indicated as "open-ended", it was a multiple-choice question. Male, female, and total percentages are given, computed to the nearest per cent. We shall include items beyond significant ranking because of their interest.

TABLE 9

ASPECTS OF WESTERN CULTURE I DISLIKE

Aspects of Western Culture I dislike and do not want for myself are (Open-ended)	Rank	Total %	Comparison	
			Male %	Female %
System of marriage	1	20	18	22
Women's dress, cosmetics	2	17	11	26
Divorce	3	14	11	19
Drinking	4	11	12	9
Emphasis on sex	5	10	8	12
Materialism	6	8	10	5
Some social customs	7	7	8	6
Food and drink, esp. meat	8.5	6	6	6
Kissing (in public)	8.5	6	5	6
Smoking, esp. women	10.5	5	4	6
Dancing	10.5	5	3	6
Colour prejudice	14.5	4	5	4
Music, esp. rock-and-roll	14.5	4	4	4
Patronizing attitude	14.5	4	6	1
Imperialism	14.5	4	4	3
Religious ideas	14.5	4	3	5
Lake of family life	14.5	4	5	2
Freedom of children	18	3	2	4
Crime, delinquency	19.5	2	2	1
Individualism	19.5	2	1	2
No dislikes		5	7	3
Not concerned		4	3	2

Misc.: night clubs, teen-age marriage, no respect for the aged, too much formality, extravagance, irreligious nature, no peace of mind.

TABLE 10

ASPECTS OF WESTERN CULTURE I ADMIRE

Aspects of Western Culture I admire and want for myself (open-ended)	Rank	Total %	Comparison Male %	Female %
Some social customs	1	12	13	11
Education system	3	11	9	14
Manners, courtesy	3	11	9	14
Friendliness, sociability	3	11	10	11
Dress, esp. male	5	10	13	5
System of marriage	6	9	11	7
Love of freedom	7	8	6	9
Books and magazines	9	7	7	7
Discipline	9	7	6	7
Freedom and status of women	9	7	3	11
Dignity of labour[9]	12.5	6	6	6
Political ideas—democracy	12.5	6	9	2
Broadmindedness	12.5	6	6	5
Social, civic consciousness	12.5	6	5	6
Free mixing of sexes, dating	16.5	5	7	2
Food and drink, ways of serving	16.5	5	3	6
Frankness, candour, ease of speaking	16.5	5	5	3
Hard work	16.5	5	4	5
Equality—sexes, classes	23	4	5	2
Punctuality	23	4	4	4
Humanitarian international relations	23	4	6	2
Standard of living	23	4	5	2
Vitality, zest, sense of adventure	23	4	4	5
Honesty, love of truth	23	4	5	2
Importance of individual	23	4	5	2
Music	23	4	3	4
Progressive industrial society	23	4	5	1
Family life, cooperation men & women	28.5	3	2	4
Economic opportunities for all	28.5	3	3	2
Intelligence, energetic mind	31	2	3	1
Religious ideas	31	2	1	4
Efficiency	31	2	1	2
Nothing		5	5	4

Misc.: Lack of inferiority complex, sense of fairness, honest government, dancing, art, cinemas, courage, sense of humor, parent-child relationships, freedom of children, respect for elders, homes (esp. the kitchens), cleanliness.

[9] "Dignity of labour" refers to the willingness to work at anything, especially in connection with manual labour.

The students' prime interest—social matters, especially in relation to sex and marriage—is reflected in aspects of Western culture disliked, politics scarcely showing. Banares and Visva-Bharati were high in scorning "materialism", and all the responses labelled "not in the least concerned" came from the Banares group. Annamalai was generally against Western marriage; St Xavier's did not mention it. But Annamalai had only one response against divorce, whereas Miranda House girls were 10/26 against it— probably because it is a reality in their lives. Bethune, Lady Irwin, Miranda House, and Baroda Home Science girls were somewhat against Western dress and cosmetics, the more conservative girls did not mention them. There was some inconsistency between responses in "disliked" and "admired"—for instance, several who were against the Western system of marriage came out for "free mixing of sexes".

It is impossible to know what students mean by "some social customs", though in interview they indicated this meant "freer mixing, more friendliness, greater freedom". The girls are impressed with Western manners (though it was a young man who told us he had learned to say "please" and "thank you" from Americans), the education system, and friendliness; the boys with Western dress, social customs and the system of marriage. Oddly, Annamalai, which had many responses against Western marriage also ranked high in favour of it—whereas Lady Irwin and Miranda girls neglected the subject. The more "progressive families" are no doubt enjoying greater liberality on this matter now. Miranda ranked highest in yearning for "friendliness", St Xavier's boys for "free mixing of the sexes". Few were interested in "political ideas—democracy" and "social, civic consciousness" outside of the more politically-minded Annamalai students. Banares accounted for most of the score on "nothing to admire".

It is natural that the girls are concerned with the freedom and status of women. As one young lady from Delhi wrote, "I admire the West because girls of my age (18) stand on their own feet, so that they have to think, act, and decide matters themselves. This definitely makes them better individuals."

The impression we receive from this data is that Indian students are more knowledgeable and perceptive as regards the West than they have generally been credited. There is much ignorance, and some students rank Pat Boone above the President, Hollywood above New York, but we detect little stereotyping, much sensitive differentiation. Those Western qualities not admired are generally those causing social and psychological trouble in the West; those qualities admired are those usually viewed with pride.

It is clear that students in those institutions which have enjoyed the presence of Western students, professors, and their families have the most human and realistic views—perhaps in this sense the "personal" is more significant than the "mass media" contact. In spite of the cinemas and cheap literature there is a somewhat balanced and rational perception of Western ways of life. Certainly the students of India are not slaves of propaganda.

4 | *The Indian Family Changes*

THE family, basic biological-political-economic-religious-social unit, undergirds any society, and a nation's cohesion or disintegration relates directly to its structure and values. Certainly no other institution so determines the good or ill health of a society and its individual members. For the most part the family tends to be conservative and thus has a stabilizing influence. But it always responds to political and economic changes in the larger society. It is functional only to the extent that it constitutes the kind of basic unit the structure of society needs.

In the history of any people, thus, we see how the nomadic-pastoral way of life changed to the rooted, feudal, early agriculture and crafts economy. Then towns and trade drew people to business and commerce, and agriculture became scientific, requiring fewer but more highly educated farmers. When advanced industry developed, the cities became the loci of power. The self-sufficient, monarchial clan thus changed to the patriarchal farm family, "low status" and dependent in many ways—but also independent in basic life necessities and in thought. It was the broad base of society, its power secure until the rising middle class usurped its foundational position. As a group it became economically and educationally backward, and farmers' sons began to demand *mobility*, began to want to be different from their fathers in occupation and status. Education and new economic opportunities made that possible, so some youth struck out, leaving their families behind them. They found new authorities in schools, factories, governments; they found new peers in classrooms, labour unions, professional organizations, social associations, political parties. So—clans break up, patriarchs lose their power. Each separate

60

family stands on its own feet, each individual tries to find and make his role instead of inherit it. India reflects this shift from joint to separate family, especially in the cities. It is a fact both rued and welcomed, but it is a fact. Joint families have been more "good" than "bad" in past centuries, but they become more like "prisons" and less like "social security units" as India changes its political and economic patterns.

Our student respondents largely represent the "progressive families", where many changes had taken place before Independence.

TABLE 11

THINGS PERMITTED TO ME AS A CHILD

As a child, up to about the age of 12, I was permitted to[1]	Rank	Total %	Comparison	
			Male %	Female %
Play with children of any caste or class	1	79**	80	76
Play with children of the opposite sex	2	76*	78	71
Go outside unaccompanied	3	69—	70	65
Choose my own clothes	4	41	39	43
Speak freely in front of adults	5	38—	35	42
Spend some money as I chose	6	33	31	35

TABLE 12

FREEDOM IN ADOLESCENCE

When I was adolescent I had	Rank	Total %	Comparison	
			Male %	Female %
More freedom	1	53*	66	34
The same freedom	2	39	29	51
Less freedom	3	14	7	23

This freedom was	Rank	Total %	Comparison	
			Male %	Female %
More than my parents had	1	48*	22	82
About the same	2	24	26	20
Less than they had	3	6	5	5

I hope to raise my children	Rank	Total %	Comparison	
			Male %	Female %
With more freedom	1	47**	49	43
As I was raised	2	39*	37	42
With less freedom	3	3	3	3

[1] Male and female ranks will not be given unless significant.
* The number of plusses indicates the number who *double*-plussed this item
— The number of minuses indicates the number who *double*-minused the item
This "strength of agreement or disagreement" does not always fit ranking.

TABLE 13
DUTIES AT HOME IN CHILDHOOD

When I was a child my duties in the home were	Rank	Total %	Comparison	
			Male %	Female %
Helping mother in the household	1	47	33	64
Taking care of my own clothes	2	45	35	58
Shopping and errands	3	36	45	22
Taking care of younger children	4	27	21	35
Helping father with his work	5	26	33	16
None	6	8	9	6

Misc.: my studies, reading.

TABLE 14
FORM OF PUNISHMENT AT HOME

The usual punishment in my home was	Rank	Total %	Comparison	
			Male %	Female %
Scolding	1	45	48	39
Beating	2	38	46	25
Forbidden to go out and play	3	35	35	34
Denied sweets or toys	4.5	13	13	13
Put alone in the room	4.5	13	10	15
None	6	6	6	4

Misc. write-ins: no affection (12 responses), given advice (16), denied food.

TABLE 15
REWARD FOR GOOD BEHAVIOUR

The usual reward for good behaviour was	Rank	Total %	Comparison	
			Male %	Female %
Praise	1	75*	73	77
Sweets	2	28	27	28
Smiling elders (write-in)	3	8	9	6
Gifts (write-in)	4	5	5	4
None (write-in)	5	2	2	2

Misc. write-ins: gentle embrace, special freedoms, "nothing expected, nothing received".

TABLE 16
OBSERVATION OF CEREMONIES

We observed the following family ceremonies [2]	Rank	Total %
Birthdays	1	76
Cradle and naming	2	63
Entering school	3	55
Shaving hair	4	48
Ear-piercing	5	40
Sacred cord (for boys)	6	35
Puberty (for girls)	7	15

Misc. write-ins: grandfather's day, parents 60th birthday, first food.

When I have a family I hope to celebrate	Rank	Total %	Comparison	
			Male %	Female %
The same ceremonies	1	33	33	34
Fewer ceremonies	2	32	34	28
More ceremonies	3	15	11	19
Abolish all ceremonies (write-in)	4	3	4	0

All the items in childhood freedoms are in opposition to most conservative Indian tradition, but the scoring was relatively even in the different groups. Strong opinion is reflected in the double-plusses and bitterness in the double-minuses—it is obvious that most of the students believe in social interaction with different castes, classes, and sex, and that some were not permitted to go out unaccompanied or speak freely in front of adults. In interviews we asked about freedom of expression, and one young lady spoke for many when she said, "Not in front of my grandmother!" Interview data tallied with questionnaire data in agreement that the freedom of children is greater than that in the past—and less than in the future !

In the item about "duties", many students left the entire item blank, indicating they had no duties. We recorded only the write-ins for "none". In interviews also, many students said they had had no duties, and several said, "But why should we—unless the family is terribly poor ? It is our parents' duty to do all these things in

[2] In addition to ceremonies connected with birth, marriage, death.

the home. Our turn will come later." Others argued against the statement, insisting that modern homes should be "democratic" in work as well as in decision-making. It is natural that boys should score highest in "shopping and errands", girls in "helping mother".

Punishment ranked higher than rewards in questionnaire totals and in interviews. Some said, "I'm afraid there's always more punishment. We are expected to be good and aren't rewarded for it." Note the significant write-ins: smiling elders, advice. We questioned "beating", having the impression that this is not a common punishment in India. We are now convinced it is, but it often consists of a slap, not so frequently a "spanking". "Beating" in anyone's language, however, is very common in schools, especially in punishing boys. (Many American Fulbright children in India have discovered this fact.)

Family ceremonies are an important part of family life—always more popular with the women than with the men. The data indicates much approval of them but also that many intend to have fewer or "to abolish them all". Some girls told us that they approved of all the ceremonies but that they knew they could not continue them. "It is one thing in a joint family where there are many women to prepare for them, many men to pay for them—but quite another thing in a busy, separate family."

TABLE 17

TYPE OF RECREATION ENJOYED BY MY FAMILY

My family enjoys the recreations	Rank	Total %
Visiting friends or relatives	1	73*
The cinema	2	71*
Music	3	70*
Reading	4	57*
Outings	5	56*
Story-telling	6.5	52
Sports	6.5	52
Going to parks	8	43
Playing cards	9	39
Going to clubs	10	25
The Ram Lila	11	22
Radio (write-in)	12	6

TABLE 18
TYPE OF RECREATION ENJOYED BY ME

I myself enjoy	Rank	Total %	Comparison	
			Male %	Female %
Reading	1	90**	90	89
The cinema	2	86**	88	81
Music	3	81**	78	82
Visiting friends or relatives	4	68*	66	68
Sports	5	65*	69	55
Outings	6	61*	55	68
Going to parks	7	45	45	45
Going to clubs	8	40	45	32
Playing cards	9	37	40	31
Story-telling	10	30	24	39
The Ram Lila	11	18	20	16

Misc. write-ins: radio, social service, meeting foreigners, politics, discussions travelling.

TABLE 19
TYPE OF FILMS ENJOYED BY ME

With respect to the cinema I enjoy	Rank	Total %	Comparison	
			Male %	Female %
Modern social drama	1	74**	74	73
The music	2	65*	64	65
Foreign films of adventure	3	60*	58	61
Foreign films about love	4	39*	35	43
Indian classical	5	35	32	39
Crime (write-in)	6	6	10	0

TABLE 20

MY FAVOURITE LEISURE READING

My favourite kinds of leisure reading are	Rank	Total %	Comparison	
			Male %	Female %
Modern Indian fiction	1	57*	52	59
Foreign adventure stories	2	50*	50	48
Science fiction	3	47*	51	39
Foreign love stories	4	45	36	56
Indian classical stories	5	41	37	47
Modern political writing	6	33	43	19
Detective (write-in)	7	8	10	4

Recreation plays an important part in Indian family life, and most of it is enjoyed "as a family", modern clubs and card-playing tending to draw the adults away from the group, sports the young people. It is common for women and children to attend the 3.30 P.M. cinema, for men to attend the evening showing; not many families go together, but they do discuss the cinemas at home together. Many attend a favourite picture time after time.

"Visiting friends or relatives" scores the highest on family recreation, but the cinema and music are strong challengers. "Radio" should have been a write-in, but is the *medium* for most of the music. The generational shift is interesting. Reading and sports go up, visiting and story-telling go down.

Cinema themes indicate the prime position of "modern social drama", the relatively low position of "Indian classical"—extremely popular a decade ago. "Crime" should have been a printed item, as should also "detective stories" in reading preferences. One student objected to the word "foreign", and wrote, "Love and adventure can never be foreign—they become one's own story".

We wish we had separated "books" and "magazines" in the items listed. It is our strong impression, verified during interviews, that most of the reading relates to periodicals. Many gave me as their "favourite" or "only" reading *The Illustrated Weekly of India*. As for "books", most of them are paper-back detective and science fiction. Indian students are not as yet "great readers", whatever their listing here seems to indicate. Very few have access to much, and libraries are scarce, inadequate, and difficult to use. Where there is good reading material available—as in good university libraries or the U.S. Information Service libraries—the students make good use of it.

TABLE 21

THINGS CAUSING HAPPINESS IN CHILDHOOD

As a small child I was especially happy when	Rank	Total %	Comparison	
			Male %	Female %
Category 1: in relation to family membership and autonomy in family				
Praised, appreciated (esp. in front of others)	1	24	27	19
Family festivals, ceremonies	2	13	14	12
When elders listened to me, when allowed to do as I wished	3.5	8	9	5
In presence of mother, father, family	3.5	8	5	11
Parents showed affection, love	5.5	7	8	5
Relatives or friends visited	5.5	7	7	6
Parents or father came home	8	5	3	8
Helping parents	9	2	2	2
Parents not fighting	9	2	3	1
Family was happy	9	2	2	1
Category 2: in relation to pleasure				
Playing with friends	1	28	30	23
Family had outings	2	21	20	22
Given gifts, sweets, books, clothes	3	20	15	27
Reading, hearing stories	4.5	5	5	4
Travelling or visiting	4.5	5	7	1
Doing something well	6	3	4	2
Going to cinemas	8	2	3	1
Singing, hearing music	8	2	2	1
Alone	8	2	1	3
Category 3: in relation to school				
Made good marks, when first in class	1	7	3	11
Rewarded in school	2	4	5	2
Entered school	4	2	1	4
Passed examinations	4	2	3	0
Had no studies, holidays	4	2	2	1
Leader of my circle at school	6	1	2	1
Leading items in all 3 categories				
Playing with friends	1	28	30	23
Praised, appreciated	2	24	27	19
Family had outings	3	21	21	22
Given gifts, sweets, books, clothes	4	20	15	27

Misc. additional items: when in school, when commanding my friends, anticipating festivals, mother made special food for me, when sent to hills for vacation, when came home from boarding school, when taken to Temple, when sharing sweets, making new friends, with Grandfather, helping teacher, not beaten for a mistake, running barefoot in the rain.

TABLE 22

THINGS CAUSING UNHAPPINESS IN CHILDHOOD

And unhappy when (open-ended)	Rank	Total %	Comparison	
			Male %	Female %
Category 1: *autonomy in relation to family*				
Scolded, punished in front of others	1	35	29	41
Not allowed to play	2	13	12	12
Not allowed to do as wished	3	11	13	6
Ignored, not listened to	4.5	5	6	3
Unjustly blamed, punished	4.5	5	5	4
Made to do something disliked	6.5	4	6	1
Not allowed to play with *my* friends	6.5	4	4	4
Beaten	8	3	4	1
Not allowed freedom	10	2	3	0
Denied sweets, food of choice	10	2	3	0
Work not appreciated, given due credit	10	2	3	0
Category 2: *family membership*				
Parents were quarrelling	1	9	11	6
Family unhappy, someone suffering	2	5	3	6
A family member died	3	3	4	1
Father or someone went away	6	2	2	3
Mother or father was unkind	6	2	3	1
I hurt my parents' feelings	6	2	1	2
Brother or sister was punished	6	2	2	1
I lost some family article	6	2	2	1
I had to leave my parents	10	1	1	1
Neglected by mother or father	10	1	1	1
Too much poverty, hunger	10	1	2	0
Category 3: *as an individual*				
Alone	1	5	3	7
Ill	2	3	3	4
Saw others suffering, begging	2.5	2	1	3
I quarrelled with friends	2.5	2	1	3
Category 4: *in school*				
Forced to study	1	5	3	6
Had bad marks, wasn't first	2	3	2	4
Leading items in all categories				
Scolded, punished	1	35	29	41
Not allowed to play	2	13	12	12
Not allowed to do as wished	3	11	13	6
Parents were quarrelling	4	9	11	6

Misc. additional items: Parents didn't love me, when among grown-ups, when father came home on leave, when in school, when I failed my exams, when teacher rejected my opinion, when I had nothing to do.

How much students' reading preferences are influenced by their family reading habits and preferences we do not know. We did have an open-ended question on favourite childhood stories, but could not categorize many of the titled responses. Fairy stories, Indian epics, folk tales, fables, English classics, stories of great heroes, local classics, and stories of adventure, love, or crime all featured, somewhat in the order given. Some students made it clear that most of these stories were "told" and not "read".

TABLE 23

THINGS CAUSING FRIGHT IN CHILDHOOD

| | | | Comparison | |
I had a childish fear of	Rank	Total %	Male %	Female %
The dark	1	36	33	39
Ghosts	2	32*	30	35
Snakes	3	31*	25	38
Burglars	4.5	26	18	35
Nothing	4.5	26	30	19

Misc. write-ins: dogs, drunkards, insects, death, the devil, madmen, Sikhs, the future.

TABLE 24

THINGS I IMAGINED IN CHILDHOOD

| | | | Comparison | |
I sometimes imagined	Rank	Total %	Male %	Female %
Becoming a famous artist, musician, painter, dancer	1	47**	45	48
Rescuing member of family from danger	2	41	46	34
Becoming a famous political leader	3	30*	36	19
Dying	4	24	15	30
Becoming very ill	5	23	15	34
Running away from home	6	20	21	18
Being a famous sannyasi (n)	7.5	15*	7	21
Being a boy instead of a girl	7.5	15*	0	36
Being a girl instead of a boy	9	5	9	0

Misc. write-ins: being a famous sportsman, being a famous philosopher, being a famous writer, being a famous scholar, being a famous orator, being a famous doctor, being an engineer, being a social reformer, being a scientist, being a professor.

Subjective memory is always revealing. We know of no generally accepted theory as regards the richness or meagreness of childhood memories, though there is some indication that the subconscious drops what one wants to forget. Many people remember a great deal, with many specific incidents, many colourful pictures; others retain only vague impressions. But both the richness and the scantiness are significant in analysing emotional life. Most of the students we interviewed seemed to have few memories. "I was just a child—mostly happy I think." "I can't remember whether I was unhappy or happy—the days were much alike."

We note the importance of family relationships in "happy" and "unhappy" memories. "Play" is high, "school" is low. Autonomy and achievement are low in happy memories, but lack of autonomy is sharply reflected in unhappy memories. There is much conflict between the "individual self" and the "family member". One young man from St Xavier's College spoke for many others in resentment of pampered treatment. "I was the only grandson in the whole joint family and was pampered, spoiled, and doted upon like a prize hen or cuckoo. I didn't need more freedom, even in adolescence. But I hope to raise my children with much more care and pains than my parents could take for me. Heaven knows they did their best, but I wish I had learned more and had not had such a pampered existence. I jolly well wish that my parents had made me learn five or six languages and that I had been given chores. I should have been taught to be social and polished—and most of all to do my own work."

Childish fears are strong, with many more girls recording their fears than boys. The fantasy life is typical in most ways, though "fame" is probably higher and "running away from home" lower than among American children. The place of political leadership in India's recent history is reflected, as is India's respect for the religious sannyasi or sannyasin.

The sex-role wish is extremely interesting to us. It has always been "normal" in India for some boys and men to have female-identification. Sri Ramakrishna, priest of Kali, for instance, was female-oriented from childhood to death—and was considered a saint, not a neurotic. This orientation may seem strange in a culture which has long subjected women, but it is consistent with the *prime* position of woman in Indian ideology. The worship of "mother" and the idealization of "pure, noble womanhood" is almost uniquely Hindu in its strength and pervasiveness.[3] On the other hand, it is new to have girls wish they were boys. As girls are mixing and competing more with boys, this trend is natural.

TABLE 25
ATTITUDE TO DECISIONS BY PARENTS

When my father made decisions regarding me	Rank	Total %	Comparison	
			Male %	Female %
I sometimes opposed him	1	55*	55	54
I never opposed him	2	33*	39	24
I often opposed him	3	6	8	4

When my mother made decisions regarding me	Rank	Total %	Comparison	
			Male %	Female %
I sometimes opposed her	1	63*	58	69
I never opposed her	2	20	24	14
I often opposed her	3	11	11	11

TABLE 26
FREQUENCY OF QUARRELS WITH BROTHERS AND SISTERS

With my brothers and sisters	Rank	Total %	Comparison	
			Male %	Female %
I sometimes quarrelled	1	75	74	74
I often quarrelled	2	17	13	22
I never quarrelled	3	9	9	8

TABLE 27
NATURE OF QUARRELS

Our quarrels were usually about	Rank	Total %	Comparison	
			Male %	Female %
Silly childish matters of no importance	1	76*	74	78
Things that were very serious to me	2	17*	15	19

[3] This is a subject we treat fully in our former research study, *The Hindu Woman*.

TABLE 28
SETTLEMENT OF QUARRELS

These quarrels were usually settled by	Rank	Total %	Comparison	
			Male %	Female %
Ourselves	1	62*	53	66
Mother	2	37*	39	34
Father	3	31	36	24

TABLE 29
PERSON CLOSEST TO ME IN THE FAMILY

In my family I felt closest to	Rank	Total %	Comparison	
			Male %	Female %
Mother	1	62***	62	61
Father	2	48*	48	46
Sister	3	31*	29	34
Brother	4	28*	33	20
Auntie	5	10	10	9

Misc. Write-ins: grandfather, grandmother, all.

TABLE 30
OPINION REGARDING ASSOCIATION WITH MEMBERS OF OPPOSITE SEX

In my opinion, adolescent boys and girls, about 12-16	Rank	Total %	Comparison	
			Male %	Female %
Should be allowed to meet or associate with members of the opposite sex, *with supervision*	1	67**	61	73
Should be allowed to do so freely, *without supervision*	2	31**	37	23
Should *not* be allowed to do so	3	8	8	9

TABLE 31
PERSON TAKING IMPORTANT FAMILY DECISIONS

In my family the major family decisions were made by	Rank	Total %	Comparison	
			Male %	Female %
Father	1	69*	65	66
Mother	2	38	33	42
All adult members	3	22	24	18
Grandmother	4	16	14	19
Grandfather	5	8	10	5
Caste panchayat	6	1	1	0

There is considerable opposition to parents—according to interview and other evidence this is a growing trend, *even with the girls*. There is more opposition to the mother than the father, perhaps because she is easier to oppose, but from 150 responses we conclude she is the chief authority figure in the home. And Grandmother outranks Grandfather ! The "pampered" St Xavier's student did not always get his way. "There was really no need to oppose father, but I did because I saw some things more clearly. He did refuse to let me attend the elite Presidency College. As for my mother, poor girl, she never made many decisions regarding me ! But I oppose her because she won't let me offer my girl-friend a lift to classes. My parents refuse to give me a car for this reason —and it's three miles !"

Contrary to some opinion, Indian children quarrel with each other frequently, and as with most children the quarrels are usually not serious and are settled among themselves. But many respondents indicated their "shame and sorrow" in having quarrelled. "I was so unhappy—really I just wanted to love them and have them love me. I don't know why we quarrelled. Perhaps we didn't have enough other things to do."

Closeness to mother scored high and is obviously an emotional matter. We do not know what "closeness" means, however, and welcome further inquiry. It is our impression that

1. There are many mother-son complexes.[4]
2. There are some father-daughter complexes.
3. There is much role-identification, girls with mothers, boys with fathers—but probably less than before.
4. Most young people "respect" their elders, but "respect" has in the past connoted "distance" and precluded "companionship". This is now changing. Many older youth do feel parents are companions. Others say quite flatly they will respect only those who deserve it. "I refuse to respect people just because they are parents, or because they are our elders."
5. Brother-sister companionship is still strong but is decreasing as both boys and girls increasingly associate with peers outside the home.
6. Aunties continue to be the favourites of some. They are rarely authority-figures, are usually loving and indulgent.

[4] A subject treated at length in *The Hindu Woman*.

There is strong opinion on "the mixing of sexes", the majority in favour of mixing *with supervision*. Girls who have brothers and boys who have sisters are especially fortunate in their opportunities to meet others in the home. "My daughter doesn't need to meet boys outside—she has a wonderful time with her brother's friends here." Indeed, "going to my friend's home" is an increasingly popular social custom. Boys and girls in college hostels "mix" or not according to the strictness of their parents' injuctions and the rules of the college. "Those whose parents 'don't know' can do as they please." But they now have a new medium of contact. Letters are still generally censored, especially in girls' hostels (though illicit note-passing is as popular as ever—and gets many in trouble). But the telephone is now often available via "an enclosed booth on the verandah", and is heavily used in some hostels. This is "access" but not "mixing".

In our discussion of "family" it seems pertinent to include some information given us by Dr Bhatia of the Child Guidance Clinic in Delhi and by Dr Gore of the Delhi School of Social Work. Areas of increasing social and psychological trouble give some indication of family mal-function under changing conditions. We were told of the following trends:

1. The joint family is breaking up, especially in the cities. There is much loneliness, much anomie. There is increased orphanhood, increased destitution of women—with prostitution being often the only economic solution.

2. The desire for vertical mobility is much stronger, especially among clerks and others in the lower middle class. Families sacrifice everything to get their children educated, hoping they will raise family status.

3. Competition is increasing, especially for jobs. One's niche is no longer assured.

4. Families are having to pay more attention to girls, as regards education and other matters. "They really need as much attention as boys."

5. Juvenile delinquency is growing (as is adult crime), though it is not nearly so serious as in Western cities. Delhi has two juvenile courts and various homes. Many boys run away from their homes, are generally found at the railway stations—"a place of opportunity".

6. The cinema is a powerful new stimulus. Many boys admit it.

7. The number of illegitimate children is still small because of

early marriage and family absorption, but it is increasing in the large cities. There is no foster parents plan, no system of adoption (outside the family).

8. Marriage strains are becoming more severe. They are greater when the women are educated and are common in professional groups. The astonishing and growing number of suicides has received considerable attention in the press. Figures released from New Delhi on May 23, 1960, indicate there were 20,731 recorded cases of suicide in 1959. "The causes, which led people to take their own lives included protracted ailments, domestic troubles, unemployment, indebtedness, financial difficulties, failure in examinations, dejection following frustration in love, infidelity of the spouse, incurable diseases, setbacks in life, and lunacy."[5] There is concern over the large proportion of women in this group. It is always been common for girls to commit suicide rather than be married to old men, but the practice of married women escaping from conditions considered unbearable is growing. The Indian Council of Social Welfare, meeting in Hyderabad on January 1, 1960, suggested that suicide attempts should not be made a penal offence and that such cases should be left to social agencies. "The conference further recommended that divorce laws should be relaxed, as this would help in reducing the number of suicides."[6]

Divorce is much against the Indian tradition, and though now permitted has little social sanction. The growing number of divorces "shocks us severely but indicates a need".

9. Probably the incidence of mental deficiency has not increased, but recognition of deficiency has, especially in hospitals. Many of these children are now helped, but there are no special schools for them.

10. The incidence of mental illness is probably increasing, although again there is better diagnosis. There are many behaviour problems, much neurotic and psychotic behaviour.

There is much brooding and sulking (as in the past), though modern schools are trying to prevent this with more activities. This is an expression of anger—it is masochistic.

There is probably a lot of active homosexuality among boys and men, a lot of latent homosexuality among girls and women teachers, especially in the hostels.

[5] *Madras Mail*, May 25, 1960.
[6] As reported in *The Times of India*, January 2, 1960.

There are some problems of sex-identification. Sikh boys, for instance, have long hair tied in ribbons—they are often not treated as "boys" until they are 12 or over.

Children know much more about the world than they did and are sensitive to it. This adds to their concerns. For instance, a six-year-old, whose grandmother died of cancer, asked "Why don't we use all the rocket money for cancer ?"

Anxiety and hysteria are common neuroses. Hysteria is much more common in women, and in rural areas is linked to superstition.

Psychosomatic illness is common—vomiting, chronic colitis' asthma, vague aches and pains, tics.

There is now some schizophrenia, even among children. There are various forms—dead, dull apathy is one kind.

Only a few ulcer cases are referred to clinics; they are considered a medical problem.

We asked Dr Bhatia what parents consider "abnormal behaviour" in their children. He listed: stubbornness, disobedience, temper tantrums, destructive action, running away from home, children that play more than study, those that defy parental authority —this happens especially with adolescent boys. "Children are generally loved and spoiled, but as soon as they are adolescent they are expected to behave as adults. They are expected to go straight from childhood to adulthood."

He said there are a good many withdrawn children in India, but they are not "behaviour problems" to parents and teachers and are seldom referred.

Some parents are, clearly, "not parents". This is a problem in any society. Some others, who fulfil their role conscientiously, apparently cannot accept defiance or disobedience. They operate with the parental virtues they were taught, do not know how to shift to increasingly democratic structures and values.

To return to our student respondents, most of whom enjoy superior homes, the sense of self and the desire for independence is strong in many. Some have to submit:

"Everyone yells and shouts in my house, and grandfather usually has to be the arbiter. My wishes are forgotten in the general din."

"My parents won't give me an allowance—I am humiliated by having to ask them for money every day."

"I am not allowed to go in for extra-curricular activities. My parents are afraid I will find bad companions, and so I have to go home directly after classes every day."

"I have to be home by dark—there can be no exceptions."

"I am being forced to become a doctor."

"My parents insist on arranging my marriage."

But some young men are getting their way:

"My parents don't approve of my wish to find my own bride, but they daren't oppose me because they want me to support them when they are old."

"My parents don't want me to become an army officer, but I shall insist."

"Of course they won't 'permit' me to choose my own wife—but I shall anyway."

"My parents are illiterate—I am my own master."

One young woman admitted that she did not dare "break social custom", but "our children will, especially if we help them". Another explained the growing liberalism. "Parents are getting more modern themselves. After all, they want us to be happy."

We submit that there is some "family disintegration" and some "family reactionary rigidity", but for the most part the Indian family is *changing* rather than breaking. If parents do not make the changes their children will educate them !

In sum, the Indian family is remarkable in its stability, in its emotional nurture. But

1. There is a lot of myth about the Indian family. Despite its sanctity it has always had its dark side and does now.
2. Authority clashes are increasing and are likely to increase still more. The paternalistic pattern becomes inacceptable to older youth when they become educated, when they learn a lot about the world, when they begin to feel they are "selves".
3. The Indian family is increasingly failing as a "social security system". Individuals and other institutions take over much of this function.
4. The Indian family is increasingly failing as an "emotional security system", though it may regain this function. Adult life is more complex than in the past, and children must be helped to *grow* into adulthood. "The innocence of childhood" may be a sweet concept, but innocence and over-protection are not guarantors of happiness.

5 | *I Want an Education*

No group could be more biased in favour of higher education than our student respondents, but we sought discrimination in their ideas and attitudes.

TABLE 32

REASONS FOR TAKING HIGHER EDUCATION

I am undertaking higher education because	Rank	Total %	Comparison Male %	Female %
I wanted it and my parents were willing	1	95**	94	97
I insisted in spite of my parents' disapproval	2	3	4	2
My parents insisted against my will	3	0	0	0

TABLE 33

REASONS FOR CONSIDERING HIGHER EDUCATION DESIRABLE

Higher education is desirable because	Rank	Total %	Comparison Male %	Female %
Knowledge is satisfying	1	67**	68	65
Education brings happiness	2	64**	60	68
It leads to the best jobs	3	58*	63	50
India needs educated leaders	4	35**	20	53
It makes for better marriage chances	5	29	23	36

78

TABLE 34
HIGHER EDUCATION AND ALIENATION FROM PARENTS

My higher education is "taking me away" from my parents because	Rank	Total %	Comparison	
			Male %	Female %
I am making my own decisions about some matters	1	45*	43	47
I will probably live and work in another town	2	35*	39	28
I have become less religious	3	14=	17	11
I am now more highly educated than they are	4	11	13	8
My parents now seem old-fashioned	5	9=	9	8
It is *not* taking me away (write-in)		22***	21	22

TABLE 35
THE MOST GRATIFYING ASPECT OF HIGHER EDUCATION

When I think about the education I have received, I am most grateful for	Rank	Total %	Comparison	
			Male %	Female %
Intellectual experiences	1	78**	80	72
Learning more about the world	2	69*	68	70
Social experiences—my association with other students	3	67*	63	71
Learning more about myself	4.5	59**	60	57
Learning how to improve and change life in India	4.5	59*	64	50
Cultural experiences—art, music, literature, etc.	6	50*	52	46
My association with professors	7	48	49	45
Recreational experiences—clubs, sports, outings, etc.	8	41	45	34

Misc. write-ins: political experiences, the job status it gives.

TABLE 36
OBJECTIONABLE FEATURES OF HIGHER EDUCATION

I have objected to	Rank	Total %	Comparison Male %	Female %
The "external examination system"	1	47**	50	41
Not enough choice in selecting courses	2	32*	34	29
Studying so hard	3	30	31	26
The "aloofness" of my professors	4.5	29*	33	24
Not being allowed to express my own ideas freely	4.5	29**	34	22
Not being allowed to talk to members of the opposite sex	6	28**	33	21
Hostel food and accommodation	7	20	20	19
The subjection of women staff and students	8	16	17	14
Having higher education in English	9	11	12	10

Misc. write-ins: the strict rules, party politics, being away from home.

TABLE 37
CO-EDUCATION

In my opinion, boys and girls should attend the same school for	Rank	Total %	Comparison Male %	Female %
Post-graduate university	1	85**	84	81
University	2	80**	77	79
Pre-school	3	76**	75	75
Elementary school	4	70**	70	67
Secondary school	5	60*	61	55
Pre-university	6	54*	52	55
All (write-in)	7	10**	15	3

And if in the same school should	Rank	Total %	Comparison Male %	Female %
Mix freely	1	85**	51	83
Be kept separate—in classrooms, library, recreation, etc.	2	10	24	9

TABLE 38

AGENCIES RESPONSIBLE FOR SEX EDUCATION

Education on sex matters— biological facts with respect to physical maturation and marriage—is	Rank	Total %	Comparison	
			Male %	Female %
The responsibility of parents and school	1	66**	61	72
The responsibility of parents only	2	30	31	26
Not necessary	3	12	15	8

Most of the students had their parents' blessings and encouragement in higher education. "They want me to have a degree—it will raise the status of the family." "They know one must have the degree nowadays, so they sacrifice to send me." Only a few had to persist over parental disapproval (undoubtedly many others had to give in to it). "As I am to step into my father's shoes in the business he feels this education is a waste of time and money, and Mother is afraid I will be led astray. But they did not refuse to send me."

How much "satisfaction" and "happiness" education brings is a moot point—"it leads to the best jobs" is less controversial— but our respondents *strongly* feel this is the case and we hope they are right. Girls are much more idealistic than boys in recognizing India's need for educated leaders, but some in each group think marriage chances are aided. "It's like a great dollop on my dowry", one sophisticated young lady laughed. As a matter of fact, much dowry money is spent on girls' education.

Many vehemently denied that higher education "is taking me away" from parents, others that they could become less religious or that their parents could seem old-fashioned. There is evidence, however, that higher education often does cause some family separation, and occasionally alienation. It is ironic that some parents who were themselves under-privileged, and who want their children to have more opportunities and sacrifice to make this possible, should then so often resent the results. It is as though they want their children to be *different* but then cannot accept the difference. As in all countries these parents complain about children "who think they know more than we do—we, their elders, who have had experience", and especially about different political or religious views. These are the parents who feel threatened; others, of course, are proud of their children's greater knowledge and new ideas, but do not hesitate to apply their own greater wisdom where it is needed.

Some young people continuously submit to the authority of instructor or printed word—incapable of doing otherwise—but the much greater proportion disagree at times, even openly. There is fear and cynicism on this point, however. Many students in interviews bitterly criticized the "system" and their instructors. "Our professors are really afraid of us," one sage young woman remarked, "but we're afraid of them, too, because they hold the whip hand. What can we do ?" A young man bitterly commented, "No, I can't argue with a professor—not even here at Jadavpur. I want to graduate." And another said, "I sometimes blindly agree—to please them. It's the easiest way."

Gratitude for many educational experiences greatly outweighs objections. The highest scores on "objections" are scarcely above the lowest on "gratitude". And educators should themselves be gratified in the prime showing of "intellectual experiences". Many students were excited by the question "learning more about myself" and came to discuss it. They indicated they had not known this was true until they saw the statement on the questionnaire. "It may really be the most important reason for being here", one girl mused.

The "external examination system" is the greatest villain, though we must keep in mind that no student likes any kind of examinations. We shall discuss this matter later, but have considerable sympathy for the students on this point. It should be a matter of concern to Indian educators that the student objections point so directly to vulnerable points in the system. "Not having enough choice in selecting courses", "the aloofness of the professors", and "not being allowed to express my own ideas freely" are serious complaints. As regards "studying so hard", several students made it clear that they didn't object to study—or hard study—but they did object to "cramming".

Not many of our respondents live in hostels, and many who do are appreciative of their accommodations. Objections run from petty complaints about food—"They never serve the kind of rice I like"—to serious charges. "One year in a Calcutta University hostel takes ten years off your life. We are all pale, thin, and terribly tired after a few months." (A 1955 survey in Calcutta revealed that 40 per cent of the students were malnourished.)

Response on English as a medium is very low, and does not reflect the magnitude of this problem. We call attention to the fact that we asked for respondents who spoke English well, and it can be presumed most are biased in favour of English.

Strong emotions are reflected in the response to "not being allowed to talk to members of the opposite sex". There is relative freedom at the Universities of Delhi and Baroda, much frustration elsewhere. The majority of students approve of coeducation, with lower scores for the secondary and pre-university levels. One student wrote, "It is not for us to decide". "Mixing", supervised or unsupervised, is strongly approved.[1] Several girls cautiously qualified their response with "if our parents consent".

Sex education is an emotional and controversial matter in any country, but our respondents are for it. There is virtually none in Indian schools, not much in homes, Indian tradition believing in "pure innocence until marriage". We found considerable objection to this approach in our early study, *The Hindu Woman*, and more in 1960.

The girls, in the addendum for women on the questionnaire, indicated that with respect to information about menstruation and reproduction,

	Female %
Some, but not enough information	38
No information	34
Sufficient information	23

The International Planned Parenthood Conference, held in Delhi in 1959, stressed the need for sex education in schools and colleges, and the Central Family Planning Board of India agreed. Marriage and family courses are now offered in a *few* colleges, but much sex education is needed at the school level, too. To quote Smt. Renuka Mukerji, senior lecturer in the Faculty of Home Science, M.S. University of Baroda, who teaches the marriage and family course there—[2]

[1] For the benefit of non-Indian readers, it is the practice in India for boys and girls to sit on separate benches or on opposite sides of the room—in classrooms, auditorium, etc. Even husbands and wives are separate.

[2] Renuka Mukerji, "A Programme in Sex Education for College Girls", *Journal of Family Welfare*, June, 1959.

"It is really surprising to find that the majority of our population enter marriage without even the rudimentary knowledge of sex. This area is shrouded with superstitions, beliefs and adverse ideas. Many graduates do not have a positive attitude towards sex life. A number of boys and girls in our country are spoiled by ignorant or perverted adults in the family or outside the family, and thus these victims develop a negative attitude towards sex. Ultimately their marital happiness is spoiled. It is universally admitted that the problems of sex are created mainly because the adults have a hushed-up attitude towards sex. It is looked down upon as something dirty, bad or nasty. When a child asks a question on sex he is not given a positive answer. . . . If proper courses in this particular area are provided in our schools and colleges, perhaps the unhealthy attitudes towards sex may disappear. . . . The majority of girls, when they come to college are blissfully ignorant about the details of the reproductory system. In the secondary schools no doubt they learn physiology and hygiene, but they do not understand the functions of the reproductory organs. They do not know how a woman becomes pregnant, and are also not clear about the physiology of menstruation. They do not have a very clear idea about these aspects of human development, and their knowledge is based on information gathered from their friends, unhealthy sources, and the secret reading of books. . . . They go through their text-books, discuss the topic with fellow students, and get erotic satisfaction from reading any literature on sex life and marriage. Often they are not able to understand what they read or discuss."

The Association for Social and Moral Hygiene, an organization dealing chiefly with "immoral traffic", in one seminar made a strong case for sex education for students in *schools* and *homes*, and prepared pamphlets for the guidance of teachers and parents. Sex education is viewed by this association as an essential "corrective" for adolescents. There is now wide agreement that children will learn the wrong things if they are not taught the right ones. This is in contrast to the traditional feeling that they can and should remain "innocent". Modern mass media precludes innocence today. Advertisements in India are now frankly sexual— "Be merry with a Merry Bra !" And sex literature, both scientific and lurid, is sold on every city side-walk, at every railway station, at every major and minor book store.

"Family planning", an important programme in India's Plans, is not officially considered a part of sex education—though it is recognized that social attitudes toward family planning should properly be set in schools. We discussed this national problem with many students and found general approval of the national programme. There is a clear distinction between the *prevention* and the *taking* of life, with no religious prohibition. The majority of students are deeply concerned over the economic implications in total nation and in individual families, and as children become economic liabilities rather than assets there is a changing view of the "sanctity of life". Most students want life "sanctified" by adequate food, education, etc. The more scientific-minded, moreover, are aware that man has upset the balance of nature by "death control"— and hence must also make "birth control" his business. There is little equivocation on this principle, but there is, understandably, considerable fear and indecision over methods of control currently used. Many students are frank in their demands "to know more about this important matter".

The inclusion of sex education in formal education—along with Home Science, manual training, and other "non-academic" subjects —indicates a growing conviction in India that education must deal with *total life*. It must be concerned with tools, skills, and attitudes as well as knowledge. This principle has not been spelled out clearly as educational policy, however, and controversy about "fit" educational content will probably grow. It seems inevitable to us—however sad—that when children are largely inducted to their adult roles outside the home, are "educated" largely in external institutions, these institutions must then assume many of the duties of the home. In vicious circle aspect, the more they do the more the home defaults and leaves it to them ! But arguments over "who shall do what" should not blind decision-makers to the needs of children. One way or the other, children must be educated to the life they will face.

6 | *Marriage*

"I won't accept a bride chosen by my parents !"

"Parent-arranged marriage is best. Our parents know what is best for us."

"I don't care what caste my wife is, but she must be educated !"

"How can one marry outside the caste community? There would be no compatibility !"

"My older sister is a spinster ! I don't want the same fate, so I'm insisting that my parents find me a husband."

"I'm *never* going to be married ! It's the only way out of an impossible dilemma."

No subject is so vital as "marriage" to Indian students. They are "at the marriage age", and they live in a moment of their cultural history when both old and new patterns are being questioned. Everything seems uncertain. Some settle for traditional certainty, others for individual rights, and a great many cannot settle on anything. "How do I know what I'll do in three or four years ?"

TABLE 39
MARRIAGE

My parents' marriage was	Rank	Total %	Comparison	
			Male %	Female %
Arranged by their parents	1	92*	91	92
A love marriage	2	8	9	5

In my own opinion, marriages should be	Rank	Total %	Comparison	
			Male %	Female %
Arranged by parents, with consent	1	78***	74	83
Love marriages—one's own choice	2	32*	31	33
Arranged by parents, without consent	3	3	4	2

TABLE 39—*Contd.*

In my own opinion, a marriage should be	Rank	Total %	Comparison	
			Male %	Female %
Within the religion	1	40*	38	41
With anyone	2	36*	39	31
Within the Indian nationality	3	34*	30	38
Within the caste	4	28	23	35
Within the sub-caste community	5	10	9	11

In considering a marriage, horoscopes are	Rank	Total %	Comparison	
			Male %	Female %
Not necessary	1	74*	79	65
Necessary	2	20	18	22

In my own opinion, the bride's dowry is	Rank	Total %	Comparison	
			Male %	Female %
Not necessary	1	66**	68	61
Wrong	2	49**	48	49
Necessary	3	4	4	5

When I am married I shall probably	Rank	Total %	Comparison	
			Male %	Female %
Have an arranged marriage	1	48	41	55
Be allowed to do as I wish	2	46	46	44
Marry within the caste	3	42	42	40
Marry within the sub-caste community	4	10	10	9
I don't know yet (write-in)		20	21	18

I am in favour of a marriage ceremony in	Rank	Total %	Comparison	
			Male %	Female %
Traditional style	1.5	51*	45	58
Reform style[1]	1.5	51*	51	48

I think most girls should marry
about the age of
(open-ended)

Responses ran from 15-25, the average 20—,
Some respondents indicated the age for urban girls should be 20-25, rural girls 16-19.

[1] A short ceremony, sometimes performed by a non-Brahmin.

The great majority of parents were married "by arrangement", and many students approve of "arrangement with consent of the couple". A few who prefer "love marriages" qualified by "with consent of parents". Some students indicated that in "doing as they wish" they will ask for their parents' help.

The majority of students want greater liberality than marrying within the caste, the boys leading the girls in insisting on "anyone". The feeling against the horoscope is considerable, against the dowry overwhelming. In comparison to the past the "reform ceremony" is gaining ground.

Various patterns of arranged marriages are emerging. At the most conservative level, the couple do not see each other before the ceremony. This practice is reported "obsolete" among the higher classes, but still exists to some extent in villages and lower urban classes. Many times the bride is very young—far below the legal age of 15 as prescribed by the Sarda Act—but absence of civil marriage licences makes control of this point impossible.

Some years ago it became common for boys to have veto power (this is "consent") and now most girls in the educated classes are also accorded this right. The veto may relate merely to "sight of face and figure" or to acquaintance. More than "acquaintance" is generally impossible—except "in relation to an old friend of the family"—for here social custom presents a dilemma to all but the most liberal. "It is wrong to reveal yourself to anyone other than a betrothed, and once you're betrothed it's settled !" "Courtship," now commonly encouraged, refers to chaperoned association before marriage, "to let the couple get to know each other before marriage".

Many students prefer "the old way". "My father will find me a bride—there is no reason why I should be looking for one on the campus", one young man said firmly. Several girl medical students at Hyderabad insisted their parents "knew them completely, perfectly", and that they could choose much better. Their confidence was their security. But a Hyderabad Muslim boy was indecisive. His brothers, themselves in the medical profession, wanted him (a prospective engineer) to marry a doctor. "A doctor wife could earn, you see. But I have to wait for the intuition sign. Yet my brothers are in a better position to think than I am—so I am not sure. Anyway they are supporting me. But I am worried about a wife with so much education—it will make trouble."

A Delhi girl described a growing practice of indirect choice. "If I know a boy I want—and think he wants me—I can ask my friends to tell their parents to suggest him to my parents. Everyone will know what is happening, but tradition will be preserved —and I'll be protected too. After all, I couldn't *really* know him at all well, but my parents would investigate his background and decide whether he'd be a good husband for me or not." We asked whether this scheme would work if the boy was in the wrong caste. "Well, *caste* wouldn't make so much difference to my parents, but his family wealth and social position would. I'd be a fool to *think* of suggesting anyone that 'wouldn't do'. But at least I'd have some say in the matter."

Others exercise their independence more boldly—against disapproval but often successfully because their parents do not want to oppose. This is particularly true of boys, some of whom openly wield the whip hand of "future support". But there is a growing number of parents who really want their children to make their own choices. They may not feel capable of choosing for them ("they are so highly educated and have so many new ideas") or they may believe in "individual rights" or "the modern age". Here the young people vary from those who have the opportunity and personal capability to do their own choosing to those who do not. One young man said he believed in choosing but not in dating. He would approve the system of another, who said, "I chose my girl—in my community—and go to visit her at her home, with her parents' consent". Several Hyderabad girls admitted they do not "go with boys" because they do not dare do so unless their parents have chosen them. *Many* students asked, "How can one *really* get to know some one ?" We commented, "Not by talking about the weather when you're together !" whereupon the girls laughed with instant recognition of familiar practice.

This transition phase has brought a new phenomenon to India— the spinster. "In India those who have tried to break with traditions have suffered." Girls who are too old (above 25) or too highly educated (above the B.A.) have denied their parents the opportunity to find them husbands. Bargaining power has gone. But it is difficult for the girls to find their own husbands (lady doctors have the best opportunity), for in their jobs and homes they must be circumspect or lose their reputations. Indeed, to be friendly to bachelors—as, for instance, colleagues in a college faculty—would often result in dismissal. The unmarried woman can now usually earn her living, but she remains an object of suspicion. It is much worse in rural areas. Community Block Development "women's work specialists" are usually nurses or trained social workers. They are much needed in the programme. But they are not welcome in many villages if young, pretty, unmarried, or widowed (a widow is inauspicious). To be acceptable, and therefore effective, they should be middle-aged, ugly, and preferably married.[2] Professional women in the large cities fare better, but many are desperately lonely and greatly restricted in their activities. "There is really no social life for unmarried people", one said sadly. And another exclaimed, "I'm going to insist that my parents refuse to to let my younger sister go to college and that they start looking for a husband now !"

A reader in Economics described his problem wistfully. "I have four daughters, whom I raised in 'the modern way'. Three have M.A.'s, the fourth is getting her M.B.B.S.[3] The oldest was married at 28, by 'arrangement', even to consulting horoscopes. The boy gave his consent, but the couple met only once before marriage. Now I am much concerned about the next two—one is 27. I really should arrange their marriages, in their interests, though I don't want to. The youngest will make her own choice, I hope, in medical school."

A candid Delhi girl put it neatly, "Indian women haven't the guts to make decisions even when their parents permit it." We do not doubt the courage—what takes more courage than marrying a stranger ?—but do recognize the cultural heritage of Indian women. Nothing in their nurture has developed—or even permitted—decision-making; everything has developed attitudes of adjustment. Adjustment to an unknown husband is possible when one marries young enough (16-17), "before the personality has rigidified", by and with that of her husband. A woman over 20, or especially 25, through no fault of her own, would find adjustment difficult. But, even in this difficulty, in this period of emotional development she probably finds more security and happiness in adjustment than independence. "I am doing what I want to !" would be cold comfort, indeed, in India. A Bombay matron is

[2] We apologize to those block workers that are neither middle-aged nor ugly. They have transcended the difficulties!

[3] Equivalent of American M.D.

one of many predicting a shift back to arranged marriages in the progressive circles where love marriages have become the vogue. "Arranged marriages will be particularly necessary for women over 25, who are too mature to adjust easily. When one makes a love marriage it's always assumed that the other will make all the adjustments. But in an arranged marriage the tradition that *both* must adjust wins out."

No resident of India fails to see the numerous (and humorous) marriage advertisements featured in some newspapers. This practice is growing, though most of our informants insist they rarely bring results. "You could never trust the information given." They are considered the last, desperate resort, an appeal to the market when romance fails.

Engineering executive, 32, Smartha Tamil Brahmin, monthly Rs. 700, foreign travelled, seeks very fair,[4] beautiful, slim, Hindu girl, any Brahmin community, up to 25, preferably with university education. No bars.

Parents of 29 year old tall and handsome covenanted Technical Officer in British Firm earning Rs. 530/month invite correspondence from rich, cultured parents of S.S.L.C. passed,[5] non-Srivatsa Tamil Vadama girls, 18-24. Reply with horoscopes.

WANTED a beautiful educated Brahmin virgin for a boy (25) getting Rs. 250/month in Government Service. No dowry.

Bengali Engineer, 27, decent salary, invites matrimonial correspondence from homely,[6] pretty working girls, below 23, or parents. Maharashtrian, Gujerati, or Bengali preferred.

WANTED Beautiful, Educated, Earning bride for graduate cultured Maratha widower, 32, well-placed officer. Caste no bar.

Educated, Beautiful, Healthy, Divorcee Maharashtrian (25) seeks matrimony with highly placed bridegroom of cool temperament.

WANTED a match for a Punjabi girl of 28-29 years, good looking, modern, independent, well versed in housekeeping.

[4] "Fair" refers to skin colour.
[5] One who has *passed* with the Secondary School Leaving Certificate.
[6] "Homely" means "accomplished in domestic arts".

Punjabis preferred. Gentlemen settled in Bombay and having no encumbrance may apply. Early marriage.

WANTED well settled non-Garg Mangli graduate for 18 years Agarwal Matric, pretty virgin. Horoscope essential.

WANTED doctor or graduate girl for Kayastha, foreign qualified engineer, aged 28. Getting Rs. 1400 per month.

Suitable independent/working virgin for handsome Khatri bachelor, 31. Well settled in life. Father an advocate.

WANTED a homely virgin for a Punjabi Khatri bachelor of 36 earning Rs. 400/month. Caste immaterial. Girl's merits the consideration.

WANTED exceptionally bright and beautiful bride from a very respectable Sindhi family for a young and promising businessman of 29 only, having steady and secured monthly income above three thousand, with still brighter future prospects. The bride must be beautiful.

Note the generally high economic and educational level, the requests for mates with specific characteristics, the other requests that repudiate caste and dowry in favour of companionship— and, often, earning capacity. "It really isn't anything new—this advertising—it's just that the newspaper is the modern go-between", one man said, but his companion retorted, "No decent people use this method !" Another explained, "I have a friend who used an 'ad' to pressure his own family into doing something. He had gone to England for his higher studies and done all sorts of things that made it impossible for his parents to find him a wife—anyway, in those days he wouldn't hear of it. Finally he really wanted to get married but couldn't find a girl himself. So he ran an 'ad', and when his uncle saw it he made the parents go out and find someone. It cost them plenty, but they couldn't permit my friend to use the newspaper method."

The newspaper "ads" reflect the dilemma of the men as much as that of older girls. Many are desperately lonely, and in all the large cities they congregate in all-male groups at restaurants, coffee houses, cinemas, parks, etc. and look around with hungry eyes. There is very little "dating" as the West knows it—Bombay

TABLE 40
FACTORS IN CHOOSING A WIFE

In my opinion, the most important factors in choosing a wife are (Men only)	Rank	Total %
Character	1	94***
Education	2	84**
Chastity	3	80**
My love for her	4	75**
Domestic training	5	71**
Beauty	6	69**
Age	7	68*
Her love for me	8	43**
Artistic accomplishments	9	41
Family wealth, position	10	18
Caste	11	17
Dowry	12	3

Misc. write-ins: health, religion, all the good qualities for which she is praised and worshipped in India.

TABLE 41
MEANING OF CHARACTER IN A WIFE

By wife's "character" I have in mind (open-ended) (Men only)	Rank	Total %
Faithful to me, loyal	1	25
Chaste, moral	2	21
Loving, affectionate	3	18
Educated, intelligent	4	14
Good-natured, amiable	5	13
Obedient, subservient	6	9
Broad-minded, modern	7.5	8
Respects my family	7.5	8
Individualistic, independent	9.5	7
Does household tasks well	9.5	7
Sympathetic and understanding	11.5	6
Gentle and patient	11.5	6
Cooperative	15	5
Religious, spiritual	15	5
Beautiful, elegant	15	5
Good manners, polite	15	5
Keeps home peaceful	15	5
Honest, truthful	18.5	4
Modest	18.5	4
A good mother	20	3
Adaptable	22	2
Sociable	22	2
A companion	22	2

Misc.: simple in words and action, "faultless perfection", one who reforms her husband, generous, courageous, humble, cultured, artistic.

permits the most. But literature, music, and advertisements shout "romance", and the love marriage has become a favourite cinema theme. Post-campus life is thus often bleaker than campus life, and the necessity for homes and companionship becomes acute.

However marriage is arranged, there are abstract preferences in selecting a mate.

TABLE 42

QUALITIES CONSIDERED UNDESIRABLE IN A WIFE

do not want a wife who is (open-ended) (Men only)	Rank	Total Male %
Immoral, not chaste	1	19
Uneducated	2	18
Ugly	3	15
Proud, arrogant, vain	4	14
Neglects housework	5	12
Cross, quarrelsome, a shrew	6	10
Disloyal, disobedient	7	9
Not devoted to me and children	8	7
More educated than I am	9	6
Can't get along with my family	11.5	5
Too timid, easily dominated	11.5	5
Talkative	11.5	5
Extravagant, loves ornaments, clothes	11.5	5
Selfish, inconsiderate	14.5	4
Too modern, Western	14.5	4
Shy in love, doesn't show affection	19	3
Unsociable	19	3
Too orthodox, old-fashioned	19	3
Stupid—an idiot	19	3
Mentally ill, unabalanced	19	3
Can't understand me	19	3
Older than me	19	3
Feels superior to me	24.5	2
Feels inferior to me	24.5	2
Suspects me	24.5	2
Dishonest, insincere	24.5	2
Too social	24.5	2
Too superstitious	24.5	2
Too rich	24.5	2
Bosses me	24.5	2
Not religious	24.5	2
Too sophisticated	24.5	2
Temperamentally different	33	1

Misc.: contradicts my views, does not keep up my prestige, is a hindrance to me, has a fairer complexion, who works in an offce, is athletic, is immodest, belongs to another caste.

TABLE 43

FACTORS IN CHOOSING A HUSBAND

In my opinion the most important factors in choosing a husband are (Women only)	Rank	Total Female %
Character	1	94**
Education	2	90**
Age	3.5	74*
Job	3.5	74*
My love for him	5	68*
His love for me	6	66*
His treatment of women	7	56*
Chastity	8	41
Handsomeness	9	38
Family background	10	25
Caste	11	24

Misc. write-in: health, intelligence.

TABLE 44

MEANING OF CHARACTER IN A HUSBAND

By a man's "character" I have in mind (open-ended) (Women only)	Rank	Total Female %
Honest, sincere	1	26
Faithful to me, chaste	2.5	25
Loves me, is devoted to family	2.5	25
Strong-willed, bold, courageous	4	19
Good-natured, patient, kind	5	16
Understands me, sympathetic	6	11
Handsome	8	7
Noble—respects higher things	8	7
Sociable	8	7
Has sense of humor	10.5	6
Mentally and physically superior	10.5	6
Respects women	13	5
Dutiful, responsible, cooperative	13	5
Generous, sacrificing, considerate	13	5
Allows me freedom	16.5	4
Doesn't think he's superior	16.5	4
Healthy	16.5	4
Broadminded	16.5	4
Self-controlled, disciplined	19	3
Forgiving, tolerant	20.5	2
Religious	20.5	2

Misc.: athletic, creative, stable, reliable, trusts me, understands himself.

TABLE 45

QUALITIES CONSIDERED UNDESIRABLE IN A HUSBAND

I do not want a husband who (Women only)	Rank	Total Female %
Flirt, fickle, chases women	1	32
Drinks (or smokes)	2	20
Uneducated, stupid	3	15
No respect for women, for me	4	13
Cruel, illtreats wife	6	12
Weak-minded	6	12
Doesn't love me	6	12
Irreligious	8.5	7
Dishonest, insincere	8.5	7
Narrow-minded, old-fashioned	10.5	6
Irresponsible about family	10.5	6
Suspects me	14	5
Ugly	14	5
Extravagant, loves money only	14	5
Has less education than me	14	5
Doesn't respond to my love	14	5
Short-tempered	18	4
Selfish	18	4
Frivolous	18	4
Very old	20.5	3
Arrogant, boastful	20.5	3
Doesn't understand me	24.5	2
Dominating, autocratic	24.5	2
Uncooperative	24.5	2
Physically weak	24.5	2
Too handsome	24.5	2
Unreasonable, obstinate	24.5	2

Misc.: feminine, younger, poor, hasn't a good job, too large a family, under the thumb of his mother, not polite, a bore, gambles, no ambition, wrong caste, can't support his family.

We knew from interviews that "character" would rank high in choosing a husband or wife oneself (we are not sure this would be the case if parents were choosing), and hence sought to have its meaning clarified. The amplification was somewhat repetitive of the first list, with personality characteristics added.

Combining all the men's responses, education, chastity, his love for her, beauty, and domestic skills seem most important. The women value education, the correct age (which many made clear meant "not too old"), job, honesty, chastity, and love and devotion. Fears are related to lack of these qualities, with drinking (and to some extent smoking), lack of respect, and cruel treatment added to women's fears, arrogance and shrewish behaviour to men's.

Obedience and subservience, a scorned characteristic for many, still has some popularity. As one boy wrote, "Women should lead perfect lives by acting in accordance with the views of their husbands". "Faultless perfection" can have many meanings.

In interviews we sought to discover whether young men—who were vociferous in their demand to have educated wives, though some felt secondary school would be sufficient—foresaw any difficulties as regards their highly educated wives' independent and possibly different ideas. A few conceded this problem would arise, some indicated their willingness to accept a life of "give-and-take", but the great majority seemed naively confident that "education makes one more reasonable", and therefore would not cause wives to take opposing views.

Some girls, both in questionnaires and in interviews, were cynical about men's trustworthiness. "Men are not to be trusted", several wrote. "We are so helpless when they deceive us", another said. But a few girls predicted that deception would not be so easy with educated wives—or, more hopefully—that men would not want to deceive educated wives.

We grouped the responses in all the above tables referring to choosing a mate, and found the following categories and percentages:

TABLE 46

FACTORS IN CHOOSING A MATE

	Rank	Total Male %	Rank	Total Female %
Personality characteristics	1	39	1	45
Relationship to mate	2	29	2	41
Family heritage [7]	3	22	3	11
Relationship to whole family	4	12	4	3

[7] With reference to items like wealth, beauty, religious background, etc. that is presumably "inheritance" more than items like "good-natured, shrewish", etc. that are presumably within one's control.

We are not sure what interpretations might be made from the comparison of male and female response, but find it interesting to note the greater female emphasis on "relationship to mate" and "personality characteristics". It is, we think, a more *personal* response.

The above data clearly supports our observation that the system of marriage in India is adjusting and changing. As one respondent said, "Most of us in our generation have to accept parent-arranged marriage, but the next generation will be freer". Changes may not bring more felicity, but they are being *demanded*. In the meantime there are inconsistencies and mixtures. "I will give my wife freedom of ideas, but she must *not* have more education than me." Men want more companionship and "equality", but they feel threatened, too. Women want more freedom and "equality", but they are understandably loathe to trade the security of dependence for the insecurity of independence.

We said previously that there is much myth connected to "the Indian family" (though we concede it is one of the best families among the cultures of the world). Much of the difficulty attendant to the Indian family today pertains to the system of marriage. "This is the single greatest fault," one woman said, "and I am convinced the family will remain as wonderful as ever if the marriage part is changed." Others, of course, will disagree—but this is a point of view that seems to be gaining ground, especially among the young people. The following three examples illustrate (but do not prove !) the minus side of the ledger. The first is in the November 22, 1959, *Amrita Bazar Patrika* Readers' Column:

Here is a tale more tragic than any story I know about the curse of the dowry system in our country. . . . The background of this story is an obscure village in the district of 24 parganas. A villager there had two daughters, Madhuri and Chhabi by name. Madhuri, the elder sister, was eighteen, fair-looking and marriageable. Her father tried his level best to arrange for her marriage in time but failed. As he was poor he could not meet the exorbitant demands of the prospective grooms. The parents lost the calm poise of their minds, and they were so worried about their daughter's marriage that sometimes they broke into hysterical quarrel between themselves. One day after such a quarrel on Madhuri's marriage, Chhabi was missing towards the evening. Later she was found hanging from a tree branch near a lonely pond. Chhabi, a twelve-year old girl . . . left a note. It claimed that her death would remove the hindrance in the way of her elder sister's marriage.

The second is an impassioned statement written by one of our

Calcutta student respondents—a young man of wealth, in love with a girl.

> Marriage is one institution in India which is an absolute mess. I have known four cases of sheer tragedy at the hands of this vicious system of arranged marriages. My grandparents married three daughters to such spendthrift, good-for-nothing gamblers and alcoholics that they are all destitute now The most evil day for my big uncle was the day of his marriage. A wife is under the pressure of everybody and is subject to harassment from every source. I shouldn't write this, but much pressure was put on my father to commit bigamy. My grandmother was the greatest influence in this pressure. I know eleven cases personally in my family where marriages were arranged. It is a sad fact that in only two cases were the marriages happy. Intrigues and counter-intrigues plague every marriage. The Indian marriage except in .0001 per cent of the cases is the lousiest and most horrible institution devised by man. If divorces were arranged, too, in India, we would have four times as many as America!

The third comes from a conversation with a gentleman from the U.P.—a man of considerable status.

> "The trouble with arranged marriage is that husbands never trust their wives, wives their husbands. This was bad enough in the old days, but it didn't matter much because neither one saw much of the opposite sex. But now! Now if a wife works in an office her husband is in an agony of jealousy and suspicion."
> "What is he really afraid of?" we asked.
> "Himself, of course ! He is feeling so much temptation that he projects the whole situation. All that has happened in modern times is that the sight-seeing has been increased but the rule is still 'hands off'."
> "But," we interposed, "the sight-seeing would be just as great if it had been a love marriage."
> "True—but the couple stays together through their mutual devotion, not through insulation from others. One's love should be, in fact, the insulation."

We stated in our first chapter that the system of marriage involves the *whole social system*, not just "who makes the decision". Traditional India has been a relatively "closed society", with no contact permitted with members of the opposite sex outside the family. Even when this was not fully possible, as in rural areas, other strict mores operated to prevent contacts, especially after physical maturation. Early marriage was one way to ensure chastity, polygamy or polyandry another.

Today, however, the society has opened up to a large extent, even though most schools are still sex-segregated. Boys and girls,

men and women, do see each other, do often speak to each other.
Most importantly, modern mass media, especially the cinema, radio,
novels, and periodicals—to say nothing of advertisements—shout
SEX. The love marriage has become a favourite cinema theme,
and audiences applaud love's triumph. Students admit enjoying
foreign films largely because of the physical contact and kissing
that is taboo—but titillating—in India. Student entertainments
on the campus increasingly deal with boy-girl themes, though very
rarely do boys and girls actually appear on the stage together—
as in traditional times, boys dress like girls, girls like boys. In
these scenes, when actors come even close to one another the
student audience hoots and whistles, and comments like "hold her
hand" float from the back.

No subject is of greater moment than "sex" on any campus we
visited. A few campuses permit "dates" during the daytime, most
do not; some do not even permit casual conversation between
boys and girls. All continue the traditional practice of sex-segre-
gation in the seating arrangement at any function. But many of
the students listen to cinema music, gossip about boys and girls,
and dream about love and romance. Many say they want to learn
social dancing, though we have found no campus that permits
it. All students have asked eager questions about "dating, courtship, marriage, and coeducation", though not all approve the
Western practice.

One piece of tradition, that of keeping the sexes apart, is going,
but another tries to persist—in keeping sex interest passive until
marriage, marriage being considered a family affair. It is inconsistent,
and it is beginning to seem incompatible to some students. Many
girls, who have been urged to higher education, are bitter that
their parents insist they become teachers of small children—in
which occupation they are presumably safe. Some students, the
girls in particular, wish their parents wouldn't assume "being with
boys" necessarily means having "evil thoughts". They speak
wistfully of wishing they could "greet" boys without having the
greeting interpreted as an invitation. "Why must my parents
think doing things with boys is *bad*? I don't think bad thoughts
when I'm with them—I'm more likely to when I'm not allowed
to be with them!" We murmured that it has ever been thus
in the world. "But that doesn't help us in India, does it? It's our
problem *now*."

It seems highly significant to us that in the "women's addendum" we received the following response:

TABLE 47

PROTECTION OF WOMEN AGAINST SEXUAL ADVANCES

With respect to the protection of women from sexual advances	Rank	Total Female %
Women generally can protect themselves by their own speech and action	1	82
Women cannot protect themselves, and therefore their families and society must protect them	2	13

This is a radical departure from tradition, and clearly indicates that the Indian girl is learning to say "no".

Logically a democratic and "open" society should have coeducation. A few schools in India and many colleges and universities are essaying coeducation. It is the secondary period that is critical. The principal of a coeducational secondary school said, "Yes, this brings some problems, but not so many as separation does". Thus there is evidence *in India* that natural, day-to-day contact results in less silly thought and action, less unfulfilled curiosity. Those who grow up in coeducation have a healthier attitude than those who suddenly experience it at the higher education level—or not at all.

The "traditional" and the "Western" systems of marriage are different in their priorities—one emphasizes the joining of families the other the joining of individuals. But they are similar in wanting this union based on *compatibility*. The traditional system ensures compatibility by (1) marriage within the community, (2) marriage at an early age "so that personalities can form together", and (3) limited contact with others. In the Western system one has to *find* a compatible mate. This presupposes contact with many so that choice can be made, and also that the contacts have sufficient length of time and depth of friendship to clarify compatibility —or the lack of it. Indian youth are increasingly allowed the *right* of decision without the *means* to make it, or they are given the means without the right of decision. It is not surprising to find some that rely desperately on the horoscope, as an Annamalai youth who said, "I have to have *some* way of knowing if we will be compatible". Nor is it surprising that others feel too insecure

to try, that they insist their parents choose for them. "After all,"
a Madras matron said, "this isn't a proper area for choice. We
don't choose the family we are born into—we adjust to it—so
why should we choose on marriage ? It's *too important to be a
matter of individual choice.* Mistakes are too probable and costly."
A Delhi girl represents another point of view. "I'm not going to
get married at all. It's the only way out of an impossible dilemma.
My parents want me to choose my own husband, but I can't subject
them to the inevitable criticism of our many relatives. So—I am
planning on a career, with side-lines of music and art to keep me
from getting too lonely."

We could offer no more eloquent testimony of the trials of
transition than the following voluntary and lengthy statement,
written by a girl with parents of different races and faiths, studying
in a "progressive" university.

Just about three weeks ago I met a young man—who is Muslim—we became
good friends as we had common interests and ideas, and our academic lines
were similar. We were able to help each other. Moreover, we got along just
fine. We understand each other and feel at ease with each other. When I
developed this friendship with him I did not think of marriage, but I did
consider the possibility of getting to like him more—as every girl does. I
also did look on him as a possible mate. Having been brought up with very
liberal ideas, and having parents from different faiths, I did not think of his
religion as being a hindrance—though different from mine. I brought him
home thrice and met him often here and there—as his family lives next to
mine. I really enjoy his friendship and find greater companionship with him
than other boys. All of a sudden my parents announced that they wanted me to
break my friendship with him, because he is a Muslim. I argued with them that
he should be judged as an *individual*, not a person from a certain faith. But
they are adamant—and refused to meet him and find out what he is like.
This has been a most terrible shock to me, as I never thought my parents
would reject a person because of his faith, especially since they are not of the
same religion, and our home has always been open to all persons. I said
that I had no intention at the moment of marrying the boy, but they refuse
to accept a boy-girl relationship based on companionship and common
interests. They insist my reputation will be spoilt—this I can't understand
or accept. I believe in judging a person according to his personality and individuality and do not believe that my being friendly with a boy who comes to
my home can spoil my reputation. I also can't accept the fact that the person
I love should not know about it. As I have to know him well enough to judge
him as my future mate—and this can come only if there is some deeper friendship—though I love him and have shown him so, there could be some hitch
some where. We might not be compatible—something might become obvious
to me only after knowing him better—and then I would have to break it off.

So, before one finds one's ideal mate there is the necessity of experimentation and coming to know many men well.

I have mentioned my case in detail because I feel that if India was old-fashioned there would have been no question of the hopelessness of my argument. And if India was modern I would not have had such objections raised. But now I think I am right. My education has given me these ideas, and I want to prove this to my parents— but somehow I can't at the same time—due to these great Indian family ties. So this is one problem of a changing India.

In sum, then, it is inconsistent to permit and encourage new political, economic, and educational patterns in the name of "progress", to insist on traditional social customs and values in the name of "morality". Morality, we submit, is relative.

7 | Woman's Place

"WOMAN is pure and noble." Traditional India has always accorded woman a high place, and, indeed "equality". "Man and woman are the two wheels of a cart", "Man and woman are the two halves of the whole". "Equality" meant "equal but *different*", and the complementary nature of male and female elements was stressed in theory and practice. Since the days of the Vedas, however, the Indian woman has largely been subjected, the "ideal" worshipped, the "real" neglected. Purdah practices were perhaps designed to shelter, but they had a restrictive effect. Thousands of women in recent centuries have had few rights, little freedom, scant personal identity. Ram Mohan Roy and other reformers recognized this plight, and particularly in the early part of the 20th century there was a conscious move "back to the spirit of the Vedas". The Independence Movement needed, used, and developed women, and today Independent India boasts more women in high places than most Western countries. India has been a differentiated, but relatively non-competitive society. Competition is now accelerating, and there is some indication that "equality" is equated with "identity" as in the West.

The problem of the Indian woman today is not that she cannot vote (she can and does), stand for office (she runs!), or command respect (she always had it). It is—as with women in most countries—that of being *herself* as she also fulfils traditional mother and wife roles. In our research study, *The Hindu Woman*, we found little "concept of self" as we of the West understand it. The ideal Hindu woman was supportive, was the perfect "helpmeet", was the self which had no meaning save in relationship to family and serving that family.

Modern, educated Indian girls and young women, however, have had experiences different from those of their mothers and grandmothers. Rising out of a non-competitive society, they have had to compete, to respond to new challenges, to stand on their own feet. They have had to use their brains as well as their hands; they have discovered new emotions; they have developed new ambitions. Few want to be anything but happy wives and mothers, but the recipe for happiness is changing. Ingredients of "educated happiness", to use the term we heard, "include self-realization through the development of the individual potential". One young lady smiled as she said, "Peeling an orange and hand-feeding it to my husband as I sit at his feet in humble adoration is not my idea of marriage! I want to be his intellectual and social companion—not his slave."

Most young Indian men would agree with her, though many want the old and new woman wrapped up in one package. A Lucknow student wrote, "Women should have more chance in every sphere of life, but the habit of opposing men—whether right or wrong—should not be developed. Women should not be emotional in their thinking." And a Hyderabad youth said, "Marriage has been a legal ceremony with very little attention paid to the personal thoughts of the young couple or to their ideas of happiness. Instead we must have 'one soul in two bodies' and love must play a part in marriage. But even then a wife must adjust her nature to fit that of her husband." It seems the new "ideal Indian woman" can exist. A Calcutta student wrote, "A woman is wife, mother, companion, helpmate, partner, housewife, and heaven knows what. Only a woman has the unique chance to be so many things. I know a girl who is."

Girls and women all too often want to have their cake and eat it too. Many want new opportunities, old securities; new freedom, old protection. This is natural, for the new freedoms are usually partial, tentative, and socially disapproved.

Let us examine students' responses on women:

TABLE 48
WOMEN AND EDUCATION

Women should be encouraged to education through	Rank	Total %	Comparison	
			Male %	Female %
University	1	84*	80	88
Secondary school	2	47	40	55
Pre-university	3	43	35	52
Elementary school	4	36	34	51

TABLE 49
POSITION OF WOMEN IN THEORY

Women are, in theory	Rank	Total %	Comparison	
			Male %	Female %
Equal to men	1	79**	80	77
Inferior to men	2	15	16	12
Superior to men	3	8	3	14

TABLE 50
POSITION OF WOMEN IN PRACTICE

Women are, in social practice	Rank	Total %	Comparison	
			Male %	Female %
Equal to men	1.5	44	42	47
Inferior to men	1.5	44	43	43
Superior to men	3	10	7	15

TABLE 51
WOMAN'S MOST IMPORTANT FUNCTION

The most important function of a woman is	Rank	Total %	Comparison	
			Male %	Female %
To be a good wife and mother	1	90***	90	88
To develop her own talents	2	38	33	44
To do community service	3	25	23	27

TABLE 52
OPPORTUNITIES FOR WOMEN

Women should have the opportunity to	Rank	Total %	Comparison	
			Male %	Female %
Become educated	1	75**	54	95
Get jobs	2	58	47	71
Join social clubs, associations	3	56	48	67
Enter politics	4	40	34	48

TABLE 53
WOMEN AND JOBS

Women should have jobs	Rank	Total %	Comparison Male %	Female %
Only if family is not neglected	1	56*	52	60
Only when the family needs money	2	51*	44	61
If they wish to work	3.5	47*	44	49
Only when unmarried	3.5	47	69	15

Many incorrectly responded more than once to "encouragement in women's education", but this student group clearly believes in unlimited educational opportunity for women. The majority of men and women believe that women are equal to men *in theory*, but in practice "inferior" comes a close second. The traditional idealization of woman is seen in the small but perhaps surprising "superior" scores.

Double responses are again reflected in "the most important function of a woman", but her major role expectation is clear. We were tempted to separate "wife" and "mother", and now wish we had. Traditionally, "mother" could have preceded, but we suspect our respondents would give strong priority to "wife".

Fewer men than women accord women's rights to education, work, etc. Many did not respond at all. The difference in ranking on "women should have jobs only when—" is significant. Men put "only when unmarried" first. On the other hand, many feel the woman's own wish is the decisive factor. The women are more realistic about work. As one put it, "Most women must work nowadays, but they aren't yet respected for it".

We asked an open-ended question, "My opinion on marriage *and* career for women is—" Many did not respond to the question at all, especially in Annamalai, Visva-Bharati, Kanja Kubja College, and Banares. Several wrote, "I have never given thought to this question". Many others misunderstood the question and wrote again on marriage, their responses generally reflecting strong opinion (1) against any force before or during marriage (many boys feel women must be free to make their own decisions), (2) for love marriages, or (3) for *all* women to marry. One girl wrote, "Marriage is a necessary evil for women—they are discarded if they don't". Another said, "Marriage is the noble culmination of our desires".

We follow with typical statements:

Marriage is a woman's career

"The best career is raising decent children and caring for her husband." (Lucknow)

"Woman's career is superior to that of a man. The true theatre for a woman is the sick chamber." (Hyderabad)

"She should be queen of her husband's heart." (Kanja Kubja) "Equal rights are necessary, but her prime duty is the household." (Kanja Kubja)

"Marriage is essential but a career isn't." (Scottish Church)

Marriage and career don't mix

"Choose one or the other." (Baroda)

"Careers for those who won't or can't marry." (Lady Irwin)

"Marriage only for most women. Those with *great* ability and interest should pursue careers and not marry." (Elphinstone)

"Her right, but too difficult." (Baroda)

"In theory but not in practice." (Elphinstone)

"It just doesn't work in India." (Madras)

"It affects her purity—society thinks she is bad." (Madras)

"Having a job leads to family quarrels and unpleasantness". (Kanja Kubja)

If it is necessary and if she can

"Her career must be one that aids the family." (Visva-Bharati)

"She should do as she is able, but when she has children how can she?" (Miranda)

"Many women will have to work to raise the standard in India." (Miranda)

"If with personal satisfaction and social approval." (Baroda)

"Let women do as they wish, except to do something offensive." (Kanja Kubja, Scottish Church)

"If the career is noble and worthwhile." (Osmania Science)

"If her parents choose the career." (Kanja Kubja)

"Only teaching and medicine." (Osmania Engineering)

"Only social service." (Lady Irvin)

"Let her choose a light career, like being a teacher, lecturer, or stenographer." (Osmania Women)

"If her children are old enough." (Elphinstone)

"If there are servants." (Baroda)

"If planned and carried out with better thinking." (Baroda)

"It depends on the husband's attitude." (Baroda)

"Marriage is an agreement. If the husband agrees it is all right." (Lady Irwin)

"Both if she can—but if she can't it will be chaos!" (Elphinstone)

Why not?

"Why not a suitable career?" (Bethune)

"Marriage with a brilliant career is possible." (Miranda)

"Career is essential, marriage is not." (Osmania Women)

"I'd hate not to be able to support myself in this world!" (Miranda)

"It's much safer for a woman to marry, but she must be able to earn her bread and butter." (Scottish Church)

"She should marry only after becoming financially independent, so she won't be entirely dependent on her husband and can care for herself if anything goes wrong." (Scottish Church)

"All women should follow careers with devotion before marriage and as they can after marriage." (Miranda)

"If we are equal to men—and I think we are—why not have a career for a few years? A career makes life more interesting." (Lady Irwin)

"Women should get married if it isn't a hindrance to their studies and interests." (Miranda)

"Women should remain single if they wish. If they *want* to marry or are helpless marriage is necessary. Marriage isn't always bad." (Miranda)

"If she wants to have a career she should, and at any job. But I hate old women who have never experienced the warm and rich emotion of raising children, of running homes, of being selfless and cheerful." (St. Xavier's)

In the above responses "marriage *is* woman's career" is overwhelmingly first, but there is much evidence that both the necessity and the wish for women to work is growing. One girl spoke for many in saying, "But first we must be freed from domestic burdens". Indian household work is arduous and complicated. Even if "gadgets" will largely remain economically scarce, it is conceivable that diets might be simplified. "I don't know *why* we prepare such a large variety of foods for every meal!"

TABLE 54

THINGS WOMEN SHOULD BE ENCOURAGED TO DO

In my opinion women should be encouraged to	Rank	Total %	Comparison	
			Male %	Female %
Walk with (not behind) their husbands	1	82**	80	82
Attend any mixed function	2	78*	75	84
Eat meals with their husbands	3	74*	72	75
Travel in mixed company	4	65*	63	66
Attend public functions unaccompanied	5	55	55	55
Sit in any area—not in women's section	6	47	45	48

TABLE 55

MODERN CUSTOMS WOMEN MAY ADOPT

In my opinion women should be able, if they wish, to adopt the following modern customs	Rank	Total %	Comparison	
			Male %	Female %
"Pony tail" hair style	1	52	50	54
Lipstick	2	51	43	61
Short hair	3	45	36	58
Tennis costume	4	38	32	45
Social dancing	5	35*—	30	40
Bathing costume	6	34—	30	39
Dating	7	28*—	24	32
Smoking	8	13— — —	13	12
Drinking	9	11— — —	7	5
None (write-in)	—	13***	15	9

TABLE 56

REMARRIAGE OF WIDOWS

With respect to the re-marriage of widows	Rank	Total %	Comparison	
			Male %	Female %
It is all right and can be done	1	73*	71	74
I don't object but society won't permit it	2	37*	38	34
I am against it	3	4	3	5

TABLE 57
ATTITUDE TO WIDOWS

In my own opinion widows should	Rank	Total %	Comparison Male %	Female %
Live and work without restrictions	1	84*	84	82
Observe traditional customs	2	13	16	9

TABLE 58
OBEDIENCE AND WOMEN

Women are traditionally "obient", first to fathers, then to husbands, and then to sons. In my own opinion	Rank	Total %	Comparison Male %	Female %
This is still necessary (except to sons)	1	47*	53	38
This is not necessary	2	38	33	44
This is wrong	3	18*	18	16

TABLE 59
STATUS OF WOMEN MEMBERS ON UNIVERSITY STAFF

Women university professors and members of staff should have	Rank	Total %	Comparison Male %	Female %
The same privileges and respect as men	1	93**	92	92
Fewer privileges	2	2	3	1

TABLE 60
WOMEN AND THE LAW OF INHERITANCE

With respect to the Inheritance Law, women	Rank	Total %	Comparison Male %	Female %
Should inherit some of the family land	1	79*	76	81
Should not inherit land	2	9	12	5

Westerners have been partially incorrect in assuming some customs, like women walking behind their husbands or eating meals later,

have necessarily connoted "inferiority". But Indians are increasingly aware that the customs do imply "a stigma", and many want
equality symbolized *in practice*. One man said, "I accept equality
completely—even to having my wife eating with me". Fewer are
willing to accept "mixed seating". This group includes many
women, who enjoy having their seats reserved for them—in
buses, trams, auditoriums, etc.

Emotions run high on modern feminine fashions and customs. As
we foresaw, objections to most of all suggested items were highest
in the more conservative institutions. However, many parents and
authorities may be surprised at the "liberal" response even there.
To illustrate, we include the scores of Annamalai, one of the most
conservative areas:[8]

lipstick	19	social dancing	4
pony tail	13	bathing costume	3
short hair	12	dating	2
smoking	10	drinking	0
tennis costume	5	none (write-in)	11

Widows are traditionally inauspicious, and according to the
most orthodox belief are the cause of their husbands' deaths.
They were, therefore, treated as outcastes within the family and
community. Their piteous plight has been widely publicized in
recent decades, and many reformers have taken up their cause.
We found almost no feeling that they are *now* considered inauspicious (as they still are in rural areas), but most of our respondents
could see little chance of their rights being fulfilled. "Men won't
marry non-virgins, and that settles it !" "It's best for them to
serve humanity and forget about marriage." Several gave them a
qualified chance. "It depends on their behaviour." "If they haven't
lost their characters." "If they are young and pretty."

We have always been interested in "women's three obediences",
as familiar to Japan and some other cultures as to India. It is true
that many who cast their vote for continuance of the idea specified
that it is no longer necessary to obey *sons*. It is also true that the
total response against the idea is greater than that for it. But we
submit this positive response is one of the inconsistencies so ap-

[8] We have reason to think some scores reflect students' acceptance of a Western
woman and hence her customs. We were on this campus for some weeks, where
we wore a tennis costume and smoked.

parent in the students' blend of old and new—or of theory and practice. As one Delhi girl put it, "Here is where *real* feelings show. Women must still be submissive. But *they don't like it*, and the educated women won't accept it much longer."

Women faculty members, whatever their present status, will be glad to see their total equality is approved. It may be a different story when they are actually in the competitive race.

The Inheritance Law is now a fact, though it was one of the most controversial aspects of the Hindu Code Bill and took years to pass. It is a definite threat to the joint family, for *intact* family land represents that family's *stability* and *perpetuity*. The dowry, consisting of movable goods (money, jewels, clothes, cattle, etc.) gives a girl her share of the family's wealth without jeopardizing its land-based position. For this reason many girls are not given land today, though the law declares their rights equal to those of their brothers.

In theory a girl's dowry is her share of her parental family's wealth (today it is often used for her higher education, or for travel), *security*, for it *sometimes* is treated as an insurance policy —to be returned to her if the marriage does not work, to be made available to her if her husband dies. Ideally it should make her prospective husband appreciate and value her, for she brings him material wealth. But in practice the dowry tends to commercialize marriage, material wealth put above other considerations. It places a market value on a girl—a price her father has to pay to get rid of her, a value for which the husband's family can bargain. The agreed "price" relates not only to the girl's desirability but also to the groom's status, increasingly determined by his education. "The palaver does not usually last long; market rates for bride-grooms find a general stability born of demand and supply. But as in every other commodity, there is inflationary spiralling from year to year. Today in the South, a youth who has managed to pass the competitive examination to get into the Indian Administrative Service can be sure of his Rs. 20,000 dowry, plus a car plus minor considerations on both sides. Every marriage season in the South, the big game hunting expeditions usually center around this class; engineering graduates and other equally desirable bridegrooms come lower in the scale. A mere graduate may be offered Rs. 7,000, a mere adult male Rs. 5,000."[9] We doubt

[9] Kaejee, "Wedding Pipes", *Madras Mail*, May 22, 1960.

whether these "market rates" prevail in all parts of India, but figures larger than these were quoted to us in Gujerat. Many parents who are against the practice feel helpless in the midst of a prevailing system and few are willing to jeopardize their children's future for the sake of principle. Indian fathers well know the burden of having daughters, especially if they are ugly, stupid, or too old ! And Indian women well know the humiliation of being exhibited to "scouting parties like some prize heifer !" There is a Dowry Bill now being considered. It has not yet been passed, and if it does there is little likelihood that it could be enforced, but it represents public sentiment against the practice. Our student respondents are much against the dowry, but as many have commented, "It is still hard to escape the system. As long as families arrange marriages they will be influenced by money."

Prostitution ("immoral traffic") is not our concern in this study. We have no data on the subject, though we did receive many comments on male students' participation on some campuses. We are concerned here only with its relationship to women's destitution. The Central Social Welfare Board recognizes this aspect of the problem, and has earmarked 19 crores for implementing the programme of providing for the reception, care, treatment, training, and employment of the victims. At the higher economic levels "prostitution" changes form. "We don't prostitute ourselves in the red-light district, but I think many of us do in the marriages we are forced to." One of the most sensitive and poignant themes in India is the marriage of young women to *old* men—usually widowers with many children.

Suicide is, we surmise, one way out. As we said before, the rising suicide rate is causing considerable alarm. A social worker offered the opinion that there would be much less suicide if (1) women had more choice in marriage, and (2) if divorces were easier.

Divorce, now legally possible, is not socially sanctioned. Yet many who had said, "There will never be much divorce in India" have been enlightened by the large amount that is taking place in urban areas. "The need is greater than I had imagined", one commented.

No experience, according to Indian tradition, more perfectly prepares Indian girls psychologically for womanhood than that of puberty. As informants for *The Hindu Woman* said, "After that one can adjust to anything—even a stranger as a husband".

TABLE 61

MENSTRUATION

I matured when I was the age of
(open-ended)

Ages from 12-14 were given, 13.5 an average

As regards information and instruction on menstruation	Rank	Total Female %
I had some but not enough	1	38
I had none	2	34
I had sufficient information	3	23

I learned these matters from	Rank	Total Female %
Mother	1	47
Friends	2	30
Books	3	20*
My sister	4	12
Auntie	5	5
A teacher	6	3

The first experience of menstruation	Rank	Total Female %
Was something of a shock	1	48
Was a very great shock	2	25*
Seemed natural	3	19

I was	Rank	Total Female %
Unhappy to enter womanhood	1	49
Happy to enter womanhood	2	26
Indifferent (write-in)	3	13

In my opinion, girls should be told about menstruation	Rank	Total Female %
Before it happens	1	61**
After it happens	2	32

When I matured I	Rank	Total Female %
Experienced no changes	1	40
Was made to help more in household	2	24
Was more restricted in going outside	3	19
Was made to change to saris	4	17
Felt very lonely	5	12
Began to fear marriage	6	10
Began to hear talk about marriage	7	5
Began to look forward to marriage	8	4

TABLE 62
RESTRICTIONS ON MENSTRUATING WOMEN

In our home a menstruating woman may not	Rank	Total Female %
Go to the Temple	1	48
Enter the prayer room or take part in religious ritual	2	45
Run about or take part in sports	3	38
Wash clothes for the family	4	25
Enter kitchen or prepare food	5	23
Take a bath	6	20
Eat food with the family	7	18
No restrictions (write-in)	8	11

These restrictions are	Rank	Total Female %
Less than in the past	1	74
The same as in the past—in the days of my grandmother	2	14

When I have daughters I intend to have them	Rank	Total Female %
Observe fewer restrictions	1	44
Observe no restrictions (write-in)	2.5	21
Observe the same restrictions	2.5	21

TABLE 63
MEDICAL HELP FOR MENSTRUAL PAIN

With respect to menstrual pain	Rank	Total Female %
One should get medical help, as with any other pain	1	74*
One must accept it—it is part of "being a woman"	2	19

TABLE 64
PROTECTION OF WOMEN AGAINST SEXUAL ADVANCES

With respect to the protection of women from sexual advances	Rank	Total Female %
Women generally can protect themselves by their own speech and action	1	79*
Women cannot protect themselves, and therefore their families and society must protect them	2	11

According to the most orthodox practice (giving way gradually for a long time), a girl on maturing changes to saris, is greatly restricted in going out of the house unaccompanied, begins to hear talk of her marriage, is trained more assiduously to household duties, and begins to observe her monthly three days' "outcaste-ism". During this period she may not prepare food, eat with the family, take part in religious ceremonies, or take a bath. "This really makes her submissive! She knows her place then."

There is considerable evidence that the experience of puberty is less restrictive now, though we suspect there is still much trauma, still much sex education that is inadequate. In our addendum for women we received the above information.

The average age of maturation given us seems high. We have no accurate data on this subject, but if these responses have any validity at all they refute the commonly held theory that girls in the tropics mature very early.

Sex education data confirms our opinion given in the last chapter. It is inadequate both quantitatively and qualitatively. Mother and other sources seem much the same as in other countries.

The majority (72.8 per cent) were "shocked" by the first experience of womanhood. 40 per cent experienced "no changes", others had various changes—but obviously less than was the case with their grandmothers. Many cannot take part in religious ceremonies. The next generation, according to these girls, will have far fewer restrictions.

It is very significant that menstrual pain is overwhelmingly considered a medically treatable pain, not woman's lot.

The biological nature and function of woman is fundamental in her differentiation from man. But her attitude toward the female role depends on whether she considers it her "animal nature" or her "procreative function". Indians do, generally, label the sex act as "animal" or "bestial", but on the other hand procreation is highly honoured. We suspect this ambivalence affects women's attitudes towards themselves.

It has perhaps been correctly stated that the traditional Indian woman has enjoyed "individuality" and not "individualism".[10] She has had emotional security and fruition of self in her mother-hood and wifehood—in giving of herself she has attained her self.

[10] We are indebted to Ruby Dube, U.S. Information Service, Delhi, for this statement.

The modern, urban, educated Indian woman has lost the joy of selfless service to a large extent—or, it may be that she is trying too hard to serve in too many new ways. She may have too many, and conflicting, roles. Can a woman be mother, wife, teacher, housekeeper, career woman, and companion-friend? "It is too hard. There isn't enough time in the day, enough physical and emotional energy in me."

The modern Indian woman is joining her Western sisters in this exhausting and frustrating quest even as she knows full well the dangers and possible damage. The hunger for new knowledge, for new experiences, for new selfhood is too great. "Freed intelligence and intelligent freedom are too intoxicating to be denied!" "*I* am now somebody!" Many have already felt the abrasive edge of frustration. Others have become insecure and have retreated. But many are balancing their multiple roles with grace and quiet strength. We have met them, have seen them in their work and in their homes. They command but do not offend; they accept but do not feel defeated; they work very hard but do not feel injured; and among their friends they laugh but do not mock. They give more of themselves than their older sisters, for they have developed selves with richer gifts.

8 | Religion and Ritual

"RELIGION is the air we breathe in India."

Most of our respondents were Hindu, and the portion on "religion" is designed for them. Others were told to respond as was appropriate.

The first two questions were open-ended, saying "The meaning of 'God' to me is ———" and "My family worships chiefly the deity ———." Almost all students responded, and to the best of our ability we have categorized their statements.

TABLE 65
THE MEANING OF GOD

The meaning of 'God' to me is (open-ended)	Rank	Total %	Comparison	
			Male %	Female %
The Supreme Power, the Almighty		44	45	43
The Supernatural, the Divine Force		9	6	13
The Creator		4	5	4
	1	57	56	60
The Father	2	12	11	12
An idea created by man; his own faith	3	6	5	6
Truth	4	4	5	1
Love	5.5	3	3	2
Nature; scientific order	5.5	3	3	2
Complete goodness, Absolute Purity	7	1	1	1
I have no idea		4	5	2
I don't believe in God		3	4	2

119

TABLE 66
FAMILY DEITY

My family worships chiefly the deity (open-ended)	Rank	Total %
Siva (the Creator and Destroyer)	1	19
Vishnu (the Preserver)	2	14
Krishna (incarnation of Vishnu, god of music, art)	3	11
Saraswati (goddess of Wisdom)	4	9
Ganesh, Ganpati (god of prosperity, good luck)	5	6
Ram (hunter, hero of *Ramayana*, incarnation of Vishnu)	6	5
Durga (consort of Siva, the Mother)	7.5	3
Lakshmi (consort of Vishnu, goddess of wealth)	7.5	3
Hanuman (monkey god, friend of Ram)	9.5	2
Muruga (son of Siva)	9.5	2
Kali (consort of Siva, goddess of destruction)	11	1
Misc.: Radha, Sita, many others.		

The Hindu Triad is Brahma (Creator), Siva (Destroyer), and Vishnu (Preserver). In recent centuries Brahma has receded in felt influence, and Siva has taken over the dialectic function of creating and destroying. Most Hindus worship God *via* Siva or Vishnu, but many also worship their incarnations or other gods.

Much more specific inquiry is needed to make definite conclusions about the "nature of God", but the chief conception of God as an "authority" is clear. We do not have many Christian responses, but in our data we can detect no difference between Hindu and Christian conceptions of God (Sikh responses are also similar but Muslim and other responses are qualitatively different); both groups favour God the Power which controls and punishes, both have some favouring God as the Father who guides, comforts, and loves. There is a distinct relationship between the worshippers of Siva and "power", the worshippers of Vishnu and the Father or Love. Most responses describe a Force that relates to the individual person speaking—to his *personal behaviour*.

The great majority of statements amplified the above two conceptions:

1. *The Supreme Authority*

   (a) The Supreme Power, the Almighty

   "The Supreme Power, omnipotent, omnipresent, omniscient."

"The Almighty, infinite, all-powerful."

"God is the Supreme Force, who commands our every action."

"The Supreme Being, who punishes us if we do wrong."

(b) The Supernatural

"The invisible Unconscious that controls us."

"The Divine Force, greater than any of us."

"The Supernatural, the Mysterious Spirit that we can never understand but which we cannot disobey."

(c) The Creator

"Our omnipotent Creator, all-perfect, great, good, and just."

"He who created everything on earth and who controls us."

2. *The Father*

"The Father who loves and guides us."

"An infinitely wise, omniscient Father, who watches over me, always ready to steady me when I slip."

In addition to the above majority descriptions, we note the following groups:

3. *Ritualistic*

"Work is worship." (H)[1]

"Worship of the Sacred Name." (H)

"Performance of sacred duty." (H)

4. *Abstract*

"Knowledge, existence, bliss." (H)

"Absolute purity." (H)

"Peace of mind." (H)

"Peace, truth, non-violence." (H)

"Happiness and peace." (Ch.)

"The true, the good, the beautiful." (H)

"Complete goodness." (M)

5. *Personal*

"Inspiration to us all." (M)

[1] Indication whether Hindu, Christian, Muslim, Zoroastrian.

"Caretaker of us all." (Z)

"Teacher of Life." (M)

"He keeps us sinless." (H)

"The Merciful and Good." (M)

"A higher Power who enlightens and strengthens me." (H)

"Strength and light of my life." (H)

"Light to my darkness." (Ch.)

"Who commands us to do good." (Z)

6. *Humanistic*

"God is a feeling of oneness with all other persons." (H)

"God is in everything, is not something outside the world." (H)

"He is our own creation—to keep us from the wrong path and to give peace of mind." (H)

"Only a fear under which we do not commit sins and try to be good." (H)

"That which gives satisfaction to the mind." (H)

"If one has faith in Him he does help you." (H)

"Self-realization." (H)

7. *Agnostic or atheistic*

"Absurd and un-understandable." (H)

"Nothing but a religious ambiguity." (H)

"Nothing! I am a confirmed atheist—10 years of Jesuit training has seen to that." (H)

It is interesting to contrast the above open-ended responses on "God" with the following multiple-choice responses on "religion". "Love of all mankind" ranks well above "faith in a Supreme Force", this question relating to the nature of "religion", the former to the nature of "God". They are not mutually exclusive concepts. We do not know what "love of all mankind" means to our respondents and welcome further inquiry. We do know this concept is fundamental in the sacred scriptures and in the teaching and writings of Ram Mohan Roy, Tagore, Ramakrishna, Gandhi, and others. But we suspect it is largely a sanctified verbalism to most people (as "Christian humility" and other concepts are in the West). Granting that it is always easier to love an abstract

TABLE 67

MOST IMPORTANT ASPECTS OF RELIGION

In my opinion the most important aspects of religion are	Rank	Total %	Comparison	
			Male %	Female %
Love of all mankind	1	80***	76	84
Faith in a Supreme Force	2	67**	66	66
Personal devotion to god	3	55*	54	56
Triumph of virtue over evil	4	54*	56	49
Comfort when in trouble	5	42—	41	43
Rules and guides for daily living	6	39	40	36
The meaning given to life	7	38*	38	38
The joy of worship	8	30	26	35
The fear of punishment for sin	9	26	27	24
Belonging to a community	10	14	12	15
The fear of evil spirits	11.5	12	13	11
Belief in reincarnation	11.5	12—	13	10

"mankind" than one's neighbour or mother-in-law, we submit neither sociological nor religious aspects of Indian culture substantiate this valued phrase. From the point of view of social science, India has been and still is a collection of separate groups —geographically, linguistically, religiously, caste-wise, class-wise —which have never felt and acted on a national kinship level (save during the Independence Movement), let alone an international kinship level (except recently with relation to "the coloured peoples of the world"). From the point of view of religion, Hinduism is basically metaphysical rather than ethical. It is fundamentally concerned with man's relationship to God. What seems to relate to fellow man—as "hospitality" and "the giving of alms"—is enjoined as a religious duty, through which one accrues credit. The charity of those about to depart life at Banares seems to prove this self-centered aspect of virtue. We are not saying that all Hinduism is religiously mechanistic or legalistic—the hospitality many of us have enjoyed is warmly humanistic. But we are wondering what "love of all mankind" really means to our respondents.

Considerable negative emotion is expressed over "comfort when in trouble" and "belief in reincarnation", the latter ranking lowest— but central to Hinduism. It may be the phrase was not understood. "Fear of evil spirits" is also low, which is not surprising in relation to educated respondents (it would be a different matter in rural areas). It is somewhat surprising to us, however, that the two groups scoring the highest responses to this item were the *science* students at Kanja Kubja College (9 responses) and Osmania College of Science (8 responses). It was at Kanja Kubja College that we observed some naivity as regards "possible conflicts over science and religion" during a group interview. We discussed among other matters the preservation of great numbers of diseased and useless cattle. These two areas—science and religion—seemed to be entirely separate and hence there was no question of conflict in most students' minds. Members of the science faculty, on the other hand, frankly stated that they found many incompatibilities. And a science faculty member at another college said, "There are conflicts between science and religion. I have the scientific point of view, but like others have to give in to home and women. For instance, every time I dissect animals—as I do almost every day— I have to purify myself when I go home. It is a great nuisance, but this is the only way to resolve the conflict!" An Indian social scientist commented, "India has a split personality as regards science and religious tradition. So we love scientific rationalizations, as 'pan is good for the digestion'."

Astrology is widely considered a science, as it also is in many other countries. Belief in it is widespread, even among many highly educated people. Horoscopes are determined from the *exact* moment of birth (any mistakes are due to an inaccurately given time of birth), and auspicious moments for important moves are similarly carefully computed. We were frequently given the following arguments proving astrology to be a science:

1. It is based on precise and complicated mathematical computations.
2. It is based on scientifically determined movements of the stars.
3. We are unable to understand it, but it is worked out by learned men who have made it their life study.

These are most unscientific arguments, but are passionately held by many. Others have an opposite view. "Complete nonsense!" "One hundred per cent superstition!"

We did not seek data on superstitions—they are fascinating but difficult to interpret. The cat and the mirror seem to have the same symbolism as in the West, but we note several others—

unfamiliar at least to us. "It is inauspicious to see a widow when
going out in front. One must then wait ten minutes." "It is bad
luck to sneeze when going out. It's better then to stay at home."
And, common in the villages of the Madras area, "If a white chicken
crosses the tether rope of a cow some catastrophe will happen".
Community Block Development officers, who have been giving
villagers day-old Leghorn chicks flown out from England, have
had some luck in surmounting the superstition, but for the most
part have had to change to Rhode Island Red chicks. As in all
countries, superstitions are especially common among the rural
uneducated—but have a strange hold, too, on some educated people.
Our student respondents generally view them negatively.

TABLE 68

FREQUENCY OF FAMILY'S VISIT TO TEMPLE

My family goes to the Temple	Rank	Total %
About once a week	1	33
About once a month	2	27
About once a year	3	21
About once a day	4	13
Never	5	5
Several times a day	6	4

TABLE 69

FESTIVALS AND RITUALS OBSERVED BY FAMILY

My family generally observes	Rank	Total %
Divali	1	83*
New Year	2	71
Dusserah	3	64*
Birthdays of gods	4	59*
Harvest Festival	5	40
Holi (write-in)	6	6

My family observes	Rank	Total %
Holy days and festivals	1	72*
Auspicious occasions	2	64
Going to the Temple	3	61
Religious ritual in the home	4	53
Going on pilgrimages	5	35
Food laws	6.5	34
Ancestor worship	6.5	34
Purification ceremonies	8	32
Priest attached to household	9	25

TABLE 70

RITUALS NOT OBSERVED BY ME

I myself do not believe in	Rank	Total %	Comparison	
			Male %	Female %
Purification ceremonies	1	55*	59	49
Priest attached to household	2	49*	45	53
Going on pilgrimages	3	44	44	43
Ancestor worship	4	40	37	44
Going to the Temple	5.5	38	40	35
Religious ritual in the home	5.5	38	42	31
Auspicious occasions	7	33	35	30
Holy days and festivals	8	28	31	22
Food laws	9	22	7	42

TABLE 71

FAMILY'S ATTITUDE TO CASTE

My family	Rank	Total %
Does not take caste seriously	1	61*
Does not practise caste	2	23
Is strict about caste observance	3	20

TABLE 72

CASTE AND RELIGION

In my opinion, caste	Rank	Total %	Comparison	
			Male %	Female %
Is not essential to religion	1	55*	54	54
Is wrong	2	40*	41	38
Is essential to religion	3	13	11	16

TABLE 73

DEMOCRACY AND RELIGION

In my opinion democracy	Rank	Total %	Comparison	
			Male %	Female %
Has nothing to do with religion	1	75**	78	69
Is affecting Hinduism	2	17	17	16

Many upper class Hindus have a priest attached to the household, but attendance at the Temple is also relatively common. Many university administrators and professors go daily if possible—at least in the more conservative areas. Going to the Temple differs somewhat from going to a Western church in that it is purely personal worship and has no social aspects. In worship the emphasis ranges from an emphasis on fear and placation, especially among the uneducated, to the joy of worship. Hinduism, as is well known, has appeals "from the kindergarten level of childish ritual" to intense, abstract intellectualism.

Most Hindu homes have prayer rooms or niches containing the family gods and conduct daily worship. Occasionally there is a special occasion, as Ganesh's birthday. Women are the chief upholders of ritual. "Holy days and festivals" rank first in observations, "auspicious occasions", "going to the Temple", "religious ritual in the home", "going on pilgrimages", "ancestor worship", "food laws", "purification ceremonies", and "priest attached to household" following in that order. Through these items we note that about 72 per cent to 25 per cent indicate family observation. But many student respondents are apparently against these practices, "purification ceremonies" ranking first. They are most tolerant of food laws. It is interesting that a much higher proportion of girls than boys are against food laws. It is the only significant difference of ranking in this item. One girl said, "Ritual is too mechanistic", but another insisted, "Without it there would be no discipline, and not much family fun". Many admit their enjoyment of ritual but their dislike of the arduous preparations.

Auspicious occasions are determined by astrology and determine every important move of the most orthodox. Even at less orthodox levels, the *exact* moment of marriage, the best days for important business ventures, the best hours for moving into a new house are determined. For instance, after the completion of the new girls' hostel at Annamalai University, the girls asked to move into it at 8.30 on a Saturday morning—it was an auspicious hour. Many do not approve of "auspiciousness" but are afraid to test it.

The majority of students' families "do not take caste too seriously", and more reject caste entirely than practise it conscientiously. Some Christian respondents indicated "some" practice of caste. It is well known that caste is much stronger in the South than in the North, that it is stronger in the rural areas than in the urban.

The students are definitely more liberal than their parents and vote overwhelmingly against caste. "It is our heritage of ancient folly!" one student wrote. Their emotion seems to relate chiefly to the *inequalities* of caste and much less to the *community* aspect. Many are loath to disregard it in marriage, for instance. The sub-caste is called a "community", and its members hold similar customs and values. Thus marrying a member of the community ensures a certain amount of compatibility. We know many modern and even foreign-educated Indians who are permitted by their parents to marry whom they please—even non-Indians—but who "would not dream of marrying outside the community". "This sounds like bigotry", one young woman admitted, "but so far as I'm concerned it has to do with *daily* living. When ritual and religious custom are as important as they are with us, it's much easier to live with those observing the same details. Even every meal—what it is and how it is served—is involved." Another woman said in her case it was less a case of ritual than that of belief. "People in a community *think* the same way."

There seems little doubt that Hinduism is rapidly rejecting caste and that as a religion "it does not need it". Students reflect this view in their response on "democracy and Hinduism", though we submit they are somewhat naive in their separation of religion and ideological system. Democracy is the latter, it is not just a political structure. It rests on basic assumptions as regards the individual that seem to be antithetical to basic Hindu assumptions.

Hinduism, an amazing religion without founder, creed, or organized clergy (except within each Temple) has been a distinct *culture* for centuries, has been the cement binding together a disunited multi-cultural people throughout countless invasions and changes. It has done this without proselytizing, without missionaries—though it has had its great interpreters. Its strength lies in the sacred scriptures and on people's *acceptance of them*. Their stories and meaning have been transmitted largely within the home—through prayers, stories, and ritual. Art, music, literature, and the dance have been *religious*. Boys have emulated Rama, girls have been brought up "as Sita". Modern Indian life threatens this transmission. In the "separate family" there are fewer older folk—as Grandmothers and Aunties—to tell the stories. There is less time for them, too, as new mass media and new occupations take over. At one time young people would have been strongly influenced by the scriptures—as, for instance, in the *specific instruction* in the *Kamasutra* and the *Laws of Manu*—but today few students know their own religious heritage, a matter of grave concern to many. At first the cinema chiefly featured religious epics, but modern social drama has pushed back this interest. Adult education leaders have seen rural reading material as "natural" for religious stories, but nutrition, sanitation, scientific agriculture, village democracy, how to raise children, and how to get along with husband or mother-in-law seem more necessary.

It would seem that much in Hinduism is being challenged. Its central structure is

Varna—caste, kin, colour, occupation.
Dharma—one's function in that caste.
Karma—one's personal destiny, as determined by performance of dharma.
Samsara—one's progress on the wheel of life, from bondage to illumination.
Nirvana—Union with the Divine, union of Atman (universal man) and Brahman (universal God).

Among the *educated*, "Varna" is strongly repudiated. As for "Dharma", modern economic and educational opportunities make it possible for people to reject inherited, prescribed roles. There is no *virtue* today in being a good sweeper because one was born a Harijan. It is stupid to "be a good Sudra farmer" if the rewards are much greater in the automobile repair shop or the veterinary hospital. Few would agree with the student who wrote, "Better is one's own dharma though imperfectly performed than the dharma of another well performed. Better is death in the performance of one's dharma —the dharma of another is fraught with evil." More are in agreement with "The only karma I'm interested in is a better life *here and now*". This *temporal* quality of destiny and life is becoming more satisfying than the eon-aged wheel of life. As one young man said, "I can't *reject* re-birth and the wheel of life, but I don't think about them. I can think only about the life I'm living now. And if I'm re-born later I'll think then about that life."

Hinduism, thus, though an absorptive religion that once developed caste and is now rejecting it, that once introduced idols and may later reject them, is meeting a central challenge in *scientific rational-*

ism. The impact of science is too new in India for anyone to judge total or future effect on country, but the impact on university students is visible now. Many students are accused of losing their religious faith. This may be true. Or it may be they are rejecting only the external trappings of tradition. Or, indeed, that they are finding new dimensions in religion—new ways of realizing the self or of serving society. Many are openly critical of a society which permits so much unnecessary suffering. "I am beginning to understand," a thoughtful adult told us, "that getting decent *laws* is probably the best way to keep people from being exploited or subjected. You have many such laws in the West. They are not put in religious terms, but they do what religion has only talked about." We are not wise enough to judge or predict on this matter, but it is our observation that religion is low on the interest scale of most students—in their conversations with us and in their reported conversations with each other.

We do not want to give the impression that we consider Indian students "irreligious". It is our observation that Indians are generally more religious than Americans, and that Indian students are generally more religious than American students. We recall, for instance, the devotions to Saraswati, graciously offered by Miranda House girls in honour of the guests—members of an international educational conference. This is just one example among many. We are saying that India is becoming both secular and scientific, that most educated Indians seem to find more of their values in the market-place, laboratory, or world scene than in the sacred scriptures.

An ultra-modern student put it this way. "When I was 14, I saw my baby sister die a horrible death that could have been prevented by scientific medicine. Everyone said 'It is the will of God'. I vowed I would devote my life to changing this inhuman excuse for neglect in my country. That is why I am going to be a doctor." And an ultra-conservative student was perhaps saying the same thing: "To serve society is to serve oneself. Realizing the Self is to enjoy bliss from within and without. To realize the Self is to realize God, and *service to men is service to God*."

9 | *Spiritualism or Materialism?*

"PRINCIPLES of life" cannot properly be separated from "religion", but we deliberately treated them separately in our questionnaire, partly to avoid the title of "religion". No item caused us more difficulty in formulation, and we are aware that the multi-choice nature of the question subtracts from its value. Many students responded positively to *every* item (we discarded their responses in the table below, feeling they give no discrimination) and others to many. In trials, however, we had had so little open-ended response—it is extremely difficult to write one's philosophy of life—that we resorted to the multi-choice method.

We had found in oral discussion that almost everyone gave "honesty", "sincerity", "cooperation", and "kindness", so put them first on the questionnaire. What these qualities mean to students in theory or practice we are not sure, but they rank high in valued life principles. "Good manners" have frequently been mentioned to me as "very important". "Respect for elders", "service to others", "doing one's duty", and "respecting people of any age", etc. are traditional values still honoured, though "respect of elders" had many protest double-minuses. Other traditional values—"obedience to authorities", "being content with life", "working for social harmony", and "sacrifice of self for others" had significant response but ranked much lower and were scored with many double-minuses. "Ambition—desire to get ahead", "initiative—using new ideas", "developing the self", "being constructively critical", and "working for social justice" are newer values. They show both support and disapproval.

We had hoped for discrimination between "social harmony" and "social justice" but did not find it. They are undoubtedly

131

TABLE 74
THE MOST IMPORTANT PRINCIPLES OF LIFE

In my opinion the most important principles of life are	Rank	Total %	Comparison	
			Male %	Female %
Honesty	1	85**	85	83
Sincerity	2	82**	79	84
Cooperation	3	80**	81	78
Kindness	4	77**	75	78
Good manners	5	71*	71	71
Respect for elders	6	68*—	65	70
Service to others	7	67*	69	62
Doing one's duty	8	66*	61	71
Respecting people of any age, sex, religion, class, caste, nation	9	64*—	62	61
Ambition—desire to get ahead	10	61*—	59	61
Initiative—using new ideas	12.5	59*—	59	58
Standing up for one's rights	12.5	59*—	60	56
Developing the self	12.5	59*—	56	60
First loyalty to all mankind	12.5	59**	61	54
First loyalty to God	15	55**—	55	53
Obedience to authorities	16	53*—	56	48
Sacrifice of self for others	18	52*	54	48
Working for social justice	18	52	56	45
Working for social harmony	18	52	56	45
First loyalty to nation	19	49*—	55	39
First loyalty to family	20	48*	42	53
Being constructively critical	21	44—	47	40
Being content with life	22	33—	27	41
First loyalty to cultural group	23	21—	17	27

Misc. write-ins: self-reliance, self-confidence, enjoyment of life.

difficult concepts to understand without elaboration. There was more discrimination in the "first loyalty" group, though many students marked more than one. It is clear that first loyalty does not go to "cultural group", and that "mankind" and "God" command more loyalty than family or nation—at least in this verbalized response. The girls were higher in "individuality", "doing one's duty", and "first loyalty to family"; the boys were higher in "service to others", "first loyalty to nation", and "first loyalty to mankind".

We were especially interested in the emotional nature of the Annamalai University responses. They showed many double-pluses and double-minuses on "individuality", "standing up for

one's rights", "ambition", "initiative", "development of self",
"first loyalty to cultural group", and "first loyalty to God". These
items were, obviously, controversial in their experience.

Many students were inconsistent in their responses. For instance,
sometimes both "obedience to authority" and "standing up for
one's rights" were checked or "doing one's duty" and "ambition—
desire to get ahead", or "developing the self" and "sacrifice of
self for others". These inconsistencies genuinely reflect, we think,
the conflicting values held by many students in these transition
times.

All in all, this response—inaccurate as we are sure it is in some
respects—does indicate (1) the strength of traditional values and
(2) the definite challenge of new values. As illustration, a Visva-
Bharati man wrote, "Do your *dharma* and leave the results to
God", and a 16-year old youth from Calcutta mused, "What is Life ?
How can I feel it under the shelter of my parents ?"

TABLE 75

JOBS HAVING HIGH PRESTIGE IN INDIA

The jobs with the most prestige in India are (open-ended)	Rank	Total %	Comparison	
			Male %	Female %
Indian Administration and Govt. Services	1	58	65	47
Doctor	2	41	36	48
Engineer	3	36	37	34
High position in good (foreign) business	4	20	18	21
Lecturer, professor	5	19	21	15
Teacher	6	13	12	14
Armed Forces Officer	7	12	9	14
Judge	8	10	12	8
Lawyer	9	9	9	8
Important political leader	11.5	7	10	4
Indian Foreign Service Officer	11.5	7	9	4
Scientist	11.5	7	9	4
Social worker (reformer)	11.5	7	6	8
Minister of State	14	5	8	2
Police officer, District Supt. of Police	15.5	4	6	2
Principal—college, Vice-Chancellor	15.5	4	4	4
(Jobs with highest salaries)	18	2	3	1
Farmer	18	2	2	2
Prime Minister, President	18	2	3	1
Secretary in Govt.	20.5	1	2	0
Housewife	20.5	1	0	3

Misc.: Athlete, Chief Justice, Member Parliament, chartered accountant, artist,
scholar, banker, cinema star, millionaire, black marketeer.

TABLE 76
THINGS HAVING A PRESTIGE VALUE IN INDIA

In India it gives one prestige to (have a)	Rank	Total %	Comparison	
			Male %	Female %
University degree	1	85*	88	79
Foreign degree	2	84**	82	84
Important job	3	65*	59	71
Speak English	4.5	57*	56	58
Automobile	4.5	57	57	55
Live in a modern house	6	55	54	55
Live in a big house	7	51	55	45
Servants	8.5	42	42	41
Expensive wedding	8.5	42	37	48
European clothes	10.5	32	36	26
Wear a lot of jewelry	10.5	32	30	34
Be modern—in religion, etc.	12	31	29	33
Belong to clubs	13	28	24	34
Wear a watch	14	22	23	21
Have autocratic manner with inferiors	15.5	11	16	3
Be conservative—in religion, etc.	15.5	11	9	13
Cycle	17	8	8	7

Misc. write-ins: good family ties, gift of oratory, elegant wife.

TABLE 77
FACTORS IN PRESTIGE

In my opinion, the 3 or 4 most important factors in prestige are (open-ended)	Rank	Total %	Comparison	
			Male %	Female %
A good education—university degree	1	43	42	39
A good job	2	25	27	22
Character and personality	3	21	24	16
Good manners	4	13	13	14
Honesty, sincerity	5	11	12	10
Family position, reputation	7	10	11	9
A foreign degree	7	10	9	11
Intelligence, efficiency, ability	7	10	9	10
Wealth	9.5	9	9	10
Be modern—move with the times	9.5	9	8	10
Sense of service, sacrifice	11	8	7	10
Sociable, get along well with all people	12	7	8	5
Expensive and modern clothes	13.5	5	5	3
Hard work	13.5	5	6	3
Kindness, friendliness	15.5	3	3	3
Broadmindedness	15.5	3	4	2
Many (influential) friends	17.5	2	3	2
Firm views, and iron will, disciplined mind	17.5	2	3	1
Confidence, self-respect	19.5	1	2	0
Religious, spiritual	19.5	1	1	1

Misc.: respect for parents, preservation of tradition, ambition, courage, patriotism, high salary, chastity, sober Indian woman as wife.

We counterpose against this expression of philosophy of life the responses related to "prestige". Prestige is only one aspect of *operational life*, but it may be central in influencing training, decisions about career, the way one lives adult life. These responses are again only verbal, but they seem to touch closely to actual life.

There is no doubt about the students' view of prime prestige in Indian Administrative and Government Services, though girls had a slightly higher response for "doctors". Doctors and engineers rank well, with those in high positions in *good* (often "foreign") business and industry fourth. College lecturing, teaching, and law follow. The ranking of male and female responses is remarkably similar and has no significant difference.

Prestige is apparently seen as aided most by education, preferably with a foreign degree, by a good job, the use of English, an automobile, large and modern houses, servants, an expensive wedding, European clothes, jewelry, a modern point of view, and club membership. These items score from 85-28 per cent of the total response and represent significant opinion. The only important difference in male and female response is that more boys favour European clothes (not surprising) and more girls club membership (somewhat surprising).

In the open-ended question on "most important factors in prestige", many items from the previous table were repeated. We included only the three highest to indicate their apparent importance, but discarded others (as "speak English") and began ranking with new factors. The first, "character and personality", gets a 25 per cent response and is significant—but is again one of the items we find ambiguous. Manners, honesty, family position, intelligence and ability, wealth, modern views, a sense of service, sociability, hard work, and expensive and modern clothes follow. Girls rank wealth and sense of service higher than boys do. Several students wrote "Simple living and high thinking"; one said that "prestige cannot be given"; and another that "there is no such thing as *real* prestige—all is false".

A prestige item that does not appear in the questionnaire but which is notably apparent in current Indian society is the prestige of famous Indian cinema stars. These idols enjoy more worship than many religious figures, and we are told the DMK political party in particular makes political use of their appeal. Some of the largest throngs of adoration we have seen this year were enjoying *darshan* from cinema stars.

It is abundantly evident that the educated young people of India are as materialistic as their Western cousins—and for the same reasons. Whether prestige is false or not, rewards and punishments in real life shape one's operational values. This does not mean the "nobler" attributes of life are entirely discarded, nor does it indicate that all that is materialistic is dross. There is nothing very spiritual about women staggering under too-heavy burdens, children spreading road tar instead of studying in school, or men driven to petty stealing in order to feed their families. Not all middle or upper class families find happiness by any means, but when life is undergirded with the necessities and some luxuries, happiness, kindness, generosity, affection, and many other attributes have a chance. Indian students know this and are directing their lives accordingly. Not many would admit to being materialistic— "spiritualistic" and "materialistic" are emotionally charged labels —but their choices are clear. If their responses reflect some false glitter we can point out that this is true in all cultures—because their forebears supplied the gilt.

10 | Politics and Parties

"POLITICS", whether noble or nasty, is a democratic nation's only structure of self-government, a people's only representation toward growth and improvement. Independent India immediately based her destiny on the will of the whole people via complete adult suffrage and has now gone through "the first idealistic stage when we're chiefly concerned about getting people to vote". Apparent now is the familiar challenge of political propaganda and machination that ever threatens true representation. Further, representation in itself is seen as inadequate. "It is stupid to vote without *intelligent* understanding." From village banyan tree to college campus, politics is the yeast of the new order. And as the party which won independence ages and weakens, controversy over new parties and new platforms grows.

No party is as yet an effective challenger to the Congress Party. Among the many parties in India those in which the student respondents indicated involvement are

The *Indian National Congress*—Nehru's party, the party in power, dedicated to democratic socialism.

The *Praja Socialist Party* (PSP)—a socialist party "left" of Congress.

The *Communist Party*—at the extreme "left".

The *Swatantra Party*—"Freedom Party", to the "right" of Congress, dedicated to less government control, more private enterprise; especially strong in the South.

The *Dravida Munnetra Kazhakam Party* (DMK)—a "local culture" party in the South, generally against the domination of the Brahmins and the North, for the creation of a separate

"Dravidisthan".

The *Bharatiya Jan Sangh* (Jan Sangh)—militant rightist group in the North, especially desiring a stiffer attitude toward Kashmir.

We are *not* concerned in this study with the political affiliation of any or all of the students—but only with any evidence of their interests and activities relating to the larger scene beyond their family and campus life. We take the position that an important aspect of being "modern" is personal involvement in national and international issues. What opinions the students reflect on these issues is of little moment here. In the following items we tried to select a few important and controversial matters—the ones most frequently seen in the news, the ones most affecting the nation.

TABLE 78

RESPECT FOR AUTHORITY

India has traditionally put authority in the "head" of the family, the "head" of the village, etc. I personally respect authority in	Rank	Total %	Comparison	
			Male %	Female %
My parents	1	83**	80	84
My nation's government	2	60*	63	53
Myself	3	47*—	51	39
My village's (city's) government	4	25	30	16
My religious leaders	5	16—	13	19
Political leaders (write-in)	6	7	10	3

Misc. write-ins: my teachers, the State government.

Family still has prime authority over the individual—and need not, of course, be in conflict with national authority. The positive response for authority in "myself" is significant. We should have included "political leaders" and "State Government" as items, but note the relatively small response in favour of village or city government and religious leaders (backed by a higher proportion of girls than boys).

TABLE 79
FAMILY'S INTEREST IN POLITICS

In my family there is	Rank	Total %
A little interest in politics	1	61
Much interest in politics	2	34*
No interest in politics	3	7

TABLE 80
MY INTEREST IN POLITICS

I myself am	Rank	Total %	Comparison Male %	Female %
Somewhat interested in politics	1	57	51	65
Much interested in politics	2	32*	42	17
Not interested in politics	3	17	8	28

TABLE 81
FAMILY'S POLITICAL AFFILIATIONS

My family supports the political party	Rank	Total %
Congress	1	59*
Swatantra	2	10
PSP	3	4
DMK	4	3
Jan Sangh (write-in)	5.5	2
Communist	5.5	2
None		8

TABLE 82
MY POLITICAL AFFILIATIONS

I myself support	Rank	Total %	Comparison Male %	Female %
Congress	1	59*	59	59
Swatantra	2	12	12	11
Communist	3	5	5	6
DMK	4.5	4	5	3
PSP	4.5	4	6	1
Jan Sangh (write-in)	6	2	3	0
None		5	3	9

TABLE 83

CHIEF POLITICAL INSTRUCTOR IN THE FAMILY

The chief political instructor in my family is	Rank	Total %	Comparison	
			Male %	Female %
My father	1	51*	45	58
Myself	2	33*	42	20
My older brother	3	11	10	12
Misc. write-ins: mother, uncle, grandmother, newspapers, books.				

There is no significant difference between family and respondent interest in politics, except that 16.5 per cent of the students compared to 6.5 per cent of the families are reported with no interest. This may be a genuine indication of less interest—certainly we discovered many students with little political concern—or it may also relate to current administrative fiats and public opinion against students' political activity.

The only difference between family and student affiliation with political party is a higher student proportion connected with the various opposition parties. The Jan Sangh ought to have been a printed item—it may warrant a higher response. The Congress party is the clear leader—an expression of opinion that tallies with actual party power.

Father is the chief political instructor in families, but the students themselves are often taking the lead, especially in the case of boys. Several respondents wrote that no *person* is the instructor and that "books and newspapers give me my information". We are aware of the great influence of political leaders, but had been seeking "instruction within the family".

TABLE 84

THE CENTRAL GOVERNMENT IN INDIA

The present Central Government of India	Rank	Total %	Comparison	
			Male %	Female %
Should be stronger, doing more for people	1	57*	57	55
Is doing a good job	2	48*	53	41
Is full of corruption	3	30*	30	29
Should let people manage their own affairs more	4	21	25	16
Is not doing a good job	5	13	15	11
Should give more consideration to my district	6	11*	13	7
Misc. write-in: should permit secession rights.				

TABLE 85
COMMUNITY DEVELOPMENT SCHEME

With respect to the Community Development Scheme	Rank	Total %	Comparison	
			Male %	Female %
It is doing some good	1	42	45	37
It is doing much good	2	37*	35	40
I know very little about it	3	27	21	34
It is useless	4	5	7	3

TABLE 86
CO-OPERATIVE FARMING

With respect to the Cooperative Farming Plan	Rank	Total %	Comparison	
			Male %	Female %
It is a good plan	1	57*	59	52
I know very little about it	2	28	20	37
It is a poor plan	3	17	23	9

TABLE 87
IMPORT RESTRICTIONS

With respect to the severe restriction on imports	Rank	Total %	Comparison	
			Male %	Female %
They are necessary and helpful	1	66*	70	59
I know nothing about these matters	2	17	12	23
They are unnecessary and harmful	3	13	13	12

TABLE 88
THE NATIONAL LANGUAGE PROBLEM

With respect to the national language problem	Rank	Total %	Comparison	
			Male %	Female %
I think Hindi should be the national language	1	56**	50	63
I think English should be the national language	2	42**	46	35
I think the local language should be used for all purposes	3	12	12	11

Misc. write-in: Bengali should be the national language.

TABLE 89

THE KASHMIR QUESTION

With respect to the Kashmir question	Rank	Total %	Comparison	
			Male %	Female %
India's position is correct	1	54**	58	48
There should be a plebiscite—let Kashmir decide	2	28*	30	26
Let the United Nations settle the question	3	16	15	16
I am undecided	4	12	5	22
Pakistan's position is correct	5	3	3	1

TABLE 90

INDIA'S FOREIGN POLICY

With respect to India's foreign policy	Rank	Total %	Comparison	
			Male %	Female %
It is preserving the peace	1	70**	75	62
We must remain friendly with China	2	43	47	36
Communism is a danger	3	36*	43	26
Colonialism is a danger	4	31*	36	22
I know nothing about it	5	10	3	20
It is leading us to war	6	3	3	4
Appeasement is dangerous (write-in)	7	1	2	1

TABLE 91

THE UNITED NATIONS

With respect to the United Nations	Rank	Total %	Comparison	
			Male %	Female %
It is doing a good job	1	62*	65	56
It should have more power	2	41*	51	27
It is useless	3	11*	9	12
I know nothing about it	4	6	2	12
China should be represented (write-in)	5	1	1	1

As is natural, boys are generally more interested in political matters than most girls. Much confidence in the current policy of the Central Government is reflected, and the response on the Co-operative Farming Plan—a plan subject to violent controversy in the press—indicates considerable party loyalty, though there is a strong expression as regards corruption. Some respondents are extremely inconsistent—as, for instance, a Communist Party adherent who votes *strongly* for the Central Government doing a good job, the value of the Community Development Scheme, the Cooperative Farming Plan, and the United Nations.

Many frankly admit ignorance about the Community Development Scheme, the Cooperative Farming Plan, the restrictions on imports, and foreign policy, but others have discriminating opinions. The emotional nature of the national language problem is reflected in responses, a militant group in the South voting for English. "Kashmir" is even more emotionally viewed. Several Banares students expressed to us their "sense of being insulted" that Kashmir was listed as a "problem". "No respecting Indian considers it a problem ! Kashmir is a part of India !" 28.3 per cent of the respondents feel Kashmir should decide the issue, however, and 15.8 per cent want the United Nations to settle the question. Most of the latter responses came, we note, from areas far from Kashmir, as Annamalai and Santiniketan. The tiny response for Pakistan's rights is not statistically significant, but it may be of interest that 7 of the 10 responses came from non-Muslims.

The Chinese border troubles have heightened interest in India's foreign policy, and it is significant that fear of Communism outranks fear of Colonialism. A number of students expressed their concern over "non-alignment", and during interviews we heard some outspoken disapproval of the official policy.

There is general approval of the United Nations, but—as is also the case in other countries—little faith in it as regards its ability to "guarantee the peace". We have found few students who know much about the U.N., and one explained cynically, "It has not been in our syllabi".

Interest in other nations and the international scene is growing, however, partly because of the large number of students studying abroad.

TABLE 92

FOREIGN COUNTRIES ABOUT WHICH I HAVE SOME KNOWLEDGE

I know a good deal about the following nations: (open-ended)	Rank	Total %	Comparison	
			Male %	Female %
U.S.A.	1	81	89	68
United Kingdom	2	69	77	56
U.S.S.R.	3	49	60	32
China	4	34	33	29
Pakistan	5	20	24	14
West Germany	6	18	24	8
Japan	7.5	16	18	12
France	7.5	16	23	5
Ceylon	9	12	15	7
Africa (esp. Ghana)	10	10	5	15
Australia	12	5	6	4
Burma	12	5	7	1
United Arab Republic	12	5	7	1
Switzerland	14	4	6	1
Italy	15.5	2	2	1
Egypt	15.5	2	5	1

Misc.: Spain, Yugoslavia, Malaya, Indonesia, Tibet, Nepal, Canada.

TABLE 93

FOREIGN COUNTRIES ABOUT WHICH I WOULD LIKE TO KNOW MORE

And should like to know much more about these nations: (open-ended)	Rank	Total %	Comparison	
			Male %	Female %
U.S.A.	1	42	43	40
U.S.S.R.	2	38	40	35
China	3	23	24	20
United Kingdom	4	19	18	19
West Germany	5	18	20	15
Japan	6	17	20	14
France	7	10	8	12
Africa, esp. Ghana	8	9	9	9
Australia	9	7	6	8
United Arab Republic, Egypt	10.5	5	7	2
Switzerland	10.5	5	7	2
Canada	12	3	3	2
Latin America	14	2	3	1
Pakistan	14	2	1	2
South Africa	14	2	1	2
Italy	16.5	1	2	1
Denmark	16.5	1	2	1

Misc.: Tibet, Sweden, Portugal, Indonesia.

TABLE 93—(Contd.)

Because (open-ended)

The many responses we have categorized thus:

1. Knowledge is important. I want to know about them. These subjects were neglected in my education. (139 responses)
2. These are the most advanced nations of the West, and we should learn from them. (U.S.A., U.K., U.S.S.R., Germany, France, Switzerland, Australia). (107 responses)
3. These are the nations advancing most rapidly now. (Japan, West Germany)
4. I want to compare America and Russia.
5. I want to know more about Russia. (I am afraid of her.) (I admire her system.)
6. I want to understand China. Why did she break the Panch Sheela?
7. These are the nations fighting against the evils of colonialism.
8. These are the nations of coloured peoples. I want to understand them.
9. I may go there to study.
10. I want to understand why the West is interested in India.
11. I am a cricket fan and want to know more about Australia.
12. I want to understand Portugal. Why don't they give us Goa?

Miscellaneous: Interest in "Denmark's content", "Egypt's patriotism", "Paris fashions", "the beautiful women in France". "These are the nations (U.A.R., Africa, Australia) where the destiny of man is to be shaped—the development of the welfare of humanity depends on them. They are highly explosive spots and may lead to the destruction of the earth."

The response to "I know a good deal about the following nations" was extremely high for an open-ended item, but the results are misleading. Many students questioned orally knew almost nothing about nations listed. There was even considerable ignorance about "nations"—various American states and universities, not to mention the U.S. Information Service, were accorded nation-status. Nevertheless, the response indicates genuine, realistic, and personal interest.

Most Indian students are justifiably proud of India's international stature, and many spoke of her international contribution in the position of peace. Especially from our interviews, however, we strongly conclude that most political positions are based on party loyalty, especially with reference to the Congress Party, which still wears the halo of Independence. Further, most political interest relates chiefly to local and special interest matters, less to national affairs, and very little to international issues. This is both normal and understandable, especially in a nation where adult interests are similar—as one can see by the newspapers. But the *degree* of national and international ignorance and indifference should be a matter of concern to educational leaders and should be reflected in new syllabi and courses of study. The current Chinese threat, for instance, is but a symbol of the complex and momentous issues that the coming generations must assuredly face. India's international involvement affects national principles and programmes, which, in turn, affect every Indian citizen. The currently proposed National Service Scheme is an example of this direct effect. Should all Indian youth be called to "national service"? Would there be any exemptions allowed? What about girls? Will this "service" be wholly military? If not, should it be under military administration? How long should the period be? At what age should it come? Can it be incorporated into college life for those who undertake higher education? These are but few of the questions related to a single issue. India is coming of age in difficult times, and her youth cannot afford "international innocence and ignorance".

11 | *My India*

SOCIAL scientists used to say, "The slowest changes are the best changes", for as they viewed the results of imposed "progress" under colonial or foreign mission administration they could easily see the resistance, the misunderstanding, the distorted results. Paternalism usually assumes that "They don't know what is good for them". In the mid-twentieth century, however, many underdeveloped peoples are themselves accusing their former guardians of "having done too little, too slowly". All over the world the newly liberated peoples are blaming these masters and teachers for having withheld progress, for having "frozen" society. Their accusations are well-founded, but they may fail to recognize an important new factor —they themselves now *want* to change. It is this attitude that makes the difference between a reluctant and an eager society. India wants to change, is *determined* to change. Few are clear about the "gestalt" of this desired New India—it is difficult to imagine a new society in its totality—but fewer deny the urgency of moving toward new political, economic, and social patterns. The central theme in India at present is the removal or the *minimizing of inequalities*.

TABLE 94
DIRECTION OF CHANGE IN INDIA

India is changing	Rank	Total %	Comparison Male %	Female %
In the right ways	1	64*	65	62
Too slowly	2	38	42	31
Too rapidly	3	34*	33	34
In the wrong ways	4	10	10	8

147

TABLE 95

CHANGES WHICH I APPROVE OF IN MODERN INDIA

I am pleased with the following changes in modern India: (open-ended) [1] Political:	Rank	Total %	Comparison	
			Male %	Female %
Political system—democracy	1	15	18	10
Foreign policy—neutrality	2	4	3	4
Fundamental rights of individual	3	3	3	1
Growth of national consciousness	4	2	2	3

Misc.: the adult franchise, women in politics, the separation of religion and politics, Nehru's leadership, socialism.

Economic :	Rank	Total %	Comparison	
			Male %	Female %
Industrial development — 5-Year Plans	1	48	55	37
Agricultural development — Community Development Scheme	2	21	19	22
Scientific research and development	3	10	14	4
Higher standard of living, wages	4	6	7	5

Misc.: atomic development, handloom industry, technical education.

Educational :	Rank	Total %	Comparison	
			Male %	Female %
Educational development	1	36	34	38
Education for women	2	3	1	6

Misc.: coeducation, technical education.

[1] We have categorized responses as best we can. In a sense all is "political" but we have indicated economic, educational, and social aspects of political decisions and development.

TABLE 95—(*Contd.*)

Social :	Rank	Total %	Comparison	
			Male %	Female %
The social awakening, social reforms	1	25	27	21
Less caste consciousness, untouchability	2	17	15	19
Less force in marriage system	3.5	5	5	6
Less tradition and/or superstition	3.5	5	5	4
Less religious dogmatism	5.5	4	6	1
Equality of the sexes	5.5	4	5	3
Feeling against dowry system	7	3	1	6
Dignity of labour	9	2	3	2
Revival of India's heritage	9	2	1	3
Family planning	9	2	2	2

Misc.: the divorce act, abolition of purdah, women's property rights, abolition of child marriage, monogamy act, widow re-marriage, prohibition.

Overall ranking :	Rank	Total %	Comparison	
			Male %	Female %
Industrial development	1	48	55	37
Educational development	2	36	34	38
Social awakening, reforms	3	25	27	21
Agricultural development	4	21	19	22
Less caste, untouchability	5	17	15	19
The political system—democracy	6	15	18	10
Scientific research and development	7	10	14	4
Higher standard of living, wages	8	7	7	5
Less force in marriage	9	5	5	6

TABLE 96

CHANGES WHICH I DISAPPROVE OF IN MODERN INDIA

And am worried about these changes : (open-ended)

Political :	Rank	Total %	Comparison	
			Male %	Female %
Corruption, maladministration	1	18	21	12
The Chinese invasion	2	8	7	8
Regionalism, communalism[2]	3	6	7	5
Communism	5.5	5	7	3
Lack of capable, honest leaders	5.5	5	7	2
Lack of national unity, patriotism	5.5	5	4	5
The language problem	5.5	5	4	5
Many useless parties	8	4	3	4
Foreign policy of non-alignment	10	3	3	2
Lack of real democracy	10	3	2	4
Lack of adequate defence	10	3	3	1
The Kashmir problem	12.5	2	2	2
Ineffiicency, red tape	12.5	2	3	1
Party strife	14.5	1	1	1
Lack of opposition party	14.5	1	2	0

Misc.: political hypocrisy—difference between saying and doing, U.S. imperialism in Pakistan, excessive nationalization, refugee problem, the inferior status of India in world, after Nehru what?, Goa, SEATO.

Economic :	Rank	Total %	Comparison	
			Male %	Female %
Unemployment	1	16	15	16
Poverty, low standard of living, hunger	2.5	14	12	16
Overpopulation	2.5	14	15	12
Deficit financing of Plans	4	4	5	2
Beggar problem	5	3	3	3
Economic disorganization	6.5	2	3	1
Inflation	6.5	2	1	2
Useless strikes	8	1	2	1

Misc.: the growing class system, cooperative farming, poor health standards and facilities, obsolete agriculture, need of more in private sector, taxes.

Educational :	Rank	Total %	Comparison	
			Male %	Female %
Student indiscipline	1	6	4	7
Low standards, deterioration	2.5	4	5	3
Illiteracy, lack sufficient facilities	2.5	4	1	6
Inadequacy in science education	4	2	3	0

Misc.: the low status and pay of teachers, the guaranteed admissions for scheduled classes.

[2] " Communalism " — anti-group feelings, especially in Hindu-Muslim relations.

TABLE 96—(Contd.)

Social :	Rank	Total %	Comparison	
			Male %	Female %
Blind Westernization of our culture	1	9	6	12
Caste feelings, untouchability	2.5	5	6	4
Backward ideas, outworn practice	2.5	5	6	2
Blind superstitions	4	4	5	4
Lack of discipline	5	5	3	2
Inequalities of wealth	6.5	2	3	1
Dowry system	6.5	2	1	3
Too much freedom for women	9.5	1	2	0
Deterioration of morals	9.5	1	2	1
Rising juvenile delinquency	9.5	1	1	2
Too conservative parents	9.5	1	1	1

Misc.: population control methods, continuance of child marriage, increase in divorce, break-up of family, extravagance of students, night clubs, card clubs, dancing, the bad effects of the cinema, no real freedom for women, girls are unable to adjust to changes.

Religious :	Rank	Total %	Comparison	
			Male %	Female %
Belief in God lessening	1	1	1	1

Misc.: science may destroy our spiritualism.

Nothing :	Rank	Total %	Comparison	
			Male %	Female %
	1	2	3	0

Overall ranking :	Rank	Total %	Comparison	
			Male %	Female %
Corruption, maladministration	1	18	21	12
Unemployment	2	17	15	17
Poverty, low standard of living	3.5	14	12	16
Overpopulation	3.5	14	15	12
Westernization of culture	5	9	6	12
Chinese invasion	6	8	7	8
Regionalism, communalism	7.5	6	7	5
Student indiscipline	7.5	6	4	7
Caste, untouchability	10	5	6	4
Communism	10	5	7	3
Lack of capable, honest leaders	10	5	7	3

TABLE 97

FURTHER CHANGES IN INDIA DESIRED BY ME

I should like to see the following further changes : (open-ended) Political :	Rank	Total %	Comparison	
			Male %	Female %
More national unity, cooperation, zeal	1	6	7	5
More capable and honest officials	2.5	3	5	1
Less talk, more work	2.5	3	2	3
More political consciousness	6	2	2	3
More efficiency, less red tape	6	2	3	1
A dictator	6	2	3	0
A more international outlook	6	2	3	0
Democracy really understood and used	6	2	1	2
An opposition party	10.5	1	2	1
A stronger army	10.5	1	2	0
China-India peace	10.5	1	2	1
End of Pakistan-India dispute	10.5	1	1	1

Misc.: more democracy in *homes*, stronger political parties, students prevented from joining political parties, more women in politics, alignment with West, one religion, one language, decentralization, abolition of linguistic states, more socialism, more cooperation with other countries.

Economic :	Rank	Total %	Comparison	
			Male %	Female %
Elimination of poverty; higher standard of living, wages	1	16	16	15
More rapid industrialization	2	13	16	8
More scientific research & development	3.5	9	7	9
Employment problem solved	3.5	9	8	9
Economic self-sufficiency	5	5	6	2
More rapid agricultural development	6	4	5	1
Food problem solved	8	3	3	3
More equality of wealth	8	3	2	4
India as modern as the West	8	3	4	2
More village uplift	10	2	2	2
Atomic development	11	1	1	1

Misc.: cooperative farming, more development of handicrafts, more machinery, urban community development, beggar problem eliminated, abolition of money-lender, better housing.

TABLE 97—(Contd.)

| Educational : | Rank | Total % | Comparison | |
			Male %	Female %
Adequate education for all, free and compulsory	1	15	10	22
Modern educational system	2	6	9	2
More technical, practical education	3	3	3	2

Misc.: nationalization of education, students given more choice of subjects, better pay for teachers, vocational guidance, more freedom of thought.

| Social : | Rank | Total % | Comparison | |
			Male %	Female %
Caste abolished	1	9	9	9
More broadmindedness, less tradition	2.5	5	4	6
Real equality for women	2.5	5	1	11
The dowry system abolished	4	4	1	8
The Western marriage system	6.5	3	3	4
More social reforms	6.5	3	3	3
More family planning	6.5	3	2	4
More honesty	6.5	3	4	1
Free mixing of sexes	10	2	2	3
More individualism	10	2	3	1
More dignity of labour	10	2	1	2

Misc.: abolition of bigamy, abolition of child marriage, more intercaste marriage, more education for women, more Western influence, less Western influence, women put in their place, women *act* equal to men, more Western punctuality, more trust, more courage, more sense of responsibility, India's culture enthroned, new household methods, more recognition of merit, more self-discipline in each citizen.

| Overall ranking : | Rank | Total % | Comparison | |
			Male %	Female %
Elimination of poverty; higher standard of living, wages	1	16	16	15
Adequate education for all	2	15	10	22
More rapid industrialization	3	13	16	8
Caste abolished	5	9	8	9
More scientific research and development	5	9	8	9
Unemployment solved	5	9	8	9
Modern educational system	7.5	6	9	2
More national unity, cooperation, zeal	7.5	6	7	5
More broadmindedness, less tradition	9	5	4	6

TABLE 98

WAYS IN WHICH THE YOUNGER GENERATION
CAN LEAD THE OLDER

The younger generation can "lead" the older generation by (open-ended)	Rank	Total %	Comparison	
			Male %	Female %
Demonstrating modern ways, showing uselessness of tradition	1	23	23	22
Scientific, rational, views and achievement	2	22	26	16
Education and knowledge	3	16	15	16
Politics based on nation, on *all* people	4	6	7	5
Following the advanced West	5	5	5	4
Broadmindedness, progressive ideas	6	4	4	3
Abolishing superstition	8	3	2	4
Creative action, intelligent initiative	8	3	5	1
Refusing to recognize caste	8	3	3	2
Recognizing and practising democracy	11	2	4	0
Being less religious-minded	11	2	2	2
Working hard	11	2	3	1

Reactionary :

"By becoming more interested in the greatness of Hinduism."

Skeptical :

"I do not know."

"We can't lead them."

"Most of us can do nothing."

Loving example :

"With sincerity, always respecting our elders."

"Persuading with love and affection."

"Gently leading them."

"Cooperating where others hesitate."

"Volunteering for what others won't do."

"Actually doing what the older generation would like to do but doesn't."

TABLE 98—(*Contd.*)

Idealism in action :

"Form a really socialistic society based on equality."

"By pure love for each other, as brothers."

"Plan and work in terms of a broad world outlook—not just India."

"By establishing peace."

"By growing up into a disciplined body with a sense of service and devotion to our country."

Firm convincing :

"Educate them with up-to-date, correct ideas."

"Convince them that conservatism is useless."

"Refuse to follow tradition blindly."

"Improve on our ancestors' exploits."

"Show new ideas through new experience."

"Introduce new ideas from other countries that are better than our own."

"Convince them through information from the world."

"Refuse to believe that the present is 'an apocalyptic vision'. We must work to make it good."

"Bring home to them the indubitable fact that ideas and institutions change, that every generation adds to the storehouse of knowledge, that civilization progresses, and that modes of living must be adapted to these changes. It is fatal to remain oblivious to change."

Independence :

"We must show the ability to be independent."

"We must learn to take responsibility from childhood."

"We should stop foreign aid and rely more on ourselves."

The above responses, almost all of which are open-ended, strongly attest to considerable student awareness of present and needed changes. A number of students told us they were grateful for having been asked these questions. "Not once have I been asked to think about these things in this way. It made me think a lot about my own country."

Not all students responded to "India is changing—", but there is overwhelming support of India's directions of change and considerable feeling that changes are too slow. In the details of change there is striking approval for industrial, educational, and social developments, nearly 50 per cent approving industrialization. One student described the "social awakening" as "realization of our backwardness and the willingness to work hard to improve". Girls are especially sensitive to social factors.

There is less worry than pride in the total number of responses, but there is more discrimination in detail. Boys are more conscious of political matters than girls, perhaps because many feel like the student who wrote, "This is supposed to be a democracy, but one gets nowhere without money and influence". The girls have more concerns in the social area, as, for instance, adequate educational facilities, marriage customs, and the Westernization of Indian culture. One commented wistfully, "Life is getting too complicated". But another was more belligerent in "We'd be all right if everyone didn't avoid responsibility!" The overall chief concerns are realistic and frank—corruption, unemployment, poverty, and overpopulation. One girl said, "I am chiefly worried about the immense responsibility our generation bears, with few realizing this fact".

Students would like to see many further changes, especially in the elimination of poverty, development of an adequate educational system, more rapid industrialization, and abolition of caste. Girls show concern over the equality of women, the dowry system, family planning, and marriage customs. Boys want more opportunities, and, as one put it, for "Man to be recognized for his deeds, not his papers".

Adults should feel some poignancy in the students' ideas regarding "how to lead the older generation", perhaps even in one angry retort "by the nose!" There is considerable evidence here that Indian youth feel kindly toward their elders but are determined to break the bonds of tradition. We do not know to what extent this verbal expression will be translated to action, but have already seen "revolution" in many homes in which parents are actively looking to their sons (and sometimes daughters) for guidance. Many adults are as anxious as their children for "a better life here and now", and may, indeed, have taught them that change is wise.

TABLE 99
SOURCES OF IDEAS ON SOCIAL CHANGE

My ideas on social change have come from my	Rank	Total %	Comparison	
			Male %	Female %
Education	1	88**	89	86
Friends	2	52*	54	49
Parents	3	46*	42	50
Professors	4	42	46	35
Reading (write-in)	5	10	15	4
Own experience (write-in)	6	5	8	1
Political leaders (write-in)	7.5	3	4	0
The actual achievements of the West (write-in)	7.5	3	4	1

TABLE 100
MEANING OF TRADITION

"Traditional" means to me	Rank	Total %	Comparison	
			Male %	Female %
The ways things always have been done	1	75*	75	74
The Hindu way of life	2	30	25	35
Superstitious ideas	3	16	16	15
The Eastern way of life	4	13	13	14
Accepting one's destiny	5	11	11	10

Misc. write-ins: old tales and beliefs.

TABLE 101
MEANING OF MODERN

"Modern" means to me	Rank	Total %	Comparison	
			Male %	Female %
New ways of doing things	1	78*	76	80
Scientific ideas	2	63*	63	62
The secular way of life	3.5	19	21	15
Making one's destiny	3.5	19	23	13
The Western way of life	5	17	18	14

Educators will be pleased to see they strongly influence their students! And parents, though still the mentors to many are giving way to peers—at least in these matters. "Reading", "political leaders", and "experience" would surely have scored higher if they had been printed items.

Students generally understand "tradition" as "the way things always have been done", many seeing it also as a "Hindu way of life". Few define it as "accepting one's destiny", though in a later response they strongly demonstrate this belief. "Modern" is "new ways of doing things", chiefly "scientifically". "The Western way of life", we are glad to note, lags behind other descriptions. "Making one's destiny" rates a 18.8 per cent response—significant in India. But there is perceptive warning given by some of the more conservative students. One Visva-Bharati student wrote, "I believe in tradition because it does not harm humanity. I am willing to accept modern ways that save, not destroy, humanity." And another said, " 'Modern' means to me the complete departure of peace of mind".

On the last page of the questionnaire we encouraged lengthier response to three items. Interpreting the statements to the first two, we find the following opinions:

TABLE 102
THE PAST AS A BUCKET OF ASHES

A famous American poet once said, "The past is a bucket of ashes." I'd appreciate your critical comment: (open-ended)	Rank	Total %	Comparison	
			Male %	Female %
The past is *not* a bucket of ashes	1	37	36	36
In some ways it is, in some ways it is not	2	23	25	19
I agree with the poet	3	22	28	14

TABLE 103
MAN'S ESSENTIAL TASK

Some people believe man's essential task is "adjusting to his environment," others that it is "controlling the environment." What do you think?	Rank	Total %	Comparison	
			Male %	Female %
It is "adjusting" to his environment	1.5	34	27	42
It is part of both	1.5	34	39	27
It is "controlling" the environment	3	14	21	5

The majority of students disagreed that "the past is a bucket of ashes", but among those who agreed, fully or partially, there were many who then responded firmly in favour of "adjustment". In fact, the most penetrating and frightening idea in the questionnaire seemed to be that of "controlling the environment", and the emotional nature of the statements indicates disturbance. Many responses are rationalizations, others seem closer to real "philosophy of life" than other definitions.

In the following excerpts relating to Carl Sandburg's phrase on the past (some students have undoubtedly studied Sandburg and have heard interpretations of this idea), there is a clear difference between those who find their status and security in relationship to India's past and those who prefer to look ahead.

The past is not a bucket of ashes:

"No—a bucket of diamonds!" (Bethune)

"The past is a bouquet of beautiful flowers!" (Annamalai)

"It may be true of America, which has no past, but it is not true of India, which has a glorious past." (Annamalai)

"To forget the past is to forget India's culture." (Scottish Church)

"Our civilization was world famous. The Vedas contained all possible knowledge, even of the present. Caste and other evils were all brought by outsiders." (Lady Irwin)

"The past is sweet—it is a precious memory-basket of mind that helps when you are suffering." (Bethune)

It is the past *alone* which reminds us of our duty." (Kanja Kubja)

"The past is experience—experience is a comb nature gives a man after he has become bald." (St. Xavier's)

"The past played an important role in my life—it has encouraged me—it has been the light which has made me what I am" (Baroda)

"A living, burning flame, all pervasive and inescapable. It seems almost to crush progress but we must keep it." (Elphinstone)

"As for my country—'the past is a bucket of ashes'—I totally disagree. The past for us was a Golden Age had not the foreigners invaded its wealth, its culture, its chastity—and plundered its growing knowledge and advancement. There was harmony and love, honesty and justice, but all was veiled when the first plunderers entered, and thereafter followed the powerful nations until India became a slave. But those days of slavery have left a deep scar on each individual, and no advancement either in freedom or education can make us forget." (Scottish Church)

In some ways it is, in some ways it is not:

The ashes will make good manure for a new crop." (Annamalai)

"Good manure for grapes!" (Scottish Church)

"Ashes are useful to clean vessels." (Elphinstone)

"Some of yesterday's buttermilk is needed to mix with new milk." (Annamalai)

"There can be no progress if we ignore the lessons of the past." (Madras)

"Man is wise only through experience." (St. Xavier's)

"Sometimes there are jewels hiding amongst the ashes." (Visva-Bharati)

"We ought to forget the past and look to the future, but the past can teach us." (Lady Irwin)

"Tradition is humanity's precious memory." (Scottish Church)

" 'Old is not gold', but it has its lessons." (Lucknow)

"One can draw inspiration and courage from it, but it is wrong to be bound by it." (Osmania Engineering)

"Don't lament it—learn from it!" (Osmania Science)

"I beg to differ. I do not believe that the past is 'a bucket of ashes', that it is not connected to the present. I should think that the present and the past are linked. It is on our past history and experience that we must base our decisions. We can build our policies only after seeing what mistakes were made. India today can be proud of her culture of the past. In our pride, in our heritage we endeavour to build on this foundation. We don't rest on our laurels—we build on our laurel." (St. Xavier's)

I agree with the poet:

"The future is, too! Live only in the present and leave other things to God." (Osmania Science)

"The past has no place in this changing world." (Osmania Engineering)

"Yes, because this is a day of science—the past was not." (Osmania Engineering)

"It would be a grievous fault to dwell under the illusion of hoary tradition and rich culture—this is gone." (Baroda)

"The past is a piece of bread that cannot be brought back by vomiting." (Annamalai)

"India, proud of her ancient civilization, always looks behind without worrying about the future—that is why India has not progressed." (Annamalai)

"India's past is hopeless!" (Scottish Church)

"The past is past—we live in the present." (Banares)

"It is the left-over of the dead old days." (Lady Irwin)

"It is 100 per cent true. We have been slaves of the past too long." (Kanja Kubja)

"It is a rich heritage, but as ill luck would have it, it is wholly spiritual." (Scottish Church)

"Better to go ahead and do something useful." (Lady Irwin)

"Things that are long past cannot be brought back in this modern world. We must forget the past and adapt ourselves to new and entirely different activities and changes." (Scottish Church)

"It is true—but I wish it weren't." (Kanja Kubja)

"It is sad to forget the past, but we must." (Miranda House)

"In my view it is true. When we compare the present age with that of the past, in spite of 'cold wars' and frenzied opinions about the world going to the dogs, in our heart of hearts we cannot deny the fact—that never has there been such an understanding between man and man as today. Knowing the other man helps one get along well with him. And this feeling has been progressing day by day. Obviously in these conditions 'the past is a bucket of ashes'." (Osmania Engineering)

In the following excerpts relating to "adjusting" or "controlling" the environment, the larger question of "challenge and response" comes to mind. It is said to be "Anglo-Saxon" to want (or understand wanting) to climb Mt. Everest "because it is there". This is too simple and inaccurate a generality, but it may be correct to say that few Indians would feel the *personal* challenge implied in the statement. "We are too philosophical—too sensible—to go to that effort, risking our lives, to prove nothing." Furthermore, physical and psychological survival in India in the past has rested on "adjustment". It may be that survival in the future will rest on "control"—though this depends on what is meant by "control". One student wrote, "Men command nature by adjusting to it", another, "In adjusting we are controlling". Many respondents understood "environment" as "nature", others as "society". It makes a difference whether one is discussing control of the physical world or of people.

The responses in favour of adjustment fall clearly into several categories:

Adjustment is moral, control is immoral:

"Man is not greater than nature." (Osmania Women)

"Control is against natural law." (Kanja Kubja)

"Never try to interfere with nature's laws." (Osmania Science)

"Control always brings diaster." (Osmania Science)

"Nature punishes those who try to control." (Kanja Kubja)

"When we control the environment we become its slaves." (Annamalai)

"Indian philosophy is based on adjustment." (Banares)

"Adjustment is man's greatness." (Osmania Science)

"Adjustment is a sign of a matured personality." (Baroda)

"Man's business is not 'bossing about' ." (Scottish Church)

"Control leads to hunger for power, egoism, absence of humanity." (Visva-Bharati)

"It is selfish to try to control." (Lady Irwin)

"Adjustment requires sacrifice, but it is ultimately satisfying." (Baroda)

"The best quality in a human being is adjusting to the environment." (Lady Irwin)

"Those who try to control fail to achieve their destinies." (Osmania Women)

"Those who do not adjust are regarded as backward." (Lady Irwin)

"Always adjust—the fittest survive this way." (Kanja Kubja)

"It is the only way to be successful or happy." (Miranda House)

It is too difficult—or impossible—to control:

"Control is neither possible nor desirable." (Scottish Church)

"Not all of us have the opportunities of Napoleon. Social injustices force us to adjust." (Visva-Bharati)

"It is too dangerous to control the environment." (Annamalai)

"Man's environment is chiefly other men. It is difficult to control them—easier to control the self." (Baroda)

"We can control our emotions but not our environment." (Bombay)

"It is easier to change the self than environment." (Osmania)

"It takes hard labour, faith, prayers, and strength of character to control the environment. It is a good theory, but too difficult in practice." (Baroda)

Control leads to frustration, unpopularity:

"We have troubles enough now without multiplying them by trying control." (Scottish Church)

"The desire to master the environment only leads to frustration." (Madras)

"By adjusting we feel comfort, we find happiness." (Madras)

"If we control, society excludes us." (Annamalai)

"Control leads to unpleasant experiences." (Annamalai)

"Life goes smoothly and happily for those who can adjust." (Osmania)

"If we are too different people will laugh at us." (Annamalai)

"When we adjust we get the cooperation of others; control brings conflict and rebellion." (Annamalai)

"Controlling means taking a risk and may mean failure and downfall." (Osmania Women)

"Adjustment is the only way to peace of mind." (Osmania Engineering)

"It's best to do as the Romans do—without losing one's personality." (Lady Irwin)

"One who adjusts is always happy, always popular." (Bethune)

"It's too lonely doing anything else. We have to adjust." (Miranda)

"Control makes a dominating character. This leads to failure in life, as 'equality' is the order of the day." (Miranda)

This is an age requiring adjustment:

"Changing too fast is not democratic." (Annamalai)

"Especially in times like this, when things are changing so fast, we must accept anything, adjust to everything." (Osmania Women)

"We are living in an age when we need to adjust." (Lady Irwin)

"Life will change—we don't have to change it—just adjust to it." (Lady Irwin)

More girls than boys are on the side of adjustment. Many of each want a combination of "adjustment" and "control", their comments grouping thus:

Take the middle road:

"Choose a golden mean." (Elphinstone)

"All excesses are bad, including adjustment." (Banares)

"One should be neither the master nor the servant." (Annamalai)

"It is always a pull between the individual and society. Take the middle of the road." (Banares)

Do whichever is possible, or best:

"Man should mostly adjust, but it is also his duty to improve his surroundings." (Elphinstone)

"We must control what hurts." (Osmania Science)

"Adjust to what is good, control when improvement is necessary." (Miranda)

"It is the dual task of mankind. Adjusting is easier, but we must control when possible." (St. Xavier's)

"Do whichever brings happiness and pleasure." (Lady Irwin)

"Embrace the good, discard the bad—control when possible." (Bethune)

"Much of life must be adjustment, but *only* adjustment means we can be deceived —as in Pakistan and China." (Kanja Kubja)

"Better to be master than slave, but sometimes controlling makes us slaves." (Osmania Engineering)

"Mostly we have to adjust. The environment is God's gift to man, but God also gave man intelligence to use for his betterment." (Annamalai)

Most must adjust, a few can control:

"Only those strong enough to alter the flow of the stream can control." (Visva-Bharati)

"Only a few have the power to control. The rest of us must adjust." (Scottish Church)

"To control is difficult. Those who do are the 'mahatmas'." (Madras)

"Only those with strong will power can control." (Osmania Women)

"The common men must adjust, but progress comes from uncommon men." (Osmania Science)

"Most people can only adjust, and do, but some control—these are the rebels and to them progress is due." (Elphinstone)

"The reasonable man adjusts to the changing environment, and the unreasonable man is always trying to adjust the environment to himself. So all progress depends upon the unreasonable man, and hence kudoes go to him." (Osmania Science)

This is an age of "control":

"I wouldn't want to adjust to every stupid thing in our environment." (Baroda)

"This is one of the times (in history) when control is necessary." (Baroda)

"Social harmony comes only from adjustment, but social progress comes from control. We need social progress." (Baroda)

"In my opinion man's essential task is both adjusting to and controlling the environment. Adjusting is what every other animal can do—only by controlling and fighting with the environment does man show his greatness as a man. But mere controlling may lead man nowhere but to discontent. Man has to adjust to his controlled environment. The environment is passive only when we demand something from it, when we come to conquer it. All the great nations in history are nations which tried to conquer the environment. I will try to control the environment more than adjust to it. Controlling needs courage and energy, but it bears fruit afterwards. When we adjust we have to be satisfied with what we get, but when we control we get whatever we want —though at the cost of much striving." (Visva-Bharati)

The minority who are in favour of "control" express themselves thus:

Adjustment is wrong:

"Adjustment means submission." (Scottish Church)

"Control lets us really live, and keeps life from being static." (Lady Irwin)

"There can be no progress if everyone adjusts." (Madras)

"Adjustment makes men slaves and puppets." (Osmania Engineering)

"Life is a struggle—we must force the circumstances—it is cowardly to yield to them." (Osmania Engineering)

"If we adjust there can be nothing new." (Kanja Kubja)

Control is essential and right:

"What else?" (Banares)

"Control is almost impossible, but necessary." (Scottish Church)

"It *has* to be." (Bethune)

"To be 'good' is to be master." (Banares)

"We can change the environment if we like. It is hard, but we must." (Kanja Kubja)

"Education needs a free, active, and creative environment. We will have to make this environment." (Lady Irwin)

"Today we are masters of everything. Control through science." (Annamalai)

"Adjustment is bygone. This is the day of science, of control." (Scottish Church)

"Man differs from animals in his ability to control." (Annamalai)

"In a time of science man controls." (Elphinstone)

"Science has shown us how to stop being slaves—even in the social world we can stop unhappy customs and traditions." (Osmania Science)

' What cannot be cured must be endured. I personally feel that most of the things in this world can be changed to suit us—if we have sufficient will power and perseverance to do it." (Osmania Engineering)

"I think that man must command and control the environment in order to prove true to his innate greatness. The term 'adjustment' implies that man is slavish to his environment, which is not at all desirable. Life is a ceaseless struggle between the two forces—man's struggle to live and the environment's attempt at domination. By 'adjusting' to the environment man loses much of his critical, inquiring faculty, and will suffer from spiritual coma. The final test for the survival of a civilization rests on man's capacity to reveal the truth of life and the laws of nature. And in doing so to establish his stand in the world. Man's happiness is derived from comfort, and this is dependent upon his capacity to benefit from his environment without losing his individuality. Hence, in my opinion, man should control and command the environment." (Visva-Bharati)

The final statement in the questionnaire reads, "If there is anything else you would like to write about 'Changing India' or about your own ideas, kindly use the space below. And thank you very much for your cooperation". Not all students responded, but among the majority who did most students were eloquent in their pride in nation and their high hopes for India's future. We include here a few excerpts, illustrating the various categories of responses:

Warning that student respondents are not "the real India":

"One thing I would like to point out. This data is being collected from those who are sharp enough to answer the questions. But never try to judge India from this. Real India lives there where you cannot approach it. These questionnaires are beyond the common people's understanding, but they are the persons who can really depict changing India, progressing India. Go and meet these people, dwell with them, understand them—and you would feel that India has been awakened." (Miranda House)

India is changing slowly, but we students cannot change it:

"*We* can't change anything. Education hasn't made it possible for me to change anything. There is no 'social responsibility' in education—it is just for myself, for my own pleasure." (Annamalai)

The two above statements are isolated in their sentiments. The majority of statements fall in the following group.

Pride, patriotism, optimism:

"The future is bright and prosperous." (Bethune)

"Long live India! (Though China may think otherwise.) (Banares)

"My holy nation is progressing towards the right way under the leadership of Nehru, my beloved prime minister." (Banares)

"We are striving forward with all that we have, and I'm sure God is with us." (Lady Irwin)

"With work and prayer we will come out of the dark ages of slavery and take fi st place among the nations." (Osmania Engineering)

"There is no reason to be complacent or despondent. The squalor is bad, but it is our squalor—and will one day be our paradise." (Elphinstone)

"India today is facing a drastic transition. Unfastened from the ties of poverty, ignorance, ill health, inertia, Indians are going to bring about an all-round revolution. They are now growing ambitious. The days of gloom are no more.

In the socio-economic structure the Five Year Plans have brought about or are going to bring about the equal distribution of wealth, economic power, and social justice. The problem of untouchability is almost done away with. Our government has improved and is introducing many prudent policies and projects in the social development of India." (Scottish Church)

"Changing India—it is not an illusion or piece of party propaganda. There is a reality behind these words, and that reality is shown not only by the steel structures in new buildings and factories. It is there also in the villages. People who never dreamed of seeing electricity or heard of radio, or savings schemes, are actively participating and enjoying these facilities. It is the big smile on the faces of these hardship-stricken poor village people that is the silver lining on the face of resurgent India. Indians are prepared to learn from others, be helped by others. But one thing that is dear to every Indian heart is their freedom. Let not any country bargain with it. I would like you to know that the essential feature of changing India is her love of independence of action." (St. Xavier's)

Disgust, skepticism:

"India is forgetting her purpose. She is trying to copy Western culture—which is not a culture at all. She is losing her faith in the 'Vedas'—which is wrong. Finally, India is going to the dogs." (Osmania Engineering)

"India is changing—yes, very slowly and gradually. But whether it is climbing the steps or going down the steps no one is sure of. India is short of money. Many grants and loans are taken from other countries for construction— dams, bridges, roads, and railways—and agricultural and industrial planning. But the money given for these works is not used for them to the last pie. Half of the money goes into the pockets of contractors and overseers. The rich become richer and the poor poorer. The dams will come down in five or ten years. Again the same amount of money is spent for repair, and thus it goes on! What I want to say is that a programme to remove poverty in India has never worked on the right path and will never work if the same conditions continue. Our ministers may give big, big lectures that they are trying their level best to remove poverty—but it is not true! The poor die as they were born!" (Baroda)

"When we decided to free India with non-violent means, I asked for the slow change we are witnessing now. I have no complaints to make about it. But I have a feeling that we are too much in the air and should come down to brass tacks. Social and educational changes have to be made, and made much, much faster. Unless this is done we can't build up the potential for all that we are planning now. In this context the use of a certain amount of social force is necessary, especially with respect to birth control. Pundits may keep on arguing about human rights and what not—but meanwhile we have to save India." (Osmania Science)

Realism: progress, problems:

"We have made great progress, but the rest of the world is advancing faster." (Madras)

"India is changing, but not in all fields and sometimes wrongly. The police force is much too cruel now." (Bethune)

"India needed to change—the upper class ruled the lower—but it has gone far enough! No more changes! The younger generation has been pushed to a life unsuitable for them. Degrees are everything, and people forget the basic principles of life." (Baroda)

"I am proud of India's progress but worried about the stability of the modern Indian home." (Baroda)

"Some changes are good, some bad, but India will always change." (Osmania Engineering)

Needs: correct attitude:

"Minds should change first—but this is not happening." (Annamalai)

"If only we had Gandhiji's ideal of tears wiped from every face." (Elphinstone)

Needs: science and education:

"We must use new methods—the old ones brought poverty, illiteracy, disease, and unemployment. Science is showing us new methods." (Annamalai)

"India is backward. She must change through science and education." (Madras)

"India must reach a higher position in the world, and can through science and education." (Annamalai)

Needs: more social welfare:

"We should use much more money for education, uplift, and helping the poor— less for the heads of state, Republic Day functions, etc." (Bombay)

"We need much more social work." (Annamalai)

"Why are we so gentle in our foreign affairs and so brutal in our own social affairs?" (Kanja Kubja)

Needs: cooperation:

"If all parties would unite we could have a constructive programme." (Annamalai)

"India can never be a great country until Indians cooperate with each other and the government." (Annamalai)

Needs: more work:

"We are progressing but *must* close the gap between theory and practice." (Bethune)

"We need more action, less talk." (Osmania Science)

"Let's practise, not profess, democracy." (Bombay)

"Many just talk—won't cooperate—won't work hard." (Baroda)

Needs: self-reliance:

"In the competitive world of the twentieth century, where all the nations are armed to the teeth and are trying to be self-sufficient, India should do the same —more than she is." (Banares)

"India *must* become self-reliant." (Osmania Engineering)

Needs: eradication of corruption:

"Erase corrupt on, liberalize education, work for cooperation among the people." (St. Xavier's)

"India needs overhauling, and that includes our corrupt government." (Kanja Kubja)

"We *must* eradicate 'influence' in employment." (St. Xavier's)

Other methods: dictatorship, Communism:

"We must have the rule of a great, able dictator—this is the only way to improve for some time." (Annamalai)

"India must take money away from its rich capitalists like Birla and Tata." (St. Xavier's)

"If the government doesn't move faster there will be a mass uprising—with an end to the middle-class aristocracy who suck the blood of the proletariat." (Visva-Bharati)

"The coming of Communism in India has enormously changed our outlook, and we think that it is very suitable for a country like India where people much need their injustices recouped. It has brought a radical change and most of the educated youths are hopefully receiving it, as it alone can make an ideal India based on equality among the people. Exposition of the narrow opportunists is no doubt a good sign. Worthy students, disgusted with the deteriorated social system, are strongly supporting Communism, which has brought fabulous changes in the U.S.S.R. and China." (Scottish Church)

The place of religion:

"India should *practise* her religion, removing poverty, caste, and illiteracy." (Scottish Church)

"We must get rid of religious bigotry and fanaticism. We should worship only perfection." (Scottish Church)

"India is now going to attain the pre-ordained Vedic period." (Banares)

"India *will* remain spiritualistic in spite of industrialization." (Scottish Church)

"Change we *must* because of our needs in all spheres, especially in our religious outlook, which to me is a little too rigid. . . . The change should be brought about by society, and not by government. The religious leaders should know their role now and should accept science and its rewards. They should be more *moralistic* (not in the older traditional meaning) rather than *ritualistic*. They should understand that the fear of God in everything is now no more there. People in conquering nature have less awe in God, but can be made to respect God by showing them the true meaning of God and religion in the love of mankind. India needs this change very badly." (Lucknow)

India's contribution to the world:

"India is leading the world in peaceful ideas—political non-alignment, peaceful uses of atomic energy, no racial discrimination." (Banares)

"We should be moulded according to the past, peaceful, and silent life. We will contribute to the world by peaceful inventions of science." (Banares)

The danger of Westernization:

"We *must* progress, but do not need to become Western." (Scottish Church)

"I hope we learn from the experience of other countries, but that we don't adopt the new blindly." (Baroda)

"The change in India has meant the growth in education, but the education is essentially Western. It has resulted in the Westernization of the educated classes, in culture and way of life. Unfortunately this acceptance of Western values appears to have undermined the old Indian values and has replaced it with a mere veneer of Western culture. The deeper and better things of Western culture have not really been absorbed. But I do believe this is only a passing phase. India will retain her individuality while combining with it the best of the Western culture." (Elphinstone)

"I think India is progressing very nicely indeed. Education, science, industry—all these have developed very well—but I do wish the people of India would try to keep some of the traditional practices, like wearing their own dress, doing 'namaste' instead of saying 'hullo', showing their respect for elders by touching their feet, etc. These are beautiful customs and they should not be swallowed up by Western civilization. It would really be a pity." (Scottish Church)

"There is a tremendous movement in India to impose Western ideals on Indian society. There is no justification for this. Each society can find its own ideals (Western society did). To judge, evaluate, and change India by using a Western yardstick is, I think, a distortion of the concept of progress. Progress should not mean a Westernization of society, but a change in social ideals to suit the self-determined needs of society." (Elphinstone)

"In social customs we are making a synthesis of our glorious past and the West." (Banares)

The question of time and timing:

"The younger generation is moving faster than the old—it will take us a century to establish ourselves." (Annamalai)

"Progress is too slow—there is too much corruption and red tape. More education would hasten progress." (Madras)

"We are going too fast—will break down in exhaustion." (Madras)

"There is improvement, but it is too slow. China has moved faster." (Visva-Bharati)

"It is a time of critical transition, the old ways discarded, the new ways not understood." (Madras)

"I am proud of India's progress, but it is too slow in the villages. These people leave everything to God—man cannot oppose." (Kanja Kubja)

The generation gap:

"I feel the gap between the two generations—in education, ideas, feelings of independence, the development of individuality, etc.—is so great that unless India has suitable education at all levels she will not be able to fill this gap. . . . People seem to realize problems but don't think of the solutions fast enough." (Baroda)

"I have just one sincere prayer—that the educated Indian parents may understand their children a little more. I wish that our feelings and love for some particular person could be considered and not neglected. Another wish is that Indian mothers could be a little more friendly with their children, especially with their daughters. If these wishes could be fulfilled it would save a lot of mis-understanding. It would be so fine if one's opinions could be respected. But I am determined to achieve all this with my ability. I am very confident of achieving my goal and can in the end promise to be a friendly mother." (Baroda)

Thanks to other nations:

"Thanks to other nations we will progress." (Scottish Church)

"India is changing faster than any nation in the world. I am proud of her progress, but I know we are dependent on big nations like America." (Kanja Kubja)

"We can do everything we plan if the U.S. and the U.S.S.R. help us." (Baroda)

The task of students:

"We will progress if students stick to their studies." (St. Xavier's)

"How can we change properly with the present educational system? We are given only academic knowledge." (Kanja Kubja)

"There should be more opportunity for Indian students to study abroad— so they can correct their misconceptions of the West." (Visva-Bharati)

"We young people are the pillars of the nation. With the help of our great leaders and the Almighty God we will achieve success." (Osmania Engineering)

"The progress of a nation depends on its people. India has just now gained its freedom, and this period of time (since 1947) is insufficient to remove the old-fashioned thinking of the older generation which suffered under the foreign yoke. It takes a whole generation to get rid of its deeprooted, silly ideas. My appeal for the most urgent need of India is the awakening of its younger generation to its responsibilities and a smooth cooperation from our old people—so that all Indians may march together towards the road of prosperity." (Osmania Science)

Idealism: mankind:

"It may be in India, America, or even Russia—but it should always be considered of utmost importance to respect individuality. The individual should be given enough scope, opportunities, and facilities to develop his potentialities irrespective of his colour, caste, or creed. There is no alternative—we must choose between the co-existence or the co-destruction of mankind. If we wish to survive let us do away with all races, all castes, all colour bars, and let us learn to be humans if we wish to live as humans." (Baroda)

Indian students largely accept and welcome "change" as a way of life—they want their nation to stand tall in the world, and they themselves want to enjoy the spiritual and material perquisites of progress. Many are penetrating in their judgment of credits and debits on the ledger of actual accomplishment and clearly see the gulf between word and deed. Perception on "delivered goods" and external matters is high. It is a different story as regards internal factors, as regards critical analysis of the Plans themselves—of their motives, their by-products, their strengths, their limitations.

Few can or dare guess what human changes are likely to accompany the political and economic changes. It is enough at present to decry inequality, the chief villain in experience. Corruption, which distorts present efforts, is "bad"—but few ask what causes its rise and what can minimize it. It is now enough to say that men should be honest even if society says otherwise in its rewards and punishments. The *real* values of a society are seen not in verbal morality but in social sanctions, in the paths to success or failure, in the human relationships that accompany the daily routines of living.

The formation and support of values in changing times is ever a fundamental problem, rarely recognized or well handled in any society. But it is *central* to a people's faith in leaving old securities and finding new ones. Indian students show considerable sensitivity to this matter of values, but they generally reflect their nation's vague and uncertain approach to this aspect of changing society. They are exposed to little but paternalistic exhortation in philosophical tone or to slick political slogans. And their own education ill fits them for their own analysis. This generation is getting very little help from their elders in matters connected with change—clearly it will have to strike out boldly.

Some are prepared to do this—they are the "unreasonable men to whom progress is due". Others are already bogged down in an attitude of adjustment. Even their education is "adjustment" rather than an active sharpening of tools for intellectual carpentry. Many can see themselves as *units* in the house of tomorrow—few can envision the architecture of this house—even fewer are applying as architects. They are, as we have repeatedly said, little different from students in any land, but their nation is in more critical phase, their education is less functional to national and personal needs. To repeat a Madras student's appraisal of this moment of Indian history—"It is a time of critical transition, the old ways discarded, the new ways not understood." Some will wait for new ways to become clear, and will follow them. Others will take a hand in shaping the new ways. But all are vitally concerned with their form and direction. We think it was more than politeness when so many students wrote at the end of their questionnaire some form, of "Thank you very much. I have learned a great deal about my country and myself. Best wishes for your project."

12 | Why "Student Indiscipline"?

"We want a holiday !"
"I demand admission !"
"The Dean should be ousted !"
"We refuse to take the examinations !"

THE students of India are shocking their elders by speaking up —and speaking up boldly, often rudely. "Student indiscipline" has become a matter of national concern, with speeches of exhortation published side by side with reports of new incidents. Some students seem bewildered, others belligerent, as they themselves confess they don't know why they act as they do. "It is in the air." Examiners are threatened on dark streets, effigies are burnt, vice-chancellors' homes are invaded, staff members are physically assaulted, university gates are locked, and speakers are hooted off platforms. "Indiscipline seems to be the order of the day."[1]

Indiscipline in the Nation

Dr Shrimali, Minister for Education, deplores the weakening moral values, and calls for "the resuscitation of traditional values, moral and cultural."[2] Others think the solution does not lie in trying to turn the clock back. Dr Chandrasekhar observes that India is experiencing transitional disorder and that consequently indiscipline has become an intimate part of the national pattern

[1] Usha Biswas, "Why Such Indiscipline in Educational Institutions?" *Amrita Bazar Patrika*, November 22, 1959.

[2] K. L. Shrimali, as reported in *The Statesman*, October 8, 1959.

174

of behaviour. "The current epidemic of student indiscipline is only a species of our national genus of indiscipline of all kinds. There is a profound lack of discipline among our Ministers—the way some of them go against rules and regulation, conventions and usages—and among our legislators—their constant manoeuvring to promote no-confidence motions against some Chief Minister or other (the results of the strains and stresses of groupism). There are the strikes and threats of strikes by the economically disinherited among the educated—non-gazetted officers, bank employees, pilots, and the like; the inevitable and accepted-as-necessary strikes of the industrial workers; and, last but not least, the strikes, fasts, walk-outs, and general rowdyism of the students. Almost every stratum of population, barring children, old people, and the rural peasantry seems to be full of disaffection."[3]

A reader continues Dr Chandrasekhar's argument by pointing out that "The social fabric as a whole is permeated with discontent, distrust, and unrest....Our youth has come to know that 'rewards' await those who defy authority. They also know that ability and merit are no longer given due consideration and that communalism and provincialism decide all issues, from admission to schools to appointment in jobs. A feeling of diffidence and frustration has gripped the entire nation, and it is no wonder that ... the students, who form part and parcel of the social set-up and 'are not some outlandish element in our national life' toe the line chalked out by their elders."[4]

Professor D. S. Sarma, in writing of dark clouds on the horizon, says, "Corruption in high places, the soaring prices of foodstuffs, the slow strangulation of middle class families, the squandermania of the Central Government, the fissiparous tendencies in many States, a growing fifth column in the country, and a general lack of honesty, efficiency, and patriotism on the part of the people are said to be some of the dark clouds. But to my mind the darkest cloud is the deteriorization which has come over our universities and which is working havoc in our colleges and schools and is threatening to destroy all moral and intellectual values in the field of education. Educational institutions form the tap-root of national life, and if they deteriorate the nation is bound to perish. . . . One hears almost daily of strikes in schools and colleges, of assaults on teachers

---

[3] Dr Chandrasekhar, *The Illustrated Weekly of India*, March 13, 1960, p. 14.
[4] Lalitha Venkata Raman, *The Illustrated Weekly of India*, April 3, 1960.

by students, of examinations postponed on account of disturbed conditions, or, worse still, of examinations conducted under police guard. But, most appalling of all is the well-known and wide-spread bribery among examiners in some universities, where marks are sold according to an established schedule. . . . Discipline in schools and colleges is largely a matter of continuous tradition. When once that tradition is broken and set aside it is very difficult to restore it, especially in a country where there is so little discipline in national life."[5]

Many who concede the national picture is dark look especially to those in education for leadership, for correction. The Home Minister, G. B. Pant, in addressing students of Nagpur University, eloquently said, "Education is first and foremost a social process. Its aims and objectives are intimately bound up with the needs and ideals of the society it is to serve. An education out of tune with the needs of the society will be atrophied by its lack of purpose. Education in relation to society has a dual role: it should help to provide the ideals of a new order, and train men and women who will bring the practices of the community nearer those ideals. For an underdeveloped country such as India, which is engaged in the reconstruction of its social order and in the development of a higher potential in its economic and human resources, education is of vital importance. Change, growth, progress—these are the consequences of pioneership, and it is the function of education to give us the pioneers we need."[6]

But the education profession seems not to be staffed with pioneers who use education to lead the nation. The profession, instead, merely reflects the national dilemma, and "the reconstruction of the social order" is not a visible aim of education. Student in-discipline, dramatically visible, should point to the inadequacy of the once-noble halls of learning, but unfortunately the real misbehaviour of many students turns attention to "their lack of morals" more than to underlying causes. Something is clearly rotten in the State of higher education. Humayun Kabir has written a pamphlet called "Letters on Discipline".[7] The "World Brother-hood All-India Committee" conducted a survey and seminar on

[5] D. S. Sarma, "Threatening Clouds", *The Hindu*, February 28, 1960.

[6] G. B. Pant, "Universities' Role in the Nation's Growth", *The Hindu*, March 13, 1960.

[7] Humayun Kabir, "Letters on Discipline", Government of India, 1958.

the attitudes and opinions of students in Bombay University on student indiscipline.[8] The Dewan Chand Trust Company conducted a survey in the Delhi area, interviewing administrators.[9] The most useful and penetrating study, in our opinion, is that of Chanchal Sarkar, special correspondent to the *Statesman*.[10] Basing his analysis on visits to ten universities, Mr Sarkar entitled his series of *Statesman* articles "Where the Demoralized Teach the Disgruntled", "Myths and Mysteries About Students", "Universities and Governments— a Bad Relationship", and "Amenities Alone Cannot Revive Universities". The author probes painful areas of pseudo-prestige, power politics, personal insecurities, and professional immorality. No mere carping critic, he makes many constructive suggestions as regards the national and professional bodies politic.

Analysis of this educational problem must involve analysis of this transition period in Indian history. Dr Chandrasekhar says, "The first and perhaps the foremost reason. . .is the radical change in values that has crept into our society—values that affect relations between parents and children, between teachers and pupils, between the state and the citizen. The old cherished values (I realize that all that is old is not necessarily good), which gave an enviable stability to our society, are disappearing, without anything tangible, tested, and acceptable to our cultural mores. . . . Certain old values can be discarded if we can replace them with new and better ones. But our society is now like a two-headed Janus—not able to make up its mind. This dilemma is reflected in practically every phase of our life. In addition to the dilemma, our public life is riddled with double standards of morals and behaviour. One leader exhorts the public to a life of simplicity and poverty, but is known himself to live in uncommon luxury. Another harangues the people against foreign and Western education, but sends his son to the United States to be educated. Yet another pleads for Hindi in everything, but sends his daughter to an English-medium school. The Gujerati citizen, who cannot tolerate his immediate Maharashtrian neighbour, talks of world brotherhood—and their counterparts all over India are no less hypocritical. This distressing and deceitful

---

[8] Report of Seminar of the "World Brotherhood All-India Committee", Bombay, as yet unpublished.

[9] Dewan Chand Trust Co., New Delhi, as yet unpublished.

[10] Published now in pamphlet form: "The Unquiet Campus", a *Statesman* Survey, 1950.

dichotomy between public utterance and private behaviour has contributed to the present rot in our national moral fibre. The lack of public integrity in our public life. . .is not lost upon our students, who, after all, look to their parents and leaders for guidance. . . . The students in their indiscipline are only following the leaders."[11]

S. Ookerjee, a participant in *Seminar's* symposium on university education, points out society's ambivalent attitude toward the intellectual. "Society looks upon education, at its best, as a means to practical ends. This attitude is, I believe, suicidal. . . .There need be no real incompatibility between theory and practice, but there is a general feeling that university education produces only book-worms and 'scholars', not men of action. . . .An obvious cause of the bulk of our student population's growing indifference to study is the constant demand which society makes on it—a demand strangely inconsistent with its belief in the uselessness of university education. The world outside the university, which can absorb into its evergrinding network of industry and commerce the labours of our young men, demands from them a scrap of paper guaranteeing their having attended a university. This scrap of paper doesn't usually indicate actual attainments, but is considered necessary in the race for employment."[12]

But the problem is not solved, as some would have it, by asking youth to heed the "wiser heads of the older and more experienced generation". In one sense students are only following their leaders, but in another they are refusing to do so—because they are losing their confidence in them, because they are beginning to have ideas different from those of tradition. The problem will lend itself to solution only when (1) the meaning of "discipline" and "indiscipline" is defined and understood in terms of modern India, and (2) the discontinuity of values between pre-Independence and post-Independence generations is recognized and handled intelligently.

In the course of this study we have asked many faculty members and other adults to describe "discipline", "indiscipline", "self-control", and "maturity". We submit these are difficult concepts to define, but insist the general meaning given to them is critical in the guidance of youth. As we have said, it is dangerous to gener-

---

[11] Dr S. Chandrasekhar, "Why This Student Indiscipline?" *The Illustrated Weekly of India*, March 13, 1960, p. 14.

[12] S. Ookerjee, "Our Universities", *Seminar*, Bombay, March, 1960, p. 31.

alize, but we have been impressed with the preponderance of the following reactions and statements:

1. Most respondents, including those faculty members involved in social sciences, were "thrown" by the request for definitions or descriptions. "Yes, that is a good question. We ask students to be 'mature', but what do we mean?" The quickest responses were the more stereotyped, the less thoughtful, but even the more deliberate and reflective responses fell largely into the following definitions:

2. "Discipline" means "observing decorum", "adapting so as to cause no trouble", "obeying the authorities". It is "conformity", and results in "order".

3. "Indiscipline" is the opposite—the failure to conform, obey, control oneself. It results in "disorder".

4. "Self-control" means controlling one's own desires in favour of social custom. It is the "elimination of desire" (central to the ancient scriptures). Lack of self-control results in selfishness and social chaos.

5. (a) "Maturity" means assuming one's traditional social role, being what society expects you to be. "This kind of person contributes to society."

   (b) "Maturity" means having the knowledge and *will*, when confronted by alternatives, to *decide* what to do, and to *carry out this decision* no matter what happens.

Note the relationship of all but the last statement to an authoritarian and stable society, in which "induction of the young into adult roles" is a question of having them do as they are told, behave as they are expected. The second definition of "maturity", which we received many times, is clear indication of a step toward personal autonomy. Only a few adults we questioned demonstrated an understanding of "maturity" that goes beyond "personal power" to include making decisions in the context of others' needs and rights or in that of values.

Two very thought-provoking statements given us by adults give further light to conflicting values felt by youth. "India has always permitted freedom of thought, but not freedom of action." Freedom of action is an essential corollary of freedom of thought— release thought and action will follow. It requires more maturity

than most students have to *discipline* the action. The other state-
ment may or may not be true, but is, also, interesting. "In the
United States people know when to work and when to play. In
India it is 'all work' or 'all play'."

The current generational shift in India reminds us who were in
the post-World War I youth group of our experiences with our
pre-World War I parents. Rapid change always brings discontinuity, always results in lack of communication between elders and
youth. It has ever been fashionable for gray heads to deplore the
wickedness of the younger generation, with failure to see the changed
conditions, the impact of new mass media, the result of much
"education" outside the home. Indian *society* is changing, and
hence Indian *psyches* are developing along new patterns. We
have repeatedly pointed out in this analysis the inconsistency of
encouraging new political-economic patterns with insistence on
retention of traditional social mores. That this is "human" and
has been done by other societies in more leisurely eras is no comfort
to an India which is deliberately telescoping centuries into decades.
Planning in some areas of society requires planning in all—if
society is not to lose its balance.

Indiscipline in the Universities

Non-Indian readers in particular will need to know the exact
nature of the indiscipline in universities—the strikes, the burnt
effigies, the processions, the demands. To mention just a few,
students in Calcutta rioted over difficult examinations and walked
out in refusal to take them; hundreds of students in Mysore
"demonstrated in unruly fashion" their right to attend the World
Youth Festival; two students of Doab College went on a hunger
strike in protest against the "rustication" (suspension) of the
president of the Students' Union on a charge of indiscipline; the
Vice-Chancellor of Banares Hindu University recently resigned,
in aftermath of last year's demonstrations and strikes over various
university policies and appointments that resulted in a three-month
closure; students are still agitating at Aligarh University, where
courts are considering the serious charges of corruption and misappropriation of funds against the Vice-Chancellor; two students
in Orissa went on a hunger strike in protest against the authorities'
refusal to permit 36 students to appear for examinations (they

had failed to keep the required minimum attendance); 400 students recently made a forced entry into the premises of the Patna Commerce College and assaulted the principal and four professors, causing grievous injury to one of them.

The State of Uttar Pradesh has had more "serious trouble" than any other area—power politics is usually given as the reason—where, in addition to troubled Banares and Aligarh the "worst cases of the year" have been Allahabad and Lucknow Universities, both closed for many weeks and under the jurisdiction of the armed constabulary. The Allahabad case started with a young man who had been refused admission in the post-graduate programme (not all can be admitted, and he had failed his B.A. examination on his first sitting). He undertook a "fast unto death" in order to force the authorities to admit him. The Vice-Chancellor, in reviewing the situation for the press on December 14, stated, "Trouble of one kind or another with the students has become a regular feature of Allahabad University. The formal life of the University has frequently been violently disturbed by the students, making it impossible for the University to function smoothly. The main feature in all such disturbances has been the insistence of students that whatever they demand must be conceded, because in all such cases there so-called demands have been backed by a show of force."[13] This hunger strike was backed by the Student Union (Student Government) executives, and soon many students were emotionally aroused over the authorities' "indifference to a valuable life". They added further demands, and some 700 students marched in procession to the Vice-Chancellor's home, shouting slogans. Several nights later 300 broke into the Vice-Chancellor's compound and thereafter "besieged him". One day a group barricaded the main university gates and prevented all from entering, "practically lynching one instructor" in the struggle. The Executive Council, which had first stood firm against giving in to force, capitulated at this point and granted admission to the student in question. This was no longer sufficient for the inflamed students, however, and the situation worsened. Civil authorities were asked to take over, and the Provincial Armed Constabulary moved in. All educational institutions in the city were ordered closed, assembly was banned, many students were arrested, and students were forced to leave the hostels and go home. When the

[13] *The Statesman*, December 15, 1960.

university eventually re-opened after a long "holiday", the Student Union was suspended, the Convocation (Commencement exercises for the previous group of graduates) was postponed. Onlookers had been pleased by the relatively firm action of the faculty in the University Teachers Association in (1) resisting the show of force, and (2) pleading for the principles of democracy, but they felt the faculty position was completely undermined by the capitulation of the Executive Council. The Council, on the other hand, faced an immediate and explosive situation, and apparently did not dare extenuate the circumstances.

- We happened to be in Lucknow when student demands and demonstrations there resulted also in violence and closure. Despite being "on the spot" we could not determine the "truth" of the situation, for unsubstantiated rumour and emotions ran wild. We could only be sure that the incident brought a smouldering situation into flame. Students were agitated by the alleged immoral conduct of the Dean of the Faculty of Arts, a man by common knowledge slated to become the next Vice-Chancellor. Under the leadership of the Student Union, they demanded that he be "ousted" and that there be an inquiry into corruption, maladministration, and moral turpitude. They burned the Dean's car in an orgy of morality—"upholding the highest moral and ethical values, which the University had failed to uphold". The allegation, openly discussed, was that the Dean had long been a "womanizer", that he had caused a girl student to become pregnant and have an abortion. The girl herself, her parents, and the doctor denied the charges—"of course they would, for otherwise the girl could never get married—her reputation would be spoiled". Rumour mounted, with many students incensed over "damaging photographs" (we found no students who had seen them) and the Dean's wife's statements (we found no students who had heard her). A few students, in discussing the matter with us in relative calmness, were sobered by "the other side of the story" and admitted it was possible their Union leaders were misinformed. "But we elected them and we must support them. *That is democracy, isn't it* ?" They further admitted the Student Union leaders had been advised by the outside politicians who had been on campus. "*But these politicians are here in our cause. They are the only ones who care about us.*" It was common knowledge that the chief "outside politician" was a powerful and disgruntled ex-Minister, a man who had once virtually controlled everything in the University and who was known to be seeking revenge against the Dean, one of his opponents. Again the police were called in and the University was closed—even to the library. When the University re-opened in the spring it was soon announced that the Dean in question had been appointed Vice-Chancellor. A relatively mild student demonstration was this time quelled by students. "Alas, the worst has happened", the students said—and all quieted down. As we said, we do not know whether any of the allegations were true or not, but we have heard people all over India state their convictions that they were, and no official or public proof was offered in refutation. We see in this "modern" crisis two aspects of tradition—(1) character assassination via charges of immorality, and (2) the principle of *loyalty*. We did not see unbiased journalistic analyses and critiques, or judicial or professional procedures. The power of the administration won over the power of the students.

The above two cases are at the more serious side of the indiscipline spectrum. The worst incidents seem always to have the complications of external and internal politics. We are told there is considerable use of paid student agitators—who mislead thousands of innocent but inflammable students. At the other end of the spectrum "indiscipline" generally takes the form of "unruly hooting" at functions and entertainments, or, as one student described common practice, "Don't obey the teachers, cut classes, and tease the girls". We sadly agree with Chanchal Sarkar that co-education in its present unnatural state contributes to the "unrest" —in terms of frustration and in terms of male opportunities to have some sport at the expense of the girls. Even a comparatively liberal and trouble-free institution as Baroda University has this difficulty. Students there had trouble explaining the reason, but one said, "It always happens at the girls' entertainments, because the boys don't like reserved seats and other privileges given to girls. But I think this is just their excuse to tease girls and have some fun." Another student said, "I think we think this is the way to act collegiate. Everyone is doing it, so why shouldn't we ?"

At Annamalai University in the "quiet South" hooting at entertainments was common this year, the students sometimes even drowning out the words of the Vice-Chancellor, a gentle and beloved administrator. If, as has been suggested, the Vice-Chancellor was not firm enough in these situations and also in those where students have successfully asked for special holidays, one has to keep in mind the recent history of indiscipline in Annamalai. Students once locked up the Vice-Chancellor, and on another occasion broke all the plant pots on the Guest House verandah and burned the display of university publications. Some see only the deliberate damage in this latter situation; others see the provocation behind it. Again the ever-vulnerable girls' entertainment started the trouble. The planned entertainment was so poor in rehearsal that authorities feared excessive rowdyism on the part of the male audience and purposely refused to give the boys a "late pass" as regards returning to their hostels. Most of the boys grumbled (these student entertainments are keenly anticipated) but stayed in their quarters. Some, however, did attend the entertainment, and when the hostel gate-keeper, under firm instructions, refused to let them enter (and, in fact, ran away with the key), the indignant boys marched to the Vice-Chancellor's home and demanded entrance to the hostel. The distraught Vice-Chancellor cried that he did not like all this trouble and said he might resign and go to live in the Temple. "Yes, resign!" some shouted. "No, please don't resign, sir!" others countered. And the ensuing argument on his possible resignation drove the unhappy administrator into his house, leaving the boys still locked out of their hostel. It was at this point they broke the plant pots and burned the publications. Their sympathizers have pointed out that authorities mishandled the situation from the first; their detractors feel that nothing excuses their crude and unlawful behaviour.

The following statements made by some students and faculty members in various institutions during interviews illustrate the complexity of the problem. Many factors contribute to the frustration, the irrational behaviour, the general "unrest":

Scottish Church College students: "We must mass for our rights." "What we do is rarely spontaneous—we are often forced by politicians." "It is a reflection of our insecurity."

St. Xavier's College students: "We couldn't strike here—there is too much discipline. Also, we have our 'Twentieth Century Club' and Debating Society for arguments."

Baroda University students: "The stones and firecrackers at entertainments are part of fighting the administration. The management isn't proper—everything is Gujerati here, and many of us aren't Gujerati." "No, we girls don't do these things—it is indecent, and we fear public opinion. The boys do it because they don't have enough work—they have to use their energy. It is something to expect every year." "We really don't have 'free mixing'. We are not allowed to sit together. We *can* walk together on the campus, but if it is always with the same person our parents object and if it is with different persons we get bad reputations!" "The Student Union isn't a nice place—most of us girls won't go there. It's just a place to make a row. The elections are dishonest, and only the dullards and rowdies get in. Sometimes goondas beat others up. There is nothing we can do about it." "Yes, we have a newspaper, but it *never* has strong editorials—it wouldn't be allowed." "The teachers are all partial in the way they give marks, and anyway they don't teach well."

Baroda University faculty member: "The students in the hostels talk only about (1) films, (2) politics, (3) girls they'd like to know, and (4) the warden."

Annamalai University faculty member: "The authorities are on the defensive. They know there will have to be changes, but they say 'in 20 or 50 years'. The greatest pressures are on caste and sex relations". "The university motto is 'With Courage and Faith'. Notice what students have written—'With Corruption and Favouritism'."

Visva-Bharati students: "We don't have much indiscipline—there are so many activities like the Mela (fair), flood relief programme, World University Service programme, excursions, dance dramas, picnics, parties, and so on." "But the professors aren't interested in teaching—they care only about their salaries."

Visva-Bharati faculty member: "Studies aren't important here—the students have too many other interests. Trying to teach well is most unrewarding."

University of Calcutta faculty members: "The hostels here in Calcutta are impossible. One year in one takes ten years off one's life." "The textbook racket is terrible." "There is a political representative of each party in every classroom." "The problem is part of the larger problem of education in India. I don't know how to educate my son—'public' schools turn out snobs, church schools bigots, and government schools dunces."

Madras School of Social Work faculty member: "Students *defy* authority because they aren't permitted to *question* authority. They want to exercise individuality and free thinking. This indiscipline is growing because the education is no good for a changing world. The youth of today knows more about other countries and isn't satisfied with what is offered."

Osmania University students: "There is much indiscipline here—though less than in the U.P. We are asked to imagine everything, without equipment. The lecturers are poor. We students are not asked anything." "We speak to professors only in emergency."

University of Madras student: "Two thousand rupees gets one a 'first class' in the examinations. It's the only way."

University of Lucknow faculty member: "We have no professional autonomy here. The textbook racket is common, and admissions, marks, examination answers, and honours are openly bought. Advancement for lecturers is almost hopeless." "I don't blame the students in this present crisis—but they can't be allowed to have their way."

University of Lucknow students: "Freedom is now important. The authorities try to check independent thinking—they think it is dangerous. They think 'disagreement' is 'lack of respect', but 'respect' has nothing to do with 'orders' or 'elders'." "Our parents agree with our feelings but not our methods. They advise us to stay out of trouble—this makes conflicts." "Rules are no problem here—there are rules, but they are never enforced." "We want to see more of the girls." "We want more personal contacts with our professors, but there are so many students it is impossible."

Bethune College faculty member: "The revised syllabi are too heavy and difficult. It is impossible to take the time for class discussion." "Cheating and general dishonesty are rising."

Miranda House College students: "Most professors don't teach well." "There is no association between professors and students." "The professors all have their favourites, and they spend most of their time on tutorials and publishing crib notes." "In writing papers we all copy liberally from books—it is quite safe to do so because the professors never read the books." "*Everything* encourages cheating". "I see absolutely nothing good in Indian education."

VV College, Hyderabad, student participant in a seminar on student indiscipline: "Students don't get good training quantitatively or qualitatively. Education is commercialized. Students want new vistas today. Professors should be people of extraordinary personalities, but many of the poorest people go into teaching. An individual student has no personality—is not an individual. He is a monkey at best and a fool at worst. He is only an imitator, is intellectually impotent. With such raw materials of professors and students much harm is done. Where there is no vision we perish—we are lost. We only think of ourselves. We don't think of India. Education is ruthlessly failing to give us (1) individuality and (2) love of our country."

A parent of a university student: "The students show no individual courage, protest only in crowds. They show no self-assertion, have no integrity of self."

We want to make it clear that some colleges and universities are not experiencing indiscipline. This is apparently true of many women's colleges, though the girls insist "they have troubles, too" (perhaps they want to join the swim). Certainly the students of the Madras School of Social Work, a small, professional, post-graduate institution, would find it unthinkable to indulge in indiscipline. There are many reasons for this, including the maturity of the students, their intimate contact with the staff, and the School's independence from externally imposed syllabi and examinations. Students at St Xavier's College, Jadavpur University, and the University of Bombay expressed their disdain for "these childish activities". There is no question that the size of the institution is an important factor—most critics do not like the unitary type of university for this reason. Yet, tiny Visva-Bharati has had its troubles. And medical and engineering students in large and impersonal institutions are rarely involved in indiscipline. They tend to be highly selected students, are secure in job prospects, are busy with their studies every day, and they are studying what makes sense to them in terms of life to follow. Clearly there are many factors here, and no single formula fits the problem.

The causes of indiscipline discovered by the survey of the World Brotherhood All-India Committee are (1) too much leisure time, (2) political participation, (3) sex problems, (4) poor student-teacher relations, (5) lack of facilities for representation of complaints, (6) inadequately handled student misbehaviour, (7) anxiety over examinations, (8) student frustrations (anxieties, separations from friends or family, hurt feelings, unsatisfied ambitions, financial difficulties, and (9) emotional immaturity.[14] The Seminar is making many constructive suggestions based upon these findings, but it is our feeling that these suggestions, excellent as they are, do not get at underlying causes of the mounting problem. Mr Chanchal Sarkar in his *Statesman* Survey, "The Unquiet Campus",[15] is much more penetrating in his analysis, taking up the problems of Student Unions and student leadership, the causes beneath "disgruntled students" and "demoralized faculty", the unhealthy political relationship between governments and universities, and the need for vision. He makes it clear that fundamental changes are in order. The University Grants Commission in its report to the Rajya Sabha in February, 1960, recognizes the "problem of student behaviour" and has appointed a committee to study it and take steps "for meeting student welfare".[16] Student welfare may be needed, but the very phrase indicates a point of view that is not likely to tackle the fundamental matters Mr Sarkar analyses.

Causes of Student Indiscipline

Many of the factors listed below have been discussed, but in the interests of organization of the multiple causes of student indiscipline we suggest the following three inter-related areas:

[14] World Brotherhood All-India Committee, Bombay, J. C. Daruvala, executive secretary—to be published.
[15] Chanchal Sarkar, "The Unquiet Campus", A *Statesman* Survey, Delhi, 1960.
[16] U. G. C. Report, *Statesman*, February 23, 1960.

A. *Political-structural*

1. The structure of most institutions of higher education, in relation to State or Central Government, is too political. This is particularly true in the U.P., where there has been so much trouble in recent months, with active control on the part of political figures, either through direct representation on syndicates or boards, or indirectly through political pressures or favours. Finance, positions, and promotions seem to be effective means of control. To quote Mr Sarkar, "The influence of Governments on universities is decisive. They supply the funds; they nominate important sections of the universities' deliberative and executive bodies; they are responsible for the legislation under which universities work; and, too often, they advise the Chancellor on the exercise of his functions, including the choice of Vice-Chancellors. . . . Governments and politicians have not only interfered with universities and destroyed their status and authority, they have also wrecked that subtle thing in them which is described as 'atmosphere'."[17]

Perhaps the most discouraging aspect of this problem is that few citizens believe it is possible to have a publicly supported institution without attendant political control. Or, in the case of institutions independent of government and when a Founder is involved, this Founder is accorded almost dictatorial rights. Professional autonomy simply is not understood, and the citing of English or American experience, where tax-supported institutions have autonomy, is not convincing.

Fortunately there is increasing realization that this political control is destructive to sound education, and the Universities of Madras and Bombay are described as "wise" in their resistance to pressures. We mention again, however, the need for legal clarification of the autonomy and rights of institutions—the rush to civil courts on many matters normally handled within universities presages further difficulty.

The internal structure of most universities is too political in another sense. Symposium participants in "Our Universities" state the dilemma that "those who have the vision are not given the power and those who have the power are not given the vision". They analyse the difficulty thus: "Within the universities a bureaucratic class has arisen which is not confined to the administration

[17] Chanchal Sarkar, "The Unquiet Campus", pp. 14, 15.

alone. It includes those teachers who specialize in university administration and assume accordingly the characteristics of professional bureaucrats. They have a say in the executive bodies of the university, the degree of their influence depending upon the personality and the constitutional position of the vice-chancellor concerned. Some among these "academic bureaucrats" get appointed as vice-chancellors. An informal development taking place is the attempt by this section of teachers to build up influential contacts in government and in the University Grants Commission. The result is that policy makers at different levels hold together as a cohesive group and work as an axis on which the whole university system revolves. What is worse, those outside the axis aspire either to 'rise' and become part of it or to receive the favours of those within it. In brief, what results in the emergence of a managerial class within the educational system whose main concern is to 'run the show'. The criteria of a well-run show is not the realization of the aims of education but the publicity that can be gained thereby. It may be said that the motivation behind our educational policy seems to be that of self-advertisement and propaganda, and not of efficiency. It is worthwhile asking ourselves if this trend is conducive to the growth of a rational system of university education which adequately meets the requirements of our emerging society."[18]

✓2. Many administrators and faculty members get their jobs and promotions solely through the route of favouritism. There are generally two factions in an institution, and it seems necessary to be loyal to one of them—with attendant flattery, calumny, and judicious silence. Many are unhappy about this dubious road to occupational security, but it is difficult or impossible to achieve security otherwise. Bases may be regionalism, religion, caste, family connections, or political party affiliation—but whatever the reasons it is "impossible for an outsider to make the grade". We have been given many instances of this unfortunate situation, including cases of professionally suitable vice-Chancellors denied posts.

The motives and machinations of administration and faculty set the tone—which *can not* be called "academic"—for the university. "If administrators and teachers in universities imagine that their

[18] I. P. Desai, R. F. Kothari, I. S. Gulati, "Our Universities", *Seminar*, Bombay, March, 1960, p. 13.

petty intrigues, their tussles for elective offices, their flattery of authority, their inability to stand up against unfair practices, their lack of interest and competence in academic matters, their attempts to instigate students for private ends and their lapses of conduct go unnoticed by students then they are deceiving themselves."[19]

✓ 3. Partly for the above reason, but also for national political reasons, many faculty members and students are heavily involved in party politics. It has been called to our attention, for instance, that any situation in which an opposition party (often the PSP) is strongly represented offers an "invitation" for Communists to take advantage of the wedge against the Congress Party. Universities are thus used by national political parties in their support or opposition to the regime in power.

✓ 4. It is probable that there are paid student agitators in some universities, again in those situations in which the regime is already challenged. "I would not hesitate to use secret police methods to locate these students", one college principal commented firmly. Whether these agitators are controlled by the Communist Party or not (and they probably are), they find Communistic "readiness" in the student body. Chanchal Sarkar quotes a vice-Chancellor: "We keep tens of thousands of young people off the streets, and instead of letting them become delinquents we turn them into Communists."[20]

We did not find the "bright red Communist tinge" on Indian campuses we had been led to expect—possibly because we were not looking for it, or did not visit the appropriate students or institutions. Most of what we did see was in West Bengal and the U.P., but even there the current "agonizing reappraisal" in light of the Chinese invasion of the Indian border was obvious. More students seemed "vulnerable" than "dedicated" to Communistic propaganda.

✓ 5. When there is political agitation directed from outside, the structure of the Student Union is "made for their purposes", and politicians use it to their advantage. As many pointed out to us, and as Mr Sarkar discovered, few Student Union leaders are among the "better students", few Student Unions are representing the student bodies. Most Unions, in fact, act only as anti-adminis-

[19] Chanchal Sarkar, "The Unquiet Campus", p. 19.
[20] Ibid., p. 6.

tration bodies. The symbol of democracy—student government —is thus distorted, and most students view both the organ and the process with distrust and cynicism. *Democracy cannot seem a noble concept to India's youth when it is thus demonstrated.*

6. Students, politically wise or naive, are taking advantage of the sanctity of the *method* of satyagraha (non-violent protest). Methods related to the recent Independence Movement and to current Labour Union movements have social sanction—it is moral to oppose authority, and in this fashion. Few elders want to oppose these methods, or know how to do so. They are paralysed by their own memories, in their adherence to Gandhian methods blinded to *motives*.

7. But the students are not always tilting at false windmills. Many "rotten and corrupt practices" have continued unchecked by administrations. "How else to stop them ?" "Many students have come to the rueful conclusion that the authorities ignore all grievances until a protest movement is mounted."[21] Many students have a strong sense of mission—that is probably all the stronger for their general frustration. If life in its larger aspects seems completely bewildering, and if one does not know how to lend oneself purposefully to this life, it is satisfying to apply zeal to local and understandable details. Few students are sufficiently clear or dedicated in their purposes to act alone, but the excitement of the mob is intoxicating. Most students are easily swept along by the current.

8. There are fewer years of elementary-secondary education in India than in the West. Usually there are 10 years of education prior to the university; in some areas an additional year has recently been added. Hence many Indian students have had less exposure to studies and to life than Western students—they often enter the university at 14 or 15, immature in years and scholarship. This situation is regarded with gravity by many educational leaders. Some universities have set a minimum age, at $15\frac{1}{2}$ or 16 (we are told this has led to widespread falsification of birth records); the World Brotherhood All-India Committee Seminar recommends a minimum age of 15. Dr Humayun Kabir would prefer "the European practice of 19" but realistically is urging 17 as a practicable aim. On the other hand, the general public disapproves these suggested changes. An increasing number of families do not want

[21] *The Statesman*, February 23, 1960.

their adolescent children "hanging around home doing nothing", and feel they have the right to place their idle children in educational institutions. The solution, we feel, lies not in imposition of minimum entrance ages of 15 or 16, but in lengthened secondary ✓ education. If boys and girls graduate from secondary school at 17 or 18, the group that continues in higher education will be more selected in quality and purpose. Many boys will go directly into occupations, many girls will go directly into marriage, or into nurses' training (where none are admitted until 17). The use of institutions of higher education as custodial institutions for idle children is indefensible. The University Grants Commission recognizes this problem and stated in its report to the Rajya Sabha, "The University should not be treated as though it were some kind of waiting room in which young men and women collect before entering upon a wage-earning career."[22]

✓ 9. It is apparently political expedient at present to promote quantitative higher education—despite official pronouncements—and thus make the "degree" possible for the thousands who seek its prestige. Even the U.G.C., which has constantly urged "quality", is ambivalent in its annual report. The Commission expressed itself "in favour of restricting university education to those who have the aptitude", but also assured the Rajya Sabha that "the growing demand for university education could be met by means of the establishment of new colleges". We agree there must be some expansion even for the deserving, but note there is always political capitulation to "the demand".[23] There are many "new" students, who come from socio-economic groups formerly denied education, some of whom do not understand or respect the academic tradition. This may in part be a good thing—ivy can cover a lot of rotten bricks—but not when there is no respect for learning or the way to achieve learning. Those students who do not merit admission to higher education *on academic grounds*—whether of high or low social status—or those who do not subscribe to academic principles and achievement, should not be in universities. Selections can be made in two ways—either before admission on the basis of secondary education achievement, or partially after admission in the dropping of those who do not or cannot perform adequately. The latter method, common in U.S. state universities, is fairer to the students

[22] *The Statesman*, February 23, 1960.
[23] *The Statesman*, February 23, 1960.

—it judges them on performance in higher education—but it is more expensive as regards tax support. Almost no Indian students are dropped because of inadequate academic performance—this, somehow is considered damaging to prestige. But many are damaged more seriously by being retained throughout, without any hopes of passing—legally. We have reason to believe much of the bribery is due to students' incapability of passing any other way. If boys and girls are not "students" in preparation, achievement, or attitude, it ill serves them or the nation to permit them to obtain inferior degrees and go out to unemployment or positions of responsibility. No nation can afford to finance this kind of "degree education", and no student is really aided by it. S. Ookerjee points out this problem in *Seminar's* symposium on University Education: "Higher education for all" is an ambiguous slogan. If it means that education should not depend on race, religion, wealth, or influence, it is right and commendable. If it means that all should scramble in, irrespective of merit, then it is a vicious fallacy, and the ones who suffer are those who are able and interested but are deprived of getting the best out of their professors due to the drag of the incompetent."[24]

10. This "degree education" is as damaging to some of the excellent students as it is to the undeserving. The most favoured "prestige positions" are clearly in the Indian Administrative Service. Degrees are essential qualifications for application, but the content of the degree may have little or no relationship to the job. Many of the most brilliant students get coveted seats in physics, a prestige subject available to the educational elite. Having obtained their physics degrees with top honours, however, many students desert physics for the I.A.S. Their scientific ability—used only for the purposes of obtaining high government positions—is lost to the purposes of science.

Others, too, use degrees merely as channels. Most social science students—in India for the most part trained for social work— want to become prestigious labour-industrial relations officers (positions firms are required by law to fill). Few have any intention of doing social work, as they are interested in their own prestige, not in the social ills of the nation.

Perhaps the most serious situation involves those who become college and university teachers. This is usually a "last resort",

[24] S. Ookerjee, "Our Universities", *Seminar*, Bombay, March, 1960, p. 33.

all better positions taken up by the graduates with high honours. The result to the profession of higher education is obvious, and is one factor in the decline of standards and in professional status.

This lack of relationship between material studied and career pursued is increasingly frustrating to students and damaging to nation. The use a nation makes of its university graduates determines how the aims and structure of higher education develop—and leads us to a consideration of the professional nature of higher education.

B. *Professional*

1.   The system of higher education in India is basically a "lecture-examination" system. It is largely foreign in its origins and non-functional in its current application. It has not undergone the changes seen in English higher education, is not based on a corps of instructors steeped in sound academic tradition, and has discarded the tutorial system inherent in both the English and the ancient Hindu systems. What is now termed "tutorial" in some institutions is mere token of the principle.

Indian education has always rested on rote learning (we have found few instructors who even question this method), but it also had the "guru"—the master-teacher who was a *personal* mentor and "father" to a small number of students. A student identified with his guru, with his chosen master, in all life values.

Any system that is "impersonal" rather than "personal" tends to become mechanized. Few human beings in any culture enjoy being units in a sea of anonymity. But in India "impersonality" is particularly inhuman. Indians respond chiefly to primary, face-to-face contacts, are relatively unresponsive to secondary, impersonal situations. It is difficult to move from the intimate warmth of family to a large and cold institution. Education without the guru is a chapter wrenched out of life—is too little an inherent part of development.

2.   The administration of most Indian universities is understandably geared to State and/or Central Government, to finances, and to popular political pressures. It is generally not also geared, however, to sound educational development, to administration-faculty relations, to faculty-student relations, and to student needs and interests. There are some happy exceptions, but most vice-chancellors are not educators. The few deans are usually accorded their

titles in relation to prestige, not in relation to their academic responsibilities toward department chairmen and toward the academic
quality and development of their division. The department chairmen,
all too often, do not assist the lecturers and readers below them. In
fact, most demonstrate their threatened security and prestige in their
undermining of colleagues' efforts, especially if these colleagues
are more highly trained or have obtained a foreign degree. Each
rung of the ladder seems occupied by someone stepping on the hands
reaching up from below. Members of a department, thus, instead
of working *cooperatively* under the direction and stimulation of
their chairmen for the improvement of service to students, refuse
to share their ideas and research, and individually pursue their
relationships to power figures in the administration pursuant to
advancement. The professional structure and attitude in most
universities is consequently discouraging intellectual cooperation
and growth. What is a "faculty?"

Dr Punya Sloka Ray, writing in the newspaper about "The Case
of the Frustrated Scholar", said, "The older academician, the man
who was once a scholar and is now merely an empty shell, is a
familiar phenomenon in India today. Often he is quite harmless.
But also quite often he is not so harmless. At best this type of man
is not prepared to listen to anything which he was not familiar with
in that bygone period when he had not yet lost the habit of inquiry.
When a young man brings up ideas, he meets them with cultivated
and dignified deafness. At worst he is jealous of any tangible achievement or constructive proposal that comes from his junior colleagues
or even his own students. He tries to stop them, if not to steal from
them. Am I exaggerating? For one thing, hair-raising stories are
current by the dozen. It may be that most of them are not wholly
true. Yet all of them express the real anxiety and despair in which
our young scholars have to live. This at least is true that altogether
too many of our younger scientists have had to go abroad for recognition. When I was offered a generous research fellowship by an
enlightened vice-chancellor, one of my former teachers publicly
expressed his fear that I might be placed at the same grade as himself
at the end of the fellowship period and, on that ground, voted against
my nomination."[25]

Many universities have Staff Clubs (varying from excellent to

[25] Dr Punya Sloka Ray, "The Case of the Frustrated Scholar", *The Statesman*
January 1, 1960.

dismal), some have Staff Welfare Committees, and a few have Teachers' Associations. But little is supplied but some fellowship and a few amenities. Few faculty members outside the "seniors" feel secure in their professional or psychological positions. This is particularly true of women staff members in a coeducational institution, but it applies also to others. With reference to student indiscipline, for instance, many faculty members have complained to us that they do not know how to handle unruly students. "If we report them to authorities we are considered 'unable to deal with students', if we dismiss them from our classrooms they easily get administrative support for their attendance, if we punish the students in other ways we get parents and courts after us. There is really nothing we can do but try to pretend everything is all right, even when it isn't. Our jobs depend on it." They are, truly, helpless in the absence of administrative support or cooperative faculty action. Faculty associations are developing, but they are rarely more than rubber-stamps for the Executive Council. Faculty rights will ultimately depend on faculty organization and cohesion.

As for faculty-student relations, there is an almost complete lack of structure. There are a few relatively ineffective Deans of Student Welfare, but no Deans of Students, no counsellors, no guidance personnel. Baroda University has instituted a Counselling Office in connection with the Department of Education-Psychology (as yet unvisited by students when we were there). We commend this move, but understand general student misunderstanding of the function of the office and their reluctance to use it. It is, in any case, designed for those students who know they need psychological help and are willing to seek it. It cannot and will not serve the general student body in their day-to-day life, in their classwork, in their extra-curricular activities, in their hostels.

Students need guidance in many ways. Perhaps their greatest need in these days of changing family, sex, class and caste relations is psychological—and the need should be met by all adults with whom they have contact, before they are "in trouble". But this is asking rather too much of this generation of adults. It is more realistic to plead for curricular and vocational guidance, easier to provide but also largely denied Indian students at present. With respect to Calcutta, Chanchal Sarkar observes, "The moral here, I think, is not that there is uncertainty about the future (that there certainly is) but that the universities fail miserably to give advice and guidance even about the opportunities and training schemes that do exist—and there are a fair number of them, even for Humanities students."[26]

3. Faculty members are often undertrained—most have only the M.A., some are under 20 years of age. We can understand this standard in relation to current shortages of teaching personnel, but we are professionally concerned by the attitude prevalent among many that no more study or research is needed as qualification for teaching in universities. Many Ph.D.'s are being obtained, but they involve no further courses—just a dissertation within a narrow field. And all too often they are obtained "because there are no jobs—one might as well get a higher degree."

Almost all faculty members are tragically underpaid, with promotions inhumanly unfair and slow. The widespread sympathy and publicity connected with "the Joseph case" relate to a sensitive, personal area:

Dr Joseph hanged himself in his room on January 6 (1960) after a frustrating 15-year career at the Indian Agricultural Research Institute. He was drawing a salary of Rs. 165 in the grade of 160-330, but various deductions at source left him with a take-home pay of about Rs. 60 per month.[27]

Dr Joseph got a Government Scholarship for advanced studies in the United States in 1954. He took a loan of Rs. 3000 from the Government to meet his expenses and returned to India three years later with a Ph.D. in entomology from Fordham University, New York, which he hoped would better his prospects.

He was contractually bound to serve the Government for three years and consequently rejoined the Indian Agricultural Research Institute on a scale of Rs. 80-220. The loan money was deducted from his salary and his net emoluments were not improved when he was recently promoted to the scale of Rs. 160-330.

Dr Joseph made a number of applications for better-paid posts, including some in other sectors of the Government, but it is alleged that many of these applications were either not forwarded or not forwarded in time by the I.A.R.I. authorities through whom they had to be routed.

Dr Joseph could not maintain his wife and five children and

[26] Chanchal Sarkar, "The Unquiet Campus", p. 8.
[27] We remind American readers that $1.00 equals Rs. 4.75.

ultimately strangled himself with a telephone wire last week.[28]

The suicide has attracted wide notice and has focussed attention on the cumbersome procedures that inhibit initiative and speedy disposal of business in Government. . . . It is pointed out that officials who are prepared to cut through red tape to get a job done stand in danger of being all too readily accused of nepotism and corruption. . . . There is a widespread feeling that initiative will continue to be at a discount.[29]

It is not surprising that many academicians are tempted to accept bribes, to spend most of their time on tutorials or the preparation of published crib notes, or to succumb to the text-book racket. Their financial distress is so severe and the temptations so easy it is a matter of great significance that most do not weaken. But it is not surprising there is much bitterness about those who continue successfully to operate in this fashion, with considerable reward and no punishment. Biswanath Banerjee, in an article on student indiscipline in *The Radical Humanist*, says, "It has got to be acknowledged openly and acted upon that a good portion of blame must be laid at the doors of those who are *not*[30] at the helm. They have by a variety of factors lost the moral ascendancy and prestige in the eyes of those over whom they are to exercise authority. The most important factor contributing to such a situation is their almost utter lack of moral and intellectual integrity as exhibited by the deplorable discrepancy between their profession and practice both moral and intellectual. No one can blink at the colossal accumulation of dirty linen in the academic world which fosters in the students a sense of cynicism and moral irresponsibility."[31]

Faculty members are in some ways over-worked. They are as regards the numbers in their classes, the papers they have to correct. But most are not as regards further study, reading, research. They rarely create courses, and if they write texts it is usually in relation to an accepted syllabus or examination—nothing else has much chance of publication. They are, in effect, *prevented from being creative*. Advancement depends more on seniority or political favour than on academic excellence. And promotion within the

---

[28] *Times of India,* January 15, 1960.   [29] *Times of India,* January 16, 1960.
[30] Italics ours.
[31] Biswanath Banerjee, "Student Indiscipline", *The Radical Humanist*, March 20, 1960.

department is often blocked by the system of "only one full professor to a department"; moving to another institution involves the permission of present institution—which can punish this "disloyal attempt" if it is unsuccessful. Dr Punya Sloka Ray speaks for all "frustrated scholars": "Teachers, even at the post-graduate level, are not trusted in this country to decide what topics and books they will teach. The policy is not to choose our teachers well and then allow them discretion, but to choose those who will come cheaply and then to trust them as little as possible. The usual defence offered for this is that the majority of our teachers are not intellectually alive and, therefore, cannot be trusted with greater leisure or freedom. Unfortunately it is only too good a defence. But should we not rather ask how these teachers could ever be expected to be intellectually alive if they have been forced to spend their youth in teaching 15 to 21 hours a week, far from any library or laboratory worth the name, and on a pay that does not allow the buying of books and journals? ... we young scholars know that the odds against us are heavy. When we consider that because of the absence of books, journals, instruments and the leisure to use them, we fall behind our contemporaries abroad year by year, that it will take us years to achieve what they do in months, that we are in a race with millstones round our necks, our hearts feel like bursting. We insist, we flatter, we beg, we compromise, we save money out of meager salaries to finance pitiful efforts. How long can a man go on in this manner and not break?"[32]

Chanchal Sarkar finds the morale of university personnel one of the most serious situations in Indian higher education today. "The most depressed and pessimistic section, I found, were the teachers. Some senior people were unashamedly fatalistic. They traced the malaise in the universities to a general decline in integrity, morals, and character in the country and thought that the old breed of teachers, students, and administrators had gone, never to return. Practical steps, like paying more in order to attract better people, or providing more amenities for students were, they thought, only feeble palliatives. Younger teachers were cynical, whether coolly so or passionately. The satisfaction of teaching large classes they rated very low, promotions they did not think came in recognition of creditable work, nor did passing large numbers through

[32] Dr Punya Sloka Ray, "The Case of the Frustrated Scholar", *The Statesman*, January 1, 1960.

'grace marks' do any good. Academic freedom and autonomy they considered myths. Among both young and old were a few who thought that it was the teacher who still had the power to attract or influence the pupil, and that a good and conscientious teacher could not be entirely ineffective. But even they pinned their belief on the individual teacher, not on the prevailing system of university administration and teaching. This, I think, is perhaps the most dangerous and painful disease in Indian university education today—*those working in it have no faith*,[33] Teachers have their shortcomings —in some cases they may even obstruct progress—but the fact cannot be blinked that, as a body, they are gravely disillusioned and apathetic."[34] Later in his series of articles Mr Sarkar says, "Life is hard for college teachers. They are considered inferior in the social hierarchy, and, saddest of all, have come to consider themselves so."[35]

University faculties, within and among universities, will probably not emerge from this vicious circle until they *organize as a profession*. Professors in any country are notoriously weak at organization, but in most countries there is some effective organization—because it is essential to self and to chosen vocation. Until the *profession* clarifies educational ends and means, and then puts professional pressure on the legislatures, it cannot expect sound educational plans and policies. It goes without saying that this is a need at all levels of education, not just at that of higher education.

There are notable exceptions to the above generalizations about faculty members and universities in India today—the picture would be totally dark if this were not true—but many of the "best" professors are discouraged and all but defeated by the system. They feel the system must change—and change radically—if academic excellence is to return to India.

4. The curriculum is too rigid. Admission is to subject— often one's second, third, or last choice—with the decision made too early. There is now a trend toward General Education and toward more electives, with Baroda University leading the way, but to date the results are discouraging. For the most part students listen apathetically to isolated lectures on various subjects, are not aided toward the integration of knowledge.

[33] Italics ours.
[34] Chanchal Sarkar, "The Unquiet Campus", pp. 7, 21.
[35] *Ibid*.

5. The medium of instruction, English, is deteriorating, and the controversial problem of appropriate medium is confused and unsettled. When the medium is not one's own language, be it English or Hindi, and when most lectures and texts are in this medium, true "education" is difficult. It has been demonstrated that many pass the examinations without really understanding the medium or the ideas—provided they have good memories. The language problem is severe, and no suggested solutions are entirely acceptable, but academic rewards for "meaningless memory" bear some scrutiny.

6. The "external examination system" is, in our opinion, the worst feature in Indian education, and it ranks high in students' criticism (though most students would be insecure with a less predictable and manipulable system suddenly given). At present, with very little variation, education in Indian universities involves lectures (even in mathematics !), texts, and examinations (usually set by unknown and distant individuals). As a rule a student's entire mark is determined by his examination. (Baroda University has instituted a plan whereby only 70 per cent of the mark relates to the examination; a few other institutions have made similar moves.) Knowledge needed, thus, is geared *only* to the examination—it is no wonder there is rarely any collateral reading suggested or voluntarily undertaken. This results in passive reception and regurgitation of facts, not to mention obsolete information.[36] There is no discussion, no Socratic method, no stimulation of thought, no inquiry, no controversy, *no creativity*. Degrees are sought, not education. It is not surprising that few students, among themselves, discuss deep or worthwhile topics. They have not been stimulated—and hence they spend their time "on idle gossip and cinema stars". "Good and mature students cannot be the product of our education which is purposeless, infested with faulty syllabi and dominated by mere examination-mindedness. No wonder, then, that our student world finds itself completely bewildered in such a climate, miserably lacks social idealism or even any personal stake in life, feels altogether rootless and without any hope in the future, has become cynical and callous, and so has no respect for anybody or anything."[37]

---

[36] Nurses in Bombay State still have to learn how to apply leeches for bleeding patients—"for the examinations", not for actual practice.

[37] "Our Student World", *The Radical Humanist*, February 21, 1960.

The role of "teacher" warrants inquiry. Is the teacher "one who knows all, is always right", and therefore not open to questions ? Is the teacher supposed to "do all the work", dictating word for word *exactly* what should be known (memorized) and *all* that should be known ? Or is the teacher a "senior learner and guide", who does instruct and explain, but who also stimulates students and self to think and inquire—and, in fact, insists on inquiry ? Should the teacher seek to produce the person-who-knows-the-required-facts, or he who has certain foundations of knowledge and concepts but who knows how to think and to find out— and wants to ? These questions bear on the fundamental question, "What is education ?" Until this question is asked and resolved, what kind of system, or what kind of changes, cannot be determined.

There are some current and proposed examination reforms, and some of the more optimistic feel that all will be changed within five years. What changes are wrought—and for what reasons— is of critical import. It is not just examinations that are involved, but a total conception of what constitutes *learning*.

The majority of Indian academicians who want examination reform (and not all do), insist it cannot come until faculties can be trusted academically and morally to set the standards themselves. But a few say, "It could not be worse than it is now—let us be bold and go through the years of chaos that would follow immediate dropping of external examinations. It would produce better results sooner than continuing with the present scheme." As it is now, professors cannot start being creative. For instance, if a professor decides to use a text or approach appropriate to his own situation, he "punishes" his students by failing to fit them for first or second degree "passes"—essential qualifications for jobs—a procedure damaging to students and also to the professor's own reputation. Further, as it is now, students will continue to cram just before the examination, do little study the rest of the time. They freely admit this is their procedure, explaining candidly that daily study is ineffective. "We would not be able to remember the facts that long. The *only* way to pass is to cram at the end."

Those institutions, departments, faculties, and students involved in new areas of inquiry and research (usually science-connected) are striking exceptions to the general picture. They are active rather than passive, are whetting their minds against the frontiers of knowledge. But they are too few—and they are lonely.

C. *Socio-Psychological*:

1. Indian parents, traditionally on the side of authorities, including educational authorities, are generally ambivalent in their positions today. Many are "on the side of their children", though they also want the children to avoid trouble. Whatever their position, they are rarely appealed to or included by university authorities in the correction or guidance of the students. This is a radical change, and has both good and bad results. We ourselves —no doubt from a Western point of view—commend authorities' treatment of youth as individuals responsible for their own actions. But the problems of educating youth are too complex to merit separation of staff and parents in consideration of principles and methods of instruction and behaviour—at least in a culture confused by change. Further, the practice of "taking sides" raises emotions and obscures rational judgment on central issues.

2. Because of the educational system as explained above, there is little or no informal association between faculty and students. Those few professors who would like to be "friendly rather than aloof" find the pressure of numbers and the suspicion of colleagues defeating. "Too much friendliness on the part of students or staff always suggests favouritism."

3. There are few other forms of communication between staff and students, via clubs, socials, or other extra-curricular activities. The great majority of organisations meet twice in the year—for inauguration and closing ceremonies, each with "distinguished speaker". Those organisations that meet more frequently, as the Student Union, have more contact with their faculty advisers, but these advisers—the students tell us—are never chosen by students, are always appointed by the administration "to act as policemen".

We have already pointed out, in connection with administration, the lack of personnel-guidance-counselling procedures. Students have no one taking "parental" responsibility for them, no one to go to for questions or a friendly discussion. When institutions are large and impersonal, life must be *personalized* in many significant ways for each individual—if he is not to feel himself an insignificant cipher in his society.

3. Hostels bear some examination. They range from "good" to "extremely bad" as regards facilities, comforts, lighting, food, etc. Much of the trouble in Calcutta stems from "impossible and

inhuman hostel conditions". A 1955 survey of hostels in Calcutta revealed that 40 per cent of the students were undernourished, that 30-35 per cent lived on less than Rs. 30 per month. Chanchal Sarkar says, "They have to be seen to be believed". The drabness, dirt, lack of ventilation, lack of sunlight or adequate electric light, and—worst of all—unhygienic and pitifully inadequate sanitation, is indefensible. Lack of funds does not excuse the stench or insect population.

The majority of hostels, however, are not this bad, and many are "better than most students' homes" in their physical aspects. The main point is that they are not conceived in any way to be "homes away from home", and medieval European concepts symbolized by the terminology of "warden" and "inmates" prevail. A hostel is a habitation which contains bed and food, is rarely a place where one is glad to go, where one is gladly received. Few wardens or deputy wardens know all their charges, few students know their wardens. Again there is impersonality.

This impersonality seems to have several effects. Those students who are the most immature, or homesick, feel utterly lost and miserable. They tend to withdraw from hostel society. Others feel much freer than in their homes and "know this is their only period of freedom before society makes them conform again". They tend to kick over the traces in every way they can, testing authority and themselves with a kind of intoxication, relatively "safe" in the anonymity of the crowd.

4. Much is currently said about the need for more extra-curricular activities, and university authorities are planning for more, especially in physical education. Many students will probably still prefer to idle away their afternoons in sleep or gossip, but if more is offered that appeals to them more will participate. There is no doubt that those students who are involved in athletics or the National Cadet Corps (an immensely successful organization) are less involved in student indiscipline, are more likely to develop their own talents. Nor is there any doubt that most students would benefit from some extra-curricular interest, be it related to student government, journalism, music, dramatics, service associations, or hobby clubs. A student panel member in Hyderabad in discussing student indiscipline spoke wistfully of American universities —"where students work hard during the week but are able to follow their natural desires on week-ends". However, we agree

with those who insist the chief cure for student indiscipline lies not in increased extra-curricular activities (which stand on other merits). They can, at best, absorb some students' extra time and energy. They will not change most of the frustrations and attitudes, and they may further keep students from putting their minds to curricular matters.

5.   There are two forms of extra-curricular activities that seem essential to modern higher education, weak in Indian universities. One is "student government", certainly not achieved in most current Student Unions. Student government is much more than student elections for officers, for a body that has certain responsibilities for entertainments, or for a body whose chief function is opposition to administrative authority. Student government should *represent* the student body, should be led by the most able students, and should carry wide responsibility for campus life—within clear limitations. No student government should conceive it possible, for instance, to ask for the ousting of a dean. But students need this experience in governing themselves.

The other needed activity is a university newspaper, used for journalistic experience but also for student expression, including protests. According to the reports of many students, the few newspapers that exist "would not be allowed to do this". This may or may not be true, but it is general student opinion.

A good student government and student newspaper (each with competent adviser) give students legitimate organs and channels for discussion, dispute, and controversy. They are, probably, central to the effective structure of democracy.

6.   "Rules" usually reap student disapproval. We found some students who do not feel their rules are too strict (the suggestion surprised them!), and others who had no objections because the rules were not enforced. But many students were outspoken and indignant. An example of the lack of communication between staff and students is seen in the Benares Hindu University's rule that all students have to be inside the campus gate by 8:45 P.M., except for one late pass a week (the hour is 8:00 in many institutions). A number of faculty members thought this rule entirely justified and necessary—"the boys should be studying, and not out at the tobacco shops, at the cinemas, or on the streets looking at women. Once a week is enough." Many boys, in expressing their dislike of this rule, did not say they wanted to be out more than once a

week, or that they wanted to haunt the tobacco shops or cinemas. They quite simply felt too adult to have this kind of rule imposed on them, and they resented being treated like children. This poses a question. Would they, if given the chance through student government, impose their own discipline satisfactorily? Are they sufficiently mature to warrant this approach? Are they capable of self-discipline? Many are extremely young and immature. Some experimentation on these lines might be tried, with special privileges permitted to the older students. Certainly "code law" is not acceptable to the adult democratic personality, nor can the democratic personality develop without experience in self-government. Some matters do not lend themselves to student self-government, but those which do should be gradually put in their hands.

7. It is important to examine the concept of "discipline" and "indiscipline" understood in universities. As we said earlier, "discipline" seems to connote obedience to authority, respect for elders, adherence to custom. It is, patently, an *external form of control*, and "indiscipline" constitutes rebellion to this control (often in socially unacceptable form). "Discipline" is rarely understood as an inner acceptance of values or as inner control. Therefore, the chief method used to achieve discipline is exhortation and punishment, with no attempt made to provide the experiences needed for *individual and social learning*. The current exhortation toward "social consciousness" is not accompanied by opportunities for the social learning that must precede it. And the more authorities exhort youth in India today the more their words are unheeded, for Indian youth are beginning to reject traditional authorities and obedience to them.

8. The chronological immaturity of most Indian students has been pointed out. There is, also, much psychological immaturity, if one compares Indian with Western university students, but it is also probably accurate to say "Indian students of today are more developed than their elders were at the same age". These statements are valid if one assumes a standard of maturity related to individuality (as many would not).

Much research is needed on this matter, but some small pieces of research in India indicate the Oedipus Complex appears in boys at the age of 12 or 13, the adolescent "declaration of independence" or "anti-authority" period at 16-19. These periods are both manifestations of early concepts of "self". We suggest a tentative hypothesis that an individualistic self-concept is beginning to develop in Indian youth today (as it could not in previous periods), but since this "self" is not generally nurtured within the home or school it appears later than in the case of American youth. We are not saying that "an individualistic concept of self" is essential to psychological maturity, though this is true in Western cultures, but do hold that an "understanding" (conscious and subconscious) of the relationship of self to society is essential to maturity. It seems clear that the family-related self of traditional India is changing to one that is more "individual" and more related to factors and institutions outside the family. Certainly our observations and data support this theory, though we urge further research.

The boys, in particular, seem to be experiencing adolescent, irrational, anti-authority feelings as they test themselves in their emerging adulthood. (American boys and girls experience this phase earlier, and largely within the home. Those who develop with the least storm and stress [not all do, of course] have many "anchors to windward"—comfortable homes, abundant food and rest, loving and understanding parents, busy lives at junior high school under teachers who have made a study of adolescent behaviour. Further, they soon become interested in girls and cars. But most importantly, they are far from actual adulthood, when they have to go out into the world and stand on their own feet.) Indian youth, either away from home for the first time, or experiencing a kind of life their parents do not share or understand, do not have much of this assistance— and they are frighteningly close to real adulthood, with its responsibilities and reality. Indian colleagues have suggested to us that "this adolescence theory is undoubtedly true, but accounts only for some of the individual reactions to authority, not to mass indiscipline". We think it does account for much of the latter, in giving many students the readiness to follow peer leadership. Adolescents the world over are known for their "peer culture", for their eagerness to participate in mass movements. Few are sure enough of themselves to act alone. They are passionate in their group loyalties, strong in self-pity, but weak in self-examination. A typical adolescent has begun to remove his psychological "self" from dependence on family, but needs the support of peer group. He is *becoming* an individual, but his "self" is still forming, is tentative, is sensitive.

We further want to suggest that very little anti-authority feeling in India is directed against family authorities—in contrast to the

U.S.—because the family is so *sacred* that such expression is unthinkable, at least at the conscious level. We are ourselves convinced there is much subconscious hostility felt toward parents, but research is needed here, to support or refute this theory. But when there is strong anti-authority feeling, and *if* it is impossible to express it in relation to family authorities, this feeling will be concentrated on school and university authorities.

This psychological immaturity explains much of our collected data. As we discovered, very few Indian students—in their homes or hostels—are involved in discussions relating to philosophy, religion, foreign policy, or any of the deeper and larger aspects of life. Chanchal Sarkar comments on Calcutta students: "I was struck by the absence of a critical approach to political and social questions. They felt deeply, were troubled and indignant, but whether they were of the extreme Left, the moderate Left, or the Right, they accepted their group's official stand—hook, line and sinker."[38] It is significant that those students who have educated and progressive families and who go to schools giving them early training in autonomy and responsibility do not have this "delayed maturity". It is possible to predict, therefore, that this age 16-19 adolescence will begin to appear earlier. But at present it seems to be a general university problem, not a secondary school problem, and it would seem appropriate to suggest that universities address themselves to it.

9. Students anywhere in the world who approach adulthood in an atmosphere of unreality are likely to feel emotionally dissatisfied. We know well in the U.S. that those students who do part-time and/ or summer work, *who are thus involved in self-support and the real work of adult society*, are the more serious and satisfied. They are acting as adults. Indian students, the boys in particular, whether rich or poor, are used to servants and service. They generally continue to get this service in the universities, and putting their own hands to the broom, cooking pot, or hammer is "out of the tradition". It is true that such work pays little (others will do it for a few annas) and it is also true that the poor need jobs, but these easy rationalizations ought not to obscure the inestimable value of self-help. Most administrators say "it would not work in India", but some recognize the problem and have instituted some student work—all too often only for "the poor".

[38] Chanchal Sarkar, "The Unquiet Campus", p. 22.

We see in the principle of self-help not so much the economic aid to the student, though that may be essential, as the *psychological* value. We have in mind the "status consciousness", so widespread and paralyzing. B.A.'s generally won't accept work "beneath their status", and this often refers to "working in the same room with non-B.A.'s". We think more students would meet the reality of post-university life, adapting to jobs normally not considered within their status, or creating jobs where none formerly existed, if they experienced more reality in the university. In other words, when one discards one aspect of tradition—that of inheriting prescribed occupational roles—one should also discard the traditional status concepts attendant to these roles. The only way to become occupationally democratic is to be occupationally democratic.

10. Without question one of the greatest areas of "unreality" in Indian university life is the disparity between sex mores and sex interest. India is not alone in this problem, but Indians have generally thought the problem would not and could not arise in India. There is little frank recognition of the situation that exists and that is "building" rapidly. We have discussed the problem of courtship and marriage at length, trying to show the difficulties of a transition period. It is incontrovertible that unless "integration" in adult life is sanctioned, "integration" in schools should not be permitted. Few recognize the *relationship of social process to social results*. Boys and girls of different backgrounds—be they racial, religious, linguistic, or economic—if allowed democratically to mix freely as they grow up, are going to accept each other democratically in adult life. And this includes the institution of marriage. It is not appropriate for a Westerner to suggest India's principles or course of action, but we cannot refrain from drawing on Western experience to point out the damage of inconsistency. Young people are sure to rebel against their elders if they are forced to results inconsistent with process.

11. The question of "freedom" is troubling many parents and administrators in India—and they have much company in the world! It is recognized in India that "more freedom should be given", and some has been reluctantly granted. But if freedom is given without guidance, without limits, it often results in licence and irrational and irresponsible behaviour (as has been so largely the case in America). Many Student Union activities have "proved" to the elders that freedom is not a good thing, as they always suspected.

Much suddenly given contact between the sexes brings some "trouble" and much silly infatuation, again "proving" to the adults that they had been right in the first place.

On the other hand, as students have been succeeding in most of their indisciplined adventures, it has been "proved" to them their methods are right. This is heady wine, indeed, and they are intoxicated by their power against confused and vacillating authorities.

These "proofs" are surface judgments, failing to take into account the nature of freedom. Freedom is not licence—it is the result of many disciplines, should not be given without the disciplines. A person "free" to drive 60 miles an hour down the highway is trained to drive expertly, has a vehicle engineered to be reliable, travels on an engineered highway that has no sudden holes or sharp curves, and instinctively drives according to traffic regulations—including keeping to the correct side of the road. Eliminate any of these "disciplines" and the driver is not "free". He is in a hazardous position. He is unsafe.

Thus, just when Indian students need more student government and "natural contact with the opposite sex", many adults are withdrawing tentative freedoms offered, not realizing their own defaults in inadequate training and guidance. When institutional values are rigid, without communication with students, without guidance toward new patterns, rebellion takes place, force meets force. And the more youth is put down by force the more it will move toward stronger rebellion. For example, no Student Union should be permitted to dictate university policy. This is quite clear, and such situations, if allowed to develop, require firm resistance. But it is not the *existence* of a Student Union that is fundamental. It is the way it is set up, how it is guided, what its members understand about its functions and limits. The elimination of Student Unions—though this may be temporarily necessary—will not solve university problems with youth.

12.   When one views the above factors, it is not surprising there is much student indiscipline, both active and latent. Indeed, from a cause-and-effect point of view, it should be expected. Modes of obedience and loyalty to superiors, functional to a vertical, hierarchical, society, are not acceptable to those moving into a competitive and more horizontal society. But modes of "responsibility" and "trust", necessary to the latter type of society, are as yet neither operative nor understood.

It seems clear that the current older generation is not helping youth with their problems of entering a new age. In fact, the older generation is baffled by youth, and as their voices grow shriller the eruptions of indiscipline become more serious. As we view the current suggested "cures" for indiscipline we are concerned by the over-emphasis on "control". Control is necessary in all institutions, and authoritarian control is necessary when things get out of hand. Immature students cannot be allowed to take over institutions or to distort their purposes. The incorrigible should be removed and the others should be subjected to discipline. But the urgency of controlling their irrational and irresponsible behaviour does not *prove* that "freedom is dangerous" or that "democracy has no place on the campus". It may, indeed, prove that new ideas of "control" are needed. We think it proves "social learning" has not been fostered, that "freedom" and "democracy" have not been understood.

"Understanding youth" is a new function in India, as it was a few decades ago in the West. Few parents or teachers even think of listening to children, of trying to determine what they think, how they feel—or why. Research and literature on the subject in India is beginning, but it is meagre and unsupported. The psychology of youth should be considered in any analyses of changes from traditional to modern life. Indian youth *is* going to become modern, *is* discarding traditional morals and customs. We are not saying that all life must have Western patterns or purposes if a higher standard of living, a democratic way of life, and other Western-inspired items are developed. But we do say that any society is a kind of organism that has to move in one piece, with some kind of consistency and wholeness. If it does not there will be unbearable strains. We have pointed out these areas of strain, but would like to summarize them again:

(a) A modern urban-industrial society cannot retain the joint family, which is functional to an early agricultural-craft economy. The separate family is functional to an industrial economy.

(b) A democratic society cannot exist unless it is composed of democratic personalities, cannot develop unless democratic personalities are nurtured. But emergent democratic personalities are a threat to traditional vested authorities—and, vice versa, are frustrated by these authorities.

(c) Attitudes functional to a vertical society, as "loyalty", are not easily transformed to attitudes functional to a more horizontal society, as "responsibility" and "trust". The latter qualities will have to be consciously developed.

(d) A society that gives up prescribed, inherited roles must permit and even encourage non-traditional or "non-status" training and experience.

(e) A society that "opens up" and increases social interaction between people of different sex, faiths, castes, etc. cannot expect to remain "closed" in its institutions, including that of marriage.

(f) Modern mass media gives new knowledge and expectations and will not permit traditional isolation and innocence.

(g) Mass education, which must undergird a modern democracy, is in itself so "impersonal" that each institution must "personalize" life for the students.

(h) Parents and other elders, if they want to help young people or retain their respect, will have to learn to understand the youth of today. They will have to "listen" as well as "tell". After all, it was they who encouraged youth to new ideas.

(i) Freedom of thought without freedom of action is inconsistent.

13 | *Democracy by Education or Exhortation*

A Miranda House student told us that Max Lerner had asked Prime Minister Nehru this year why Indian students are so lacking in "social consciousness". Mr Lerner later told us he had used the phrase "social dynamism". He is reported in *Time* to have said that "a healthy discontent is the key to social dynamism", and that "the lack of this quality is what ails India". He was enormously popular with students in his provocation of those "who spout Gandhi's idealism but refuse to get their hands dirty".[1]

"Social consciousness", "social responsibility", or—to use Max Lerner's term, which is superior in its connotation of movement and growth—"social dynamism", is an essential ingredient in a mature democracy and to its chances of maturing. We have pointed out the serious lack of mutual responsibility and trust in Indian society today. Corruption is rising, exposure is feeble or absent. Discontent there is over this situation, but where is the social dynamism? Few will speak up, "stick their necks out", stand up and be counted. Corruption cannot be routed until the citizenry—of campus, city, state, or nation—refuses to live in discontent and is willing to do something about it. Suggestions are offered aplenty, but "It is impossible in India" is a rationale both popular and paralysing.

What is there in the Indian culture that might help to explain this apparent paralysis in social moral action? We have discussed the following points at some length with various Indian friends and have had partial agreement from some, total agreement from others. We offer them for the purpose of further inquiry and discussion.

1. Indian history records the story of a sub-continent that has

[1] *Time*, April 25, 1960, p. 44.

never been united in national terms—until now. Separate groups developed, warred with each other, repulsed or accommodated invasions, but continued to speak their own languages, worship in their own faiths, eat their own foods, and maintain their own customs. Even the British Raj, as is well known, did not unite India psychologically—instead it took advantage of divisions, of differences.

2.　Indian culture has been throughout the centuries essentially "Hindu culture", a way of life prescribed by a religion metaphysical in content and social influence. As we said before, ethics—the philosophy of the relationship of man to man—has been negligible in comparison to the philosophy of the relationship of Man to God. The Hindu religion is predicated on the union of Man and God, on man's separateness from other men. Elaborate and precise ritual emphasize this aim.

3.　The patriarchal family has nurtured the paternalistic personality, and colonialism further sustained it. One obeys the "father" or rebels against him.

4.　Families have generally not trained children to autonomy, to responsibility other than obeying their elders or doing their family duty. In the Hindu joint family one is old before holding the authority of decision. One is never a "self" in terms of individuality.

5.　Responsibility (as duty) and trust are strong features *within the family*, the in-group, have not generally transferred to out-groups. Children grow up seeing these qualities demonstrated only within the family, come to feel them only toward family. (This is now changing, as children and youth identify with peer groups—as in N.C.C. unit, athletic team, etc.)

6.　The concept of *karma* is individualistic in the sense that each person's position and destiny is his own business. Others' plights are their earned or deserved retribution for past sins. To give alms or aid to them is "credit" for oneself, improving one's own *karma*, but essentially one should not interfere with the destiny of others. To what extent this is consciously or unconsciously felt, or to what extent it is an easy rationalization, we do not know.

7.　The concept of "good and evil" does exist in India, contrary to the opinion of many. At the abstract level, what has been handled in the field of "morality" in the West has been in the area of "aesthetics" in India. At the more visible level, "good and evil" in India is different from that rooted in the Puritan-influenced West, is much like David Riesman's "other-directed" principle, where "it's wrong if you get caught". There seems to be no sense of *personal guilt*—always distressing to many Westerners, who are prone to atonement through guilt.

There is strong recognition of good and evil in Hinduism. The triumph of good over evil is the theme of the epic *Ramayana* and of the popular Nataraja representation of Siva in the Cosmic Dance. Further, there is specific enjoinment in the scriptures against lying, stealing, killing, etc. Concepts of sin are related to those of forgiveness—Siva can forgive anything, Vishnu may forgive anything but violence and evil. To what extent these concepts are pervasive and influential we cannot determine. But it is clear at the level of common Hindu practice that wrong-doing is easily balanced by "credit" or erased by "purification". There need be no punishment, for absolution is mechanical and easy.

Furthermore, wrong-doing in the form of lying, stealing, or bribing—*if done for kin*—is minor compared to the *right-doing* of helping family. Nepotism and favouritism have had positive value, are only now becoming bad words. It has been family against the world.

8. It appears that Hindus have not felt religious pressure or encouragement to speak out boldly on social matters. If one looks to the excessive distortions of Christianity, a one-way religion, one finds a narrow bigot. He is not to be admired for his rigidity, but in his "sureness" is a man who stands up to be counted, no matter what others think, whether he is successful or not, whether he is outvoted or not. In his excess he is a zealot, who may be socially obstructive, but he is not afraid to make his voice heard. When one looks to the excessive distortion of Hinduism, a *religion of tolerance*, one sees persons who do not need to clarify their own minds on thoughts or position. "There are many ways, there is no need to pit my principles against those of others." This lack of clarification seems to produce *indifference*. It is not socially obstructive—or constructive.

9. Hinduism, based chiefly on the *Vedas*, *Upanishads*, and *Bhagavad-Gita*, is a religious system that is all-inclusive, exhaustive, and infinite in time and place. All was considered, nothing can be new—not even modern science or the air-and-space age (the gods rode around in air cars). As such, it does not actively prevent change (we note religious silence on the subject of birth control),

but neither does it seem to help its people meet changing conditions in terms of specific clarification or application of principles. (We do not refer to the ultra-conservative religionists, who in any society resist change.) Hinduism has no creed, no organized clergy throughout the country, no conferences, no theological schools, no doctrinal publications, no sermons, no children's classes. It does have ashrams—retreats—where groups of people live together and conduct their devotions, and it does have leaders who have their disciples and followers, but these are small groups of self-seekers. In other words, in comparison to other major religions, it exercises no authority, guidance, or discipline through a religious structure with interpreters on such difficult subjects as sex relations, birth control, divorce, the changing roles of men and women, minority groups, inter-caste relations, the changing form of government, foreign policy, etc. That it does have great "force" is undeniable, for through the sacred scriptures Hinduism has been the chief cement of a vast people throughout many troubled centuries. It has sustained its strength and numbers through its appeal to Indian people, not through proselytizing. It may be that its chief disciplinary effect on individuals has lain in the daily visual reminder of "rewards and punishments" on the wheel of life in the visible existence of rajahs and beggars, sadhus and goondas. Or it may be that the force of family and community—for little is private save worship itself—has been sufficient to deter the backslider. Each man has an individual *karma*, but his reputation is both personal security and family duty.

There has been little of the protestant spirit in Hinduism, though Buddhism, Jainism, and Sikhism are conscious departures from some aspects of Hinduism. The Arya Samaj and Brahmo Samaj "interpretations" or "reforms" have come closer to protestant movements, and the great social reformers Ram Mohan Roy, Rabindranath Tagore, and Mahatma Gandhi did protest against many aspects of deteriorated Hinduism. With Gandhi in particular we see the first *modern* contribution to Hindu doctrine. His interpretation of *karma yoga*—social action—is a significant development. Hinduism has moved from invocation of the sky-gods, to speculation on the meaning of self, to discourses on the relation of self to God, to the *relation of self to society*.

The influence of these men is great, but far from understood or accepted, and all have been more or less given the place of "saints"—

people capable of superhuman virtue. Their gospel is personal only
to those who seek and accept it. *This may be Hinduism's greatness.*
But in terms of disciplined guidance of a whole people in times of
social confusion it seems a limitation.

10. Thus Hinduism, a philosophy and way of life that has sustained a people pursuant to physical, psychological, and philosophical survival throughout the centuries of feudalism and colonialism, that has helped people to *endure*, to *accept in resignation*—
seems not to serve a people toward progress and change.

Change can come only from discontent, from a dissatisfaction in
things as they are, from a determination to bring about improvement.
An individual *karma* today cannot be isolated from the destiny of the
larger society. An Indian's security and destiny, which has lain
chiefly in family and caste, lies increasingly in the institutions of
education, government, business and industry, etc. Until one feels a
relationship of *self* to *public* or extra-family institutions, until
these institutions *become personal* because they affect the person, the
necessary sense of kinship or co-destiny cannot be carried to community, nation, or world. Thus, "social responsibility" or "social
dynamism" will come only when individuals understand that their
security and destiny are related to the concepts and structures
developed in their society.

It is possible that traditional Indian culture is chiefly non-functional to the modern concepts of science, secularism, and democracy,
but it does contain significant aspects of compatibility.

1. The sense of kinship has not been totally confined to family.
Kinship terms, like Grandfather, Grandmother, Father, Mother,
Auntie, Brother, and Sister, are frequently used for friends, neighbours, or even total strangers. (We note the contrast to Mac, Joe,
Mister, Lady and Buddy—common in the U.S.) It is as though
outsiders, when accepted, are taken into the family. This is one of
the strongest and warmest bases in Indian society, and one that is
extending, not diminishing. Gandhi was "Bapu" to many, Nehru
is "father" to thousands—not because "children" address superiors,
but because grown men and women accord this relationship.

2. The sense of personal duty has deep roots. Democracy couched in terms of "vote as you please" makes little sense to many
Indians, but democracy described in terms of "duty toward others"
strikes a responsive chord. This sense of duty is enlarging from
family and village to nation and even to peoples in other lands.

3. The "love of all mankind", central to Hindu philosophy, is central also in the consciousness of today's educated Indian youth. We think this noble but abused phrase—it is "the brotherhood of man" in the West—has remained largely a verbal sentiment in the world because it has, had so little chance of implementation. More people identify with others as more cooperative *structures* and *programmes* are developed. It may be that national and international democracy has ushered in the first moment of history when this principle has a chance.

There are debits and credits, then, in Indian culture as regards the social dynamism that must undergird democracy. But Indian students are reflecting much more than their own culture. They are reflecting the conjunction of Indian and world history. As India joins the nations of the world as a co-partner rather than as a servant, she also joins a global community that is struggling to become a global society. It cannot make up its mind whether to have a "competitive" or "cooperative" society, and if peace obtains it is more likely to do so out of common fear than common sense. No student in the world today can be permitted the innocence or naivity of yesterday's schoolrooms. Every boy and girl feels the tension of a future that presses hard upon the past. The present is as fleeting as "today", for "tomorrow" is sure to be different. In India students daily see the bullock cart on the ground, the Viscount or the Boeing 707 in the air; the *charkha* in the classroom, the atomic reactor in the exhibition; the kite-flying near the village banyan tree, the N.C.C. units drilling on the maidan. The "wisdom of the ages" seems threadbare to them, but the more perceptive wonder if the Pied Piper's tune about the brave, new world does not lead to the same river of oblivion.

Indian students may seem more indisciplined than responsible, but they are much like students all over the world. This is an appropriate phase in their lives for radical thought and expression. We are more concerned about the many not engaged in radical thought than about the few indulging in radical action. If democracy is to have a fighting chance in India the students will have to fight for it. The older generation which won India's independence seems threatened by the democracy they introduced. An idea attractive to an exploited people in terms of "freedom" is less attractive in its imposition of "limitations". How many people in the history of this world have shouted "liberté, egalité, fraternité!" without understanding or intending to live by these principles! Slogans are easily broadcast, but attitudes and habits change slowly. *It is nothing less than democracy that is at stake in India today.*

If we academicians think a matter so political is not our business, we are deluding ourselves. An educational system is always a function of national political philosophy, and is shaped to implement it. An educated person is one who operates with knowledge and skill within his society. He has no role, no power, unless this is true. This is not to say that an educational system should be the tool of politicians—we have said otherwise, strongly—but that when a people, a *whole people*, chooses a political philosophy it must then guarantee the aims and concepts of this philosophy by *living them*. Some say "Education is *preparation* for life", others "Education *is* life". It is both, and the profession of education needs to be clear about it.

There are some Indians who maintain that democracy is consistent with India's tradition and therefore does not need emphasis. Most Indian historians neatly puncture this doubtful theory, pointing out that Vedic society is not like modern Indian society, that the ancient village panchayats do not resemble the Lok Sabha. India has long understood and used the principle of consensus, but consensus in a relatively small, homogeneous group of relatives and neighbours is quite a different matter from consensus in a large and hetero-genous society. "Authority" in the former situation was centralized, hereditary, and respected; in the latter it is dispersed, delegated, and suspected. "Government by consent of the governed" is not the same as "government by participation"—and it is not democracy.

We have not heard much about "democracy" this year (chief wishes are for India to be "modern" or "progressive") save to question its virtue or applicability. Some insist, "Democracy is impossible in India", others that "Democracy won't work in India now". The majority do not want to agree, but they are baffled by people's inability to appreciate their system, their inability to behave as responsible citizens. Power tends to corrupt, whether it is in the hands of the few or the many. But no nation is safe unless power is understood and administered responsibly, and Indians know their nation needs a responsible citizenry.

India's future citizens cannot be exhorted into social respons-ibility—they need opportunities for social learning. Democracy is not a static idea or system, to be adopted if it seems attractive, to be discarded if it seems not to work. It is a *process* based upon *principles*. It cannot arrive full-blown, has to be developed in each nation, *in each individual.*

India is achieving much "egalité", for this need has long been paramount. And now has come the stage for recognizing the need of "fraternité", of the feeling of brotherhood that brings social responsibility. But fundamental to both of these aspects of democracy is "liberté", the need of individual man crying out not only against injustice but *for* the chance to grow freely, live freely. A man cannot accept equality if he does not possess stature; he cannot be responsible for others if he does not have strength to offer. Freedom, then, is what liberates man from bondage to others and equips him to live as an individual who contributes richly to his society.

Individuality and sociality are thus inseparable. One's self-concept relates to one's other-concepts. In a democratic society each person is encouraged to be an individual, is respected as an individual. This does not mean that he is selfish, that he lives without consideration or respect for others. Quite to the contrary, for no man lives in a vacuum. If he wants a society in which he is respected, he must respect others in that society. A society is not the sum of separate men but is built on the relationships among these men. Thus a man is a better family-member and citizen of community and nation if he has personal *identity*, if he is encouraged to *grow*, if he is given the opportunity to *contribute* his ideas and skills. Whatever human dignity he possesses, expressed in his individual and social life, is made possible by the freedom to *grow* and *be.*

Freedom is not licence or the absence of control—it is the rejection of imposed authority in favour of inner control and authority, often delegated through elected representatives. Only a mature person seems able to operate in freedom, and yet a certain measure of freedom is essential to the maturation process. A boy does not learn how to spend money wisely by having his father always do it for him. A girl does not learn how to choose her clothes appropriately by having her mother continuously do it for her. Children can learn something from their elders' precepts, but to learn wisely and well they have to have personal experience also. They have to face their own temptations, to learn to choose, to discover their own mistakes, to recognize their own successes.

Educational authorities, therefore, should not be diverted by arguments for or against freedom, but should direct their energies to supplying the freedoms that are appropriate to the situations. University authorities might ask themselves:

"How could this trouble have been averted?"
"Do the students have justifiable grounds for their feelings?"
"Have we tried to understand them?"
"Have we helped them to understand us?"
"How much and what kind of freedom is healthy on our campus?"
"How can we help our students to use this freedom constructively?"

No democracy can develop unless these mutual principles of individuality and social responsibility are encouraged and nurtured. No democracy can be sustained unless they are protected. This is not abstract philosophy, sentimental altruism, or mystic "sense of service". It is a scientific matter of cause and effect. A healthy society is composed of individuals who make it healthy, who themselves are healthy. As we have stated before, self-government is not mere national self-determination, mere political sovereignty—it is "putting the self into government". If people do not use their own powers they will never get beyond the stage of "welfare state democracy", which has done little but substitute domestic for foreign paternalism. Government to them will remain "the" government—distant, impersonal, something to be cheated—so different from "our" government, essential to self, using the self.

One cannot suddenly be democratic at 21, or even 51. The democratic personality is one that has *become* democratic through growth and experience. Infants are safe only in an authoritarian situation, for they are helpless and must be protected. But unless they are given the opportunity to develop as individuals with their own ideas, feelings, and authority, they will always remain "infants" who need fathers. They will have paternalistic personalities—able to follow and obey, perhaps to rebel, but never to assume responsibility for themselves and others. Their mentors and guides should understand the task of bringing them from one conceptual system (authoritarian) to the other (democratic) in some kind of consistent continuum. This is not easy, for the adult tutors may be rigidly authoritarian—but it is possible when the ends and means of democracy are understood and accepted. Teachers are always able to teach well what they believe.

Families and schools, in which children are nurtured, need to be clear about the type of society their children will experience, what kinds of adult roles this society needs, and how youth should be inducted into these roles. Children need to be trained to earlier autonomy, within and outside the home, if they are to develop democratic personalities, become democratic citizens. We learn what we do—no one has demonstrated this principle better than Gandhi.

This is not idle theory. We recall the late years of the colonial period in India, when many Indian friends complained bitterly about the "unfair and foreign-imposed" laws—such as driving on the left side of the road, rotating wood-cutting plots in the hills in the interests of conservation, and using the city latrines. "Why should we submit to laws like these?" It was clear that a people had been tragically prevented the experience of deciding and imposing their own social legislation. Acceptable social legislation is the result of social learning that has led to social responsibility.

What kind of social learning is possible for children? When children are involved in some accident, do they try to right the situation themselves, or do they at once look to authority? Perhaps they would do less of the latter if they were encouraged to the former. Or, given a social situation in which children should "get along with one another", do they refrain from cruelty because they have been taught it is wicked to hit or to slander, or because they themselves have learned it is an unproductive and unhappy procedure? Have they been given the opportunity to do their own learning? Is the art work "tracing and copying", or is it free and creative? Are the various objects children make "for the purpose of manual coordination" useful and meaningful objects—or mere "exercises" to be displayed in classroom cabinet? Creativity in any form of expression should come from the emotional and social experience of the creator, linking him to life rather than separating him from it. Whether one grows up a "copier" or "creator" depends largely on how he has been encouraged to express himself.

Some of the better schools in India are encouraging this kind of social learning. The New Era School in Bombay is successfully living democracy. Classes, castes, and sexes are working together—and the work of "servants" is minimized. All boys and girls learn to ride cycles safely, take a first aid course, go camping a number of times, learn about the flora and fauna around them and not just in the texts, and learn first-hand about other Indian communities and United Nations neighbours. They plan and execute many of their own activities, discuss their own principles and discipline. They work out these principles by living them—and *their parents like the results*. They have had the right kind of freedom. The Sardar Patel Vidyalaya in New Delhi also has a programme of self-development and social responsibility the parents approve. Their motto is apt: *Ahain Brahm* (The Whole Universe in Me).

These schools demonstrate the compatibility of being "modern" and also Indian. Vinod Sena writes in *Campus*, "The basic fact that confronts us today is an unmistakable lack of vitality and virility in our centres of education. . . . India today is vitally in need of universities that can take up this triple challenge posed by modern life, and yet we seem to be fatally blind to this necessity. Starting at least two centuries after the West on the path of mechanization, we have committed ourselves to a rate of progress that not only demands more, and still more emphasis on research and specialization, but one whose speed may, if proper safeguards are not established, lead to an abrogation of our culture instead of an expansion of it. We are posed with a challenge not just to our economic future, but also to our future as a people with a distinct and ancient culture, with a marked identity."[2]

The Radical Humanist pleads for a new educational reorientation and reconstruction. "First, no plan can give us the desired results if educational reconstruction at the university level is not rooted in the level of secondary education, which, in turn, has to be rooted in the plan for a newly oriented primary education. A democratic training of minds, emotions, and character must begin early in the schools. Secondly, no improvements in the educational sphere can be possible if its wider social context is not simultaneously improved, because when placed in an undesirable social milieu even the best education is bound to degenerate into something harmful. . . . And since a beginning has to be made somewhere, we must begin with the few serious democrats available in this country. They must increase their numbers in every sphere of life without losing any time. In this connection, the responsibility of the few

[2] Vinod Sena, "University Education: A National Challenge", *The Campus*, Delhi, January, 1960.

democratically oriented teachers is the heaviest, because they alone can work in this field. They must be prepared to bear all the burdens and sacrifices of a pioneering renaissance work. They have to leave the imprint of their personalities on their students; they have to ignite the fire of a new social idealism in them."[3]

We commend this view of the total social situation and total educational problem. But sacrifice and social idealism are not enough. The educational profession needs to clarify some of its easily-voiced principles. What is *authority* in a democracy? Is authority external or internal to self? What is *discipline*? Does it lie in external or internal controls? And what is *maturity*? Growing old, or growing wise?

With clarification should come implementation, which at the university level should have emphasis on student responsibility for campus life (which does not include dictating university policy on professional matters). Those students who say "There is nothing we can do about campus corruption" will never be effective citizens of the larger community. Those who will not stand up for their own beliefs in concern over their reputations (or their families' reputations) will never be able to contribute creatively to a changing society.

Exhortation is the least effective method pursuant to attitude formation or change. It may even do harm, for it lulls the exhorter into thinking that the problem has been solved. "Talk" is the occupational medium of those of us who teach, but it is also our occupational disease. One-way talk rarely persuades anyone, and Indian students are clearly tired of it. It is good that Indian students are becoming less passive and submissive. Their ideas, even when irrational, are important. But if their elders do not welcome and guide their ideas and energy, the indiscipline will grow, the controls will have to be tightened, and India's future leaders will become rebels—or mice.

<hr>

[3] "Our Student World", *The Radical Humanist*, February 21, 1960.

14 | *The Cosmic Dance*

NATARAJA, the dancing form of Siva, symbolizes the story of civilization to millions of Indians—and others who seek its meaning. It is the depiction of the *victory of good over the evil of ignorance,*[1] the prostrate figure of temptation beneath the foot of Nataraja looking up with an impudent and far-from vanquished expression. Evil is rarely shown in India as demoniac and inhuman, is usually seductive, attractive, and completely human. The symbolization also connotes, we think, both the perpetual *struggle* in this victory and the *joy and grace* attendant to its success. And, finally, it represents the *infinity of time* in which humanity exists. This current critical period in Indian history is but a moment of consciousness in the unconscious void. India is changing, as it always has, but it will remain India.

This moment differs from many others, however, in its consciousness. India wants to change, is trying to change. In recent history we have had several examples of purposeful change. Russia became the U.S.S.R. not only through a political and military revolution, but also through a long social revolution that was finalized in a scientific (and brutal) programme. The new Soviet Man was produced by the deliberate cutting of the transmission belts of the old culture as new ones were fashioned. Autocracy was ousted in favour of totalitarian democracy. The Church, a threat to political power and a cultural agent of the past, was attacked and derided— and is allowed to exist today only to the extent it does not become a rival authority to government. The home was disrupted and demoralized, until a new generation of parents could be considered loyal and reliable tutors. And the school was child-centered until

[1] It is significant that "there would be no need for Siva if this evil did not exist".

these children grew up to become the authoritarian mentors the new regime later enthroned. These fundamental and traumatic changes did not produce a second revolution not only because they were accomplished by force but also because they were accompanied by an economic ideology that brought actual economic progress. The threat to the modern U.S.S.R. is not dissatisfaction of its citizens in comparison with life under the Tsars—but in comparison to life in the West. The Soviet Man is loyal and proud behind the Iron Curtain—but vulnerable. It is too early to know how the experiment of change is affecting China, but the dialectic of progress and inhuman brutality sounds familiar.

Internal revolution has not been the only stimulus to social change. World War II ushered in a new pattern—that of victors refusing traditional "loot" in favour of the opportunity to mould defeated nations to alliance. Money and effort were poured into Germany and Japan, not taken out. Germany may not be radically changed psychologically—as she was not during the Weimar Republic—for transmission belts to the past were scarcely disturbed. Japan, scornfully considered an inferior people by the West (as Germany was not), received more attention on the part of the Allied Occupation Forces. With less science and more humanity than was used in the U.S.S.R., Japan's future was pinned to a democratic constitution and to the American pattern of education. The Constitution, among other things, gives young people the right to make their own marriage choices, and girls, for the first time in Japanese history, have access to higher education. Much theory and practice in Occupation was naive, all was hurried. Most of the actual change in Japan probably relates to the general Japanese determination to become different, to become modern. Japanese children grow up in homes, schools, and communities that believe in change and implement their belief concretely.

Externally forced change may not be a good thing, and "scientific change" can offend human tolerance. India fits neither of these patterns of external Occupation or internal Revolution. But unless India directs her change more scientifically, high hopes may remain a mirage. What that is "new" is desirable, or undesirable? What that is "old" is harmful, or helpful? Can a "new society" obtain unless the transmission belts of the past are modified, unless new cultural agents are built? The chief "new" agent in India is government, now democratic. But can this agent alone lead a citizenry toward new values—new thinking and acting? What roles are the other cultural agents playing? It is generally conceded that the Hindu religion is not aiding its adherents to new patterns, and that, in fact, it deters progress. It is also manifest that most Indian families, beyond urging children to education, are operating more according to traditional than to new values and customs. This leaves much to the schools, perhaps the only institution which can undertake the immense task of developing a new society based on new personalities.

It does not seem that the schools recognize this task, however. They recognize neither the responsibility nor the nature of their role. Responding to the need of supplying more education for more children, and including more scientific and technical education, they are not considering *values*, *attitudes*, and *attitude change*. They are concerned with certificates, degrees, and employment— but not with psyches, the nature of the emergent society, and a modern Indian philosophy of life. They are not, in short, getting at the root of the problem, which is to shift a people from a vertical to a more horizontal society through developing in each person the concepts and habits of democracy. This involves developing "selves", who will become *participants* rather than *recipients*.

That this concern is recognized by some in India is obvious. When there is so much violence in a "non-violent society", when there is so much "misbehaviour" in a well-mannered culture, this is evidence of widening cracks in a non-functional culture. Indian society is in transition, from a geographically and socially *stable* society based on family-village-caste communities that are *personal* to one that is *mobile* and based on an urban-industrial *impersonal* society. The basic personalities of individuals reflect a rejection of external controls without the beginning of internal controls. It is not surprising so much is "out of control". When morals break down it is a favourite rationale to blame the populace for losing its religion. *The Radical Humanist*, in an article entitled "Social Change and Moral Values",[2] comments on the report of the government-appointed Committee on Religious and Moral Instruction. The Committee analyses the ills in the educational system and in Indian society as a whole as due to the disappearance of the hold of religion on the people. They recommend (1) "the deliberate inculcation of moral and spiritual values from the earliest years", (2) the teaching

[2] *The Radical Humanist*, March 13, 1960, p. 123.

of these moral and spiritual values in educational institutions, (3) stress in this instruction on good manners, social service, and true patriotism, (4) inclusion of this education in the home, and (5) practical measures for educational implementation. But the *Radical Humanist* article points out that the actual problem of social change relates to rural-urban migration, the introduction of modern ideas of health and education, a shift in social organization, and socio-political tensions resulting from the adult franchise. It has been found in the Community Development Programme that the problem is not "the increasing acceptance of secular ideas and the disappearance of religious values, but rather problems growing from the rigidities of the dominating cultural and religious values. . . . The spiritual crisis of contemporary Indian society is basically due to the initial encounter of an essentially religious and traditional society with the problems of a technological civilization. . . . The problems of a modern technological society cannot be faced by traditional institutions and values, but by absorbing the spirit of the modern age, which expresses itself in scientific terms and faith in human potentialities. . . . What we need is a scheme of education for democracy, aiming at the inculcation of the spirit of rationality and freedom with which to face the tasks of mature citizenship. Systematic and indiscriminate doses of dogma and beliefs will not help the individuals realize what is best in themselves and bring about in their character the desired creative orientation in this period of social and spiritual transition."[3] This is, we think, another way of saying what Vinoba Bhave put so simply—"The age of politics and religion is giving way to science and spiritualism."

India has already discovered that in eliminating a "caste society" she has helped a "class society" to develop. This is one of the major dilemmas of the world. As inequalities are battled largely through economic development and opportunities, economic power becomes the new ruler. Money, so benevolent to those who have not had enough, is often used tyrannically by others to continue exploitation or privilege. "Equality" is always the dream of those suffering "inferiority", but equality seems not to satisfy people once they have it—they work and scheme then to achieve "superiority". The history of the world might be written in terms of the bourgeosie downing the aristocracy, the proletariat downing the bourgeoisie, the proletariat then becoming "middle class"—at which point people

[3] *Ibid.*, p. 123.

forget "utopia" and compulsively strive to become "upper class".

Another major dilemma confronting all peoples of the world is that in finally routing most "exploitation"—that immoral practice in which a few enjoy privilege at the expense of the many—"manipulation" is allowed to take over. If power is in the hands of the masses, the way to control the masses is through control of their minds and emotions. Manipulation is not new, of course, but it has taken new form with the use of new tools in modern mass media and the science of psychology. Whether one speaks of politics, selling goods, or education, when there is manipulation, against whom can one rebel? There is no "force"—and man should be able to withstand "persuasion".

Clearly, "getting enough of what one wants", whether it is independence, education, or employment, may end some problems but brings new ones. Few people in sober thought would maintain that "progress" is always civilizing, that "civilization" is always humanizing. In the rush for "a better way of life" people sometimes pause in nostalgic memory of the simplicity that is vanishing—but gone it is. The road ahead is complex.

Man today faces new conditions. For the first time in human history the forces of destruction have no practical limits; it is scientifically possible for a few to destroy all. "Fear" is the goad to the global morality that alone can control these forces. But there is another side to the coin. "Hope" attends the forces of unlimited construction. Men can somehow accept starvation if all around are starving, too; they can accept the "justice" of death if there is no known cure for the malady; they can live with menial occupations if there are no alternatives. But human acceptance and expectations change as knowledge offers keys to new rooms. The have-nots stir, often in bitterness. First they seek patrimony, but if they are to stand on their own feet they must then turn to participation. Men struggle to make "hope" become "reality", to keep "fear" from becoming "disaster". Ignorance is certainly not bliss, but neither is knowledge. As men know more they find more to worry about, more to want.

This, then, is the world the youth of today faces—in India, in the U.S., in all other nations. It is the world their elders prepared for them, with all its dangers, with all its promise. This coming generation will face critical problems that are both global and personal. They will be called upon to make moral decisions more fundamental than they anticipate, than we, their elders, have handled. They face the urgency of war and peace, a new problem in its totality and terror. Is "space" to be filled with orbiting military machines triggered to exterminate continents on command? Or can it become a highway of adventure and exploration of new frontiers? Is the moon to become a military outpost of Washington or Moscow— or can it remain a symbol of peace and romance? Is man's home his castle—or is an underground shelter his cave?

What about the control of atomic energy? Will this fuel cook meals and smelt iron for all the peoples of the world—or will it take the place of oil as major political pawn in international power politics?

Will the nations of the world unite through some form of inter-national cooperation, or will chauvinistic nationalism divide them further? Is "democracy", in fact, possible in the international scene, or is it "for domestic use only?"

How can the world end the immorality of over-production in some areas, under-consumption in others? Is it possible to work out some kind of humane sharing without upsetting the world of finance? Food and other necessities of life are handled in the profit-and-loss area, but are fiscal matters as holy as human life?

Is mass media a useful or destructive tool? The "freedom of speech" was designed to protect men's rights to think as they wish, speak as they wish, and society within reach of any human voice could always act as a sponge for the lunatic fringe. But the "freedom of speech" ought not to give men, and indeed whole governments, the right to sway millions via subtle appeals to the subconscious transported electronically—often to things not believed by the speakers at all, but broadcast in the interest of sales or politics. The loud-speaker has altered man's voice—it has given him false courage, anonymity, and magnified power.

Can societies learn to control their populations within the limits of their resources? Can "birth control" balance the rising "death control"? If not, what will happen to "the sanctity of mankind"?

Finally, in this world into which we are launching youth, are material things merely tools for "the good life", or have they already become "the good life"? No Western export is more en-thusiastically received than "conspicuous comfort". When the chromium-plated world of material satisfaction is, in fact, so satisfying to many, is there any likelihood they will be stirred by the kind of discontent that turns minds toward search of emotional or spiritual satisfaction?

These are sharp questions, but they are not exaggerated. Educators all over the world should balance their intellectual fares against these challenges, should prod their charges to the strength of response. Moral decisions require moral courage, but it is one thing to muster a raw physical courage to go out into the dark unknown—and another to go out with maps, lights, and knowledge. The more bases for judgment one has, the more *conviction* will go with the judgment, the more sound the judgment will be. Youth should be trained to the kind of courageous conviction a surgeon demonstrates as he begins a dangerous operation. If he is a great surgeon he is humble in the face of life and death, but he operates with sure hands and brain because he has been educated to this task. His response to the challenge is effective.

Few students in the world are capable of effective response to such challenge as we have posed, but Indian students—as they are educated in India today—seem less prepared than many, at least in comparison to those in the West. Through no fault of their own, they have little analytical or deductive ability. Enormously intelligent and *teachable*, they are more *receptive* than creative. They are not used to treating ideas as important in themselves, do not think in terms of concepts—though it does not take long for some to be led eagerly in this direction. Few read *Thought*, many are devoted to *The Illustrated Weekly of India*. Their ability, often quite extraordinary, is "mathematical" in an arithmetic rather than a rational sense. They are excellent at cataloguing and classifying, weak at criticizing. (One can observe these qualities everywhere in Indian life—in art, architecture, and literature, for instance. A Hindu temple is a catalogue of items rather than an organic whole.) Indian students, then, trained as memory machines, have facts without knowledge. The "mystic" quality many also possess may be one way of handling the unknown. Indian students are not really following Saraswati, goddess of wisdom, for along with their society they are too busy following Lakshmi, goddess of wealth. They live in a world where security lies in economic, not intellectual, status.

The new world is, indeed, so complex and frightening that everyone wants "security". Youth, and especially Western youth, are seeking security in the crowd. It is called The Age of Conformity, and "how to be an individual in mass society" is the critical question of our time. David Riesman has illustrated this problem in *The Lonely Crowd*,[4] and with reference to his "tradition-directed", "inner-directed", and "other-directed" character types, it seems to this observer that Indian youth is moving directly from tradition-direction to other-direction—from "security in family" to "security in bureaucracy", without experiencing inner-direction or "security in self". The social philosophy of "adjustment", so apparent in Indian culture, lends itself easily to other-direction. Whether the progression described by Riesman is natural or inevitable we do not know, but we do suggest that a society that does not experience inner-direction—and, indeed, retains some measure of it—may not have the spirit of innovation or the drive essential to national progress, and may not have the belief in personal values that is partial corrective to mass conformity. Other-direction is based on operational expediency rather than values. That it works well is no credit to any modern society.

Riesman's analysis is so pertinent to a discussion of changes in Indian society that it seems appropriate to outline some points:

TRADITION-DIRECTION

Geared to geographic and social *stability*,
In an *agriculture-craft* economy (*economy of scarcity*),
Individuals are related to *hierarchical family-clans*,
Their *roles inherited and prescribed.*
Their *values* are those of *tradition*, transmitted by *family precept* and guidance.
They are *controlled* by this tradition, as if they were "free" within the clear
   limits and restricted activity of a *play-pen.*[5]
Their emotions re: wrong and right-doing are *shame* and *pride.*

INNER-DIRECTION

Geared to geographic and social *mobility*,
In an *early-industrial* economy of *production*, an *economy of scarcity.*
Individuals act *independently* of their families,
Finding and *making their roles.*
Their *values are personal*, as transmitted by *conscience* (set by parents).
They are *controlled* by conscience, as if free to move anywhere with "*gyroscope*".
Their emotions re: wrong and right-doing are *guilt* and *self-righteousness.*

---

[4] David Riesman, *The Lonely Crowd*, Doubleday Anchor paperback, 1953.
[5] The "play-pen" construct is ours, the "gyroscope" and "radar" are Riesman's.

OTHER-DIRECTION

Geared to even greater *mobility*,

In an *industrial economy* of *abundance* and *consumption*.

Individuals act independently of their families but not of their chosen *organizations*—they are *"organization men"*,

Who *adapt their roles* to those demanded by the organization.

Their *values* are those of the *organization*, as understood through the *"radar"* of perception. They are free to move anywhere, provided their radars accurately reflect *expedient action*.

Their emotions re: wrong and right-doing are *anxiety* and *security*.

Riesman makes it clear that few individuals and societies are "pure" in their characteristics, but it would be difficult to describe traditional India more accurately than with tradition-direction. The dominant character type is changing today because the economy is changing—because Indian youth want mobility.

The United States has developed largely through inner-direction, for Americans had largely discarded old-world tradition when they moved to a new continent which presented new conditions. It was a land for pioneers, and especially when the industrial revolution arrived men had to be mobile geographically and socially. With the "gyroscope" of conscience a man could move anywhere and become anything. He was often alone but rarely lonely. It was an age of innovation, of "rugged individualism", and of laissez-faire. Henry Ford, senior, a good example of a successful man in this period, almost single-handedly invented and built an automobile and a new system of economics. He is reputed to have said of customers, "They can have any colour car they want as long as it is black", and he continued to be impervious to suggestions of accommodation. His rugged individualism built the Ford Motor Company, but it later nearly lost it, for before Ford died it was apparent that customers' wishes were economically important in an economy of abundance. The company regained its stature by supplying public needs as determined by the "radar" of market research.

We mention this case because it so beautifully illustrates the changes that took place in the American economy and society. Henry Ford was freer than his forebears, but in terms of an economy of abundance and consumption he was not free enough—his gyroscope control was too restrictive. People did not want to buy cars that satisfied Henry Ford—they had their own views—and the company had to reflect their sentiments in their products in order to sell. Americans, especially youth and those living in the major cities, learned how to "sell themselves". People became market commodities as subtle or high-pressure advertising techniques spread from Madison Ave. across the nation. No American writer has better illustrated the success and the sorrow of other-direction than John Marquand, as, for instance, in his novels *Point of No Return* and *Sincerely Willis Wayde*. An other-directed youth today who seeks a job does not stand ruggedly on his own ability— he achieves employment less on what he knows than whom he knows, and how he responds to him. Obeying the signals of his "radar" he speaks and acts as he finds appropriate to the situation. Sadly, this procedure usually works. But even more sadly, those who seek to bolster "selves" in conformity lose these "selves". It is a lonely crowd.

No item better illustrates the differences in these character-structures than that of "emotion as regards wrong and right-doing". "Stealing", for instance, is immoral and illegal in any society. A tradition-directed person who steals feels *shame*, for he has disgraced his family, has affected its reputation. If he resists the temptation to steal he feels *pride* in having kept the escutcheon bright. An inner-directed person who steals feels *guilty*, for he has sinned and he knows it. When he resists he feels *self-righteous* in his victory over temptation. An other-directed person who steals feels *anxiety*—perhaps someone did see him after all. But in resistance he finds *security*, for he has obeyed the dictates of society and no policeman will seek him out.

Or, let us look at roles. The tradition-directed person inherits prescribed roles that are clear and relatively attainable, though not necessarily likable. The inner-directed person, an independent innovator, makes his own roles. And the other-directed person adapts to organization-roles, "doing as the Romans do".

The United States enjoyed its developmental period in isolation and with a land thinly settled and richly endowed by nature. Its citizens did not worry about "security" until shaken by the 20th century Depression and world wars. India, overpopulated and undernourished, is trying to industrialize in a time of national and international tension. Comparing *past* U.S. and Indian aims and methods:

U.S.	INDIA
Individual success	*Social harmony*
ambition	cooperation
initiative	compromise
courage	sacrifice
rights	duties

Both societies are now changing—to what they are not sure—though strong residues of former characteristics remain. As we have found in this study, the "individual self" is beginning to appear in Indian society, but the further development of self is far from certain. To quote an Indian colleague, "It is too difficult to be a 'self'— society punishes one too severely. Why suffer?" We are not wise enough to say what is desirable for India or the U.S. in the way of individuality or sociality, but we do think that human beings in any society will have to fight for their individuality in this emergent world if they are to remain *human*. Collective security is a good thing—and necessary in this world of naked power—but only if it *shores up the self*, not if it drowns it.

Charles Frankel stated in the *New York Times*,[6] as he put the U.S. television scandals into social perspective, that the reasons for immorality are (1) the emphasis on success, (2) the domination of the market place, and (3) the weakness or absence of institutions that solidly embody public purposes and that exist to protect or advance them. He might have been writing about most modern societies.

Looking again at Indian society in transition, it is apparent that *social harmony* (based on duty), personal peace of mind (based on acceptance), and security–dependence (based on family) are going out, that *social progress*, personal anxiety, and insecurity–independence are coming in. India's political decisions will determine her social nature. *Is the "welfare state" to be means or end*? Will there be *government by consent* or *government by participation*?

India is undergoing stages familiar to world social history. "Equality" is the utopia of those who have not had it. Then "security" becomes the cry, for in any egalitarian society—in contrast to a hierarchical—favoured positions are crowded by competition. Those who live in an era of the common man soon see the need of "uncommon men"—and "individualism" becomes the need.

[6] Charles Frankel, *New York Times*, November 15, 1959.

In this searching and striving the first villains are the "rulers". As they are ousted the "politicians" take over the devil's mantle. But soon it is apparent that the "public" is both ignorant and avaracious. And if more villains are needed, there are the "teachers" who ought to put everything to rights, the "students" who mis-behave, and the "parents" who do not control them. This "devil theory" is a world favourite, and particularly popular of late with citizens of the U.S. and U.S.S.R. who like to feel righteous in viewing the evil of others. It is soothing to those who point their fingers, but it always obscures the deeper issues.

India's problem is not "student indiscipline", "corruption," or "party politics"—it is the deeper problem of social change. Does culture make the man, or does man make the culture? It is a con-tinuous circle, and both movements continuously function:

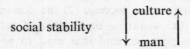

In a time of social stability, culture largely makes the man:

social stability
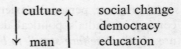

In a time of social change, especially when man enjoys democracy—a system based on his wishes—and education which liberates his mind, man largely moulds culture:

culture ↑	social change
↓ man	democracy
	education

India is in this stage—she is forsaking *resignation* and feels *dis-content*. It remains for this discontent to be organized and directed into *social dynamism*. India's problem is that of racing the motor, not of the motor itself. The renaissance of this rich civilization is certain, but its nature is being influenced by the global struggle between Saraswati and Lakshmi.

Epilogue

Back to Brooklyn

MY "passage to India" is ending, and as I make plans to return to my students at Brooklyn College in New York City I am struck by similarities. Brooklyn College is one of four tax-supported, tuition-free institutions of higher education provided by New York City for its residents. Most of the students have parents that came from "the old country" of Europe, many of whom had little education. The students, therefore, are socially mobile, and especially those who enter the higher professions have moved far from family custom. This opportunity produces strains, for 85 per cent of the students are Jewish, their family life as traditional and close (therefore sometimes confining) as Hindu family life.

But much is different, and in this difference I want to offer hope to Indian students and professors who are currently cynical about Indian education. Influence or bribery could *not* obtain admissions or any other favours for students or faculty. Students enter on their own merits (secondary school records plus an entrance examination) and stay on their own merits. They are given a great deal of help if they need it, via personal counsellors, the Psychological and Counseling Department, and remedial classes. There are many avenues open to them, and they themselves have to choose areas of specialization within the first two years of general instruction. A large number do part-time work to help defray expenses, but most find time also for co-curricular activities in student government, journalism, dramatics, music, athletics, or clubs. Those who graduate in four years with the B.A. have had a rich experience academically and socially. Many go on to further study in distinguished universities, others go directly to work. They certainly are able to stand on their own feet—largely because they began doing so years ago. A distinctive feature of American higher education is "discussion and argument", and Brooklyn College students are more argumentative than most! They brook little inadequate information, accept no theories passively. Teaching there is sometimes like an "intellectual battle".

The faculty members are hired on the basis of their ability to contribute to this kind of education. Many are "minority members" —Negroes, for instance, and even women! Though carefully selected according to training (Ph.D.) and experience, they have to *win* tenure (after three years) and each promotion via colleagues, reports on their teaching and other abilities. A faculty committee judges them on their scholarship as demonstrated by research and publication, their teaching ability, and their personalities. But they are helped, too. From the moment of their employment they are so immersed in inquiry and experiment they do not lack for intellectual stimulation. Time and energy are the problems! Hundreds of committees work on new courses, new programmes, new ideas—and then battle them through departments if they can. Nothing is accepted without the deepest scrutiny. The institution vibrates with intellectual cross-currents. It is the faculty, grossly overworked, that constantly votes for classes to be kept small (usually below 30) so that discussion has a chance—though larger classes would mean fewer classes for this same faculty.

Does this sound like an academic utopia? It may, for it is an institution academically conceived and operated. Academic freedom is the very air we breathe, whether we dispute a point with President Gideonse (a distinguished economist and practising professor) at the cafeteria lunch table, or argue with our students over cups of coffee. Certainly it is a good place to grow intellectually—we never stop learning.

I mention Brooklyn College, not to compare, but to make four points. (1) It *is* possible for tax-supported institutions under a government to have this professional nature, this professional autonomy. (2) This did not happen overnight. It was many years a-building and must be *fought for daily*. (3) Teaching in this kind of institution is *difficult*. It requires every ounce of energy, patience, skill, and sense of humour one can muster. It is, in fact, *exhausting*. I am reminded of the Madras State teaching of English programme, run by the British Council, which I observed in an old compound near Madras. The secondary teachers "in training" had just seen groups of children learning well and learning with enthusiasm, and were discussing methods and results in a seminar. All seemed "convinced" by the classrooms under the tamarind trees—where neither teachers nor pupils used, paper, or slates, but spoke English together as they used leaves, sticks, themselves, and *activity*. "But", one somewhat bewildered seminar member said, "it is so hard to teach this way! I would get so tired". He could not have described the situation better. Response to constant challenge is tiring. But, (4) it is the only kind of teaching and learning that is *alive*. It *uses life*, does not meekly talk about it.

To return to similarities, for whatever we do we are in the same educational boat, we in Brooklyn College face all the problems of mass education in a bureaucratized urban-industrial society. We call our college "an educational factory"—though we do not like others to use this phrase! We have the insecure, the lazy, and the incompetent in our academic community. We have an over-emphasis on marks, with resultant cheating. We try to teach "how to think" more than "what to think", but rewards go to the latter, especially when it agrees with us. It has been said that Brooklyn College students are prone to "wit without wisdom". And most of us feel—for all our efforts—that we do not really prepare our students for the life of tomorrow. The difference in our similarities is, I think, that of degree. We are more successful in our aims than not, and this stimulates even greater effort. We are more hopeful— therefore more helpful. It will be the same in Indian universities when the conditions of teaching and learning are improved.

Now, as I finish my writing in these beautiful hills of Kodaikanal, the only "home town" I have known—I can look out of the window and see the trees I used to climb—I look around anew at the peaceful lake and ageless hills and wonder if I can make the return to New York City. There I shall hear the roar of the subway instead of the roar of the monsoon wind in the eucalyptus trees. I must put away the bicycle and walking cane that have helped me to appreciate nature intimately. I must stop eating mangoes bought from vendors I knew years ago—and learn again to open tins of frozen orange juice bought at the supermarket. When I walk the impersonal city streets I shall remember with affection the many aging men and women who have greeted me here in the bazaar, inquiring about parents and sons. This year, technically a "professional mission", has been a journey into my past and into myself. It is difficult to bridge two worlds of place, two worlds of time—and I am grateful to have had this opportunity to "touch home base".

MARGARET CORMACK

Kodaikanal, India,
June, 1960.

Questionnaire on Social Change

Dr. MARGARET CORMACK

Number ....

University ....

FULBRIGHT PROFESSOR

SOCIAL CHANGE IN INDIA

(University Student Questionnaire)

This questionnaire deals with many aspects of "traditional" and "modern" ways of life, particularly as they affect university youth.

Please be frank. All information will be kept confidential.

Section A deals with data—please write in or underline appropriate information.

Sections B - N deal with 100 incomplete statements. Read the statements carefully. Sometimes you are asked to *describe customs*, and sometimes to give your *personal opinions*. Please respond to *all items* (writing in your own responses wherever appropriate), by putting at the left:

+ a. for agreement   — c. for disagreement
++ b. for strong agreement   — — d. for strong disagreement

A. DATA

a. Age ....   j. Mother's education ....

b. Sex ....   k. Joint or separate family ....

c. Marital status ....   l. No. brothers ....

d. Town, city, State ....   m. No. sisters ....

e. Religion ....   n. Degree subject, yr. ....

f. Caste ....   o. Intended career ....

g. Father's job ....   p. Pocket money/month ....

h. Mother's job ....   q. Dress (sari, salwar, dhoti, trousers) ....

i. Father's education..............

r. My travel in India has included ....

....

241

s. My travel and experience outside India has been ....
....

t. My contact with Western culture has come through (underline responses):

travel	Western professors	..........Info. Service
Western friends	cinemas	....
books and maga-	radio	....
zines		
correspondence	U.S. Information Service	....

u. I have been influenced by Western culture in my

dress	reading	....
food and drink	political ideas	....
social customs	music preferences	....
ideas on marriage	religious ideas	....

v. Aspects of Western culture I dislike and do not want for myself are:
....

w. Aspects of Western culture I admire and want for myself are:
....

x. Western nations that have been greatest in their influence on me are:
....

B. EDUCATION

1. I am undertaking higher education because
   a. my parents insisted, against my will.
   b. I wanted higher education, and my parents were willing.
   c. I insisted, in spite of my parents' disapproval.
   d. ....

2. Higher education is desirable because
   a. it leads one to the best jobs.
   b. knowledge is satisfying.
   c. it makes for better marriage chances.
   d. education brings happiness.
   e. India needs educated leaders.
   f. ....

3. My higher education is "taking me away" from my parents because
   a. I am now much more highly educated than they are.
   b. I have become less religious.
   c. I will probably live and work in another town.
   d. I am making my own decisions about some matters.
   e. my parents now seem old-fashioned to me.
   f. ....

4. With respect to my professors and text-books
   a. I always agree with them, because they are right.
   b. I sometimes silently disagree.
   c. I sometimes openly disagree.
   d. ....

5. When I think about the education I have received, I am most grateful for
    a. intellectual experiences—learning facts, thinking.
    b. social experiences—my association with other students.
    c. my association with professors.
    d. cultural experiences—art, music, literature, etc.
    e. recreational experiences—clubs, sports, outings, etc.
    f. learning more about the world.
    g. learning how to change and improve life in India.
    h. learning more about myself.
    i. ....

6. I have objected to
    a. studying so hard.
    b. the "external examination system."
    c. hostel food and accommodation.
    d. not being allowed to talk to members of the opposite sex.
    e. having higher education in English.
    f. not being allowed to express my own ideas freely.
    g. not having enough choice in selecting courses.
    h. the "aloofness" of my professors.
    i. the subjection of women students and staff.
    j. ....

C. FAMILY LIFE

7. As a child, up to about the age of 12, I was permitted to
    a. go outside the house or compound unaccompanied.
    b. play with children of any caste or class.
    c. play with children of the opposite sex.
    d. spend some money as I chose
    e. choose my own clothes.
    f. speak freely in front of adults.

8. When I was an adolescent, about 12-16,
    a. it was the same.   *c.* I had less freedom.
    b. I had more freedom.   *d.* .. ..

9. This freedom was
    a. more than my parents had   *c.* about the same.
        as children.
    b. less than my parents had.

10. I hope to raise my children
    a. as I was raised.   *c.* with less freedom.
    b. with more freedom.   *d.* ....

11. When I was a child my duties in the home were
    a. helping my father with his work.
    b. helping my mother in the household.
    c. shopping and errands.
    d. taking care of my own clothes.

e. taking care of younger children.

f. ....

12. The usual punishment in my home was
    a. a beating.   *e.* ....
    b. being put alone in a room.   *f.* ....
    c. being denied sweets or toys.
    d. being forbidden to go out and play.

13. The usual reward for good behaviour was
    a. praise.   *b.* sweets.   *c.* ....

14. We observed the following family ceremonies:
    a. cradle and naming.   *e.* sacred cord (boys).
    b. ear-piercing.   *f.* puberty (girls).
    c. shaving hair.   *g.* birthdays.
    d. entering school.   *h.* ....

15. When I have a family I hope to celebrate
    a. the same ceremonies.   *c.* fewer ceremonies.
    b. more ceremonies.   *d.* ....

16. As a small child I was especially happy when
    a. ....
    b. ....

17. And especially unhappy when
    a. ....
    b. ....

18. When my father made decisions regarding me,
    a. I never opposed him.   *c.* I often opposed him.
    b. I sometimes opposed him.   *d.* ....

19. When my mother made decisions regarding me,
    a. I never opposed her.   *c.* I often opposed her.
    b. I sometimes opposed her.   *d.* ....

20. I sometimes imagined
    a. running away from home.   *g.* becoming a famous political leader.
    b. rescuing a member of my   *h.* becoming a sannyasi or sannyasin.
        family from danger.
    c. becoming very ill.   *i.* being a boy instead of a girl.
    d. dying.   *j.* being a girl instead of a boy.
    e. becoming a famous artist,   *k.* ....
        musician, dancer, or painter.
    f. becoming a famous cinema star.

21. With my brothers and sisters
    a. I never quarrelled.   *b.* I sometimes quarrelled.   *c.* I often quarrelled.

22. Our quarrels were usually about
    a. silly childish matters of no   b. things that were very serious to me.
        importance.

23. These quarrels were usually settled by
    a. my father.   c. ourselves.
    b. my mother.   d. ....

24. In my family I felt closest to
    a. my father.   c. a brother.   e. auntie.
    b. my mother.   d. a sister.   f. ....

25. I had a childish fear of
    a. nothing.   c. ghosts.   e. snakes.
    b. the dark.   d. burglars.   f. ....

26. My favourite stories were
    a. ....
    b. ....

27. *In my opinion,* adolescent boys and girls, about 12-16,
    a. should not be allowed to meet or associate with members of the
        opposite sex.
    b. should be allowed to do so, with supervision.
    c. should be allowed to do so, freely and without supervision.

28. In my family the major family decisions were made by
    a. my father.   d. my grandmother.   g. ....
    b. my mother.   e. all adult members.
    c. my grandfather.   f. the caste panchayat.

29. *In my opinion,* family authority should be the responsibility of
    a. ....

D. CO-EDUCATION

30. *In my opinion,* boys and girls should attend the same school for
    a. pre-school.   c. secondary.   e. university.
    b. elementary.   d. pre-university.   f. post-graduate.

31. And if in the same school should
    a. mix freely.   b. be kept separate—in classrooms
                                     library, recreation, etc.

E. SEX EDUCATION

32. Education on sex matters—biological facts with respect to physical matur-
    ation and marriage—is
    a. not necessary.
    b. the responsibility of parents   c. the responsibility of parents and
       only.   schools.

F. MARRIAGE

33. My parents' marriage was
        a. arranged by their parents.　　*b.* a "love marriage"—their choice.

34. *In my own opinion,* marriages should be
        a. arranged by parents, without the consent of the couple. .
        b. arranged by parents, with the consent of the couple.
        c. "love marriages"—the couples' own choice.

35. *In my own opinion,* a marriage should be
        a. within the sub-caste community.
        b. within the caste.　　　　*d.* within the Indian nationality.
        c. within the religion.　　　*e.* with anyone.

36. In considering a marriage, horoscopes are
        a. necessary.　　　*b.* not necessary.　　　*c.* ....

37. When I am married I shall probably
        a. marry within the sub-caste　*c.* have an arranged marriage.
            community.
        b. marry within the caste.　　*d.* be allowed to do as I wish.

38. *In my own opinion,* the bride's dowry is
        a. necessary.　　　*b.* not necessary.　　　*c.* wrong.

39. I think most girls should marry about the age of
        a. ....

40. I am in favour of a marriage ceremony in
        a. traditional style.　　　　*b.* reform style.

(Men only—the next 3 questions)

41. *In my own opinion,* the most important factors in choosing a wife are
        a. caste.　　　　　　　　*g.* character.
        b. family wealth and position　*h.* chastity.
        c. dowry.　　　　　　　　*i.* domestic training.
        d. age.　　　　　　　　　*j.* artistic accomplishments.
        e. education.　　　　　　　*h.* my love for her.
        f. beauty.　　　　　　　　*i.* her love for me.
                        j. ....

42. By a wife's "character" I have in mind
        a. ....
        ....

43. I do not want a wife who
        a. ....　*c.* ....
        b. ....

(Women only—the next 3 questions)

41. *In my own opinion,* the most important factors in choosing a husband are

a. caste.	g. character.
b. family wealth and position.	h. chastity.
c. age.	i. treatment of women.
d. education.	j. my love for him.
e. job.	k. his love for me.
f. his handsomeness.	l. ....

42. By a man's "character" I have in mind
   a. ....
   ....

43. I do not want a husband who
   a. ....   c. ....
   b. ....

G. POSITION OF WOMEN

44. Women should be encouraged to education through
   a. elementary.   c. pre-university.
   b. secondary.   d. university.

45. Women are, *in theory,*
   a. equal to men.   b. superior to men.   c. inferior to men.

46. In *social practice* they are
   a. equal to men.   b. superior to men.   c. inferior to men.

47. The *most* important function of a woman is
   a. to be a good wife and   c. to do community service.
       mother.
   b. to develop her own talents.   d. ....

48. Women should have the opportunity to
   a. become educated   d. join social clubs and associations.
   b. get jobs.   e. ....
   c. enter politics.   f. ....

49. Women should have jobs
   a. only when unmarried.
   b. only when the family needs the money.
   c. only when their work doesn't result in neglect of family.
   d. if they wish to work.

50. *My own opinion*, about marriage *and* career for women is
   a. ....
   ....

51. *In my own opinion*, women should be encouraged to
   a. attend any "mixed" function, as feast, lecture, cinema, etc.
   b. attend public functions unaccompanied if they wish.
   c. sit in any area—not in a women's section.
   d. eat meals at the same time as their husbands.

    e. walk with (not behind) their husbands.
    f. travel in mixed company.
    g. ....

52. *In my opinion*, women should be able, if they wish, to adopt the following modern customs:
    a. short hair.   *d.* tennis costume   *g.* drinking.
    b. "pony tail" hair. *e.* bathing costume. *h.* social dancing.
    c. lip-stick.   *f.* smoking.   *i.* dating.

53. With respect to the re-marriage of widows,
    a. it is all right and can be done.
    b. I do not object, but society will not permit it.
    c. I am against it.
    d. ....

54. *In my own opinion*, widows should
    a. observe traditional customs and restrictions.
    b. live and work without restrictions.

55. Women are traditionally "obedient", first to fathers, then to husbands, and then to sons. *In my own opinion*,
    a. this is still necessary.   *c.* this is wrong.
    b. this is not necessary.   *d.* ....

56. Women university professors and members of staff should have
    a. the same privileges and respect as the men.
    b. fewer privileges.

57. With respect to the Inheritance Law women
    a. should inherit some of the family land.
    b. should not inherit land.
    c. ....

H. RELIGION

58. The meaning of "God" to me is
    a. ....

59. My family worships chiefly the deity
    a. .... *b.* ....

60. My family
    a. is strict about caste observance.
    b. does not take caste too seriously.
    c. does not practise caste observance.

61. *In my own opinion*,
    a. caste is essential to religion. *c.* caste is wrong.
    b. caste is not essential to   *d.* ....
       religion.

62. My family observes the following festivals:
    a. Harvest festival.   d. Divali.
    b. New Year.   e. Birthdays of the Gods.
    c. Dusserah.   f. ....

63. My family observes
    a. food laws.   g. going to the Temple.
    b. purification ceremonies.   h. priest attached to household.
    c. religious ritual in home.   i. ancestor worship.
    d. holy days and festivals.   j. ....
    e. auspicious occasions.   k. ....
    f. going on pilgrimages.

64. I myself do *not* believe in
    a. food laws.   g. going to the Temple.
    b. purification ceremonies.   h. priest attached to household.
    c. religious ritual in home.   i. ancestor worship.
    d. holy days and festivals.   j. ....
    e. auspicious occasions.   k. ....
    f. going on pilgrimages.

65. My family goes to the Temple
    a. never.   c. about once a month,   e. once a day,
    b. about once a   d. about once a week.   f. several times a day
       year.

66. *In my opinion*, the most important aspects of religion are
    a. personal devotion to God.   h. joy of worship.
    b. belief in reincarnation.   i. fear of punishment for sin.
    c. love of all mankind.   j. fear of evil spirits.
    d. the triumph of virtue   k. meaning given to life.
       over evil.
    e. comfort when in trouble.   l. belonging to a community.
    f. faith in a Supreme Force.   m. ....
    g. rules and guides for daily   n. ....
       living.

67. *In my opinion*, democracy
    a. is affecting Hinduism.   b. has nothing to do with religion.

I. POLITICS & GOVERNMENT

68. In my family there is
    a. much interest in politics.   c. no interest in politics.
    b. a little interest in politics.

69. I myself am
    a. much interested in politics   c. not interested in politics.
    b. somewhat interested in politics.

70. My family supports the political party

| *a.* Congress | *c.* DMK | *e.* Communist |
| *b.* PSP | *d.* Swantantra | *f.* .... |

71. I myself support
    | *a.* Congress | *c.* DMK | *e.* Communist |
    | *b.* PSP | *d.* Swantantra | *f.* .... |

72. The chief political instructor in my family is
    | *a.* my father | *c.* myself. |
    | *b.* my older brother. | *d.* .... |

73. The present Central Government of India
    a. is doing a good job.   *e.* should let people manage their own affairs more.
    b. is not doing a good job.   *f.* should give more consideration to my district.
    c. is full of corruption   *g.* ....
    d. should be stronger, doing more for the people

74. With respect to the Community Development Scheme,
    a. I know very little about it.   *c.* it is doing some good.
    b. it is doing a great deal of good.   *d.* it is useless.

75. With respect to the Co-operative Farming Plan,
    a. I know very little about it.   *c.* it is a poor plan.
    b. it is a good plan.

76. With respect to the national language problem,
    a. I think the local language should be used for all purposes.
    b. I think Hindi should be the national language.
    c. I think English should be the national language.
    d. ....

77. With respect to the severe restrictions on imports,
    a. I know nothing about these matters.
    b. they are necessary and helpful.   *c.* they are unnecessary and harmful

78. With respect to the Kashmir question,
    a. India's position is correct.   *c.* there should be a plebiscite—let Kashmir decide.
    b. Pakistan's position is correct.   *d.* let the United Nations settle the question.
    e. I am undecided.

79. With respect to India's foreign policy,
    a. I know nothing about it.   *d.* we must remain friendly with China.
    b. it is leading us to war.
    c. it is preserving the peace.   *e.* communism is a danger.

f. colonialism is a danger.

g. ....

80. With respect to the United Nations,
    - *a.* I know nothing about it.
    - *b.* it is doing a good job.
    - *c.* it is useless.
    - *d.* it should have more power.
    - *e.* it should have less power.
    - *f.* ....

81. I know a good deal about the following nations:
    - *a.* ....
    - *b.* ....
    - *c.* ....
    - *d.* ....
    - *e.* ....
    - *f.* ....

82. And should like to know much more about these nations:
    - *a.* ....
    - *b.* ....
    - *c.* ....

83. Because
    - *a.* ....
    ....

J. RECREATION

84. My family enjoys recreations like
    - *a.* reading.
    - *b.* story-telling.
    - *c.* music.
    - *d.* sports.
    - *e.* the cinema.
    - *f.* Ram Lila.
    - *g.* playing cards.
    - *h.* outings.
    - *i.* going to parks.
    - *j.* visiting friends or relatives.
    - *k.* going to clubs.
    - *l.* ....

85. I myself enjoy
    - *a.* reading.
    - *b.* story-telling.
    - *c.* music.
    - *d.* sports.
    - *e.* the cinema.
    - *f.* Ram Lila.
    - *g.* playing cards.
    - *h.* outings.
    - *i.* going to parks.
    - *j.* visiting friends or relatives.
    - *k.* going to clubs.
    - *l.* ....

86. With respect to the cinema, I most enjoy
    - *a.* Indian classical stories.
    - *b.* modern social drama.
    - *c.* the music.
    - *d.* foreign films about adventure.
    - *e.* foreign films about love.
    - *f.* ....

87. My favourite kinds of leisure reading are
    - *a.* Indian classical literature.
    - *b.* modern Indian fiction.
    - *c.* modern political writing.
    - *d.* foreign adventure fiction.
    - *e.* foreign love stories.
    - *f.* science fiction.
    - *g.* ....
    - *h.* ....

K. PRESTIGE

88. The jobs with most prestige in India are
    - *a.* .. ..
    - *b.* .. ..
    - *c.* ....
    - *d.* ....

89. In India it gives one prestige to
    a. have a university degree.
    b. have a foreign degree.
    c. have an important job.
    d. live in a big house.
    e. live in a modern house.

    f. have servants.
    g. have a cycle.
    h. have an automobile.
    i. speak English.
    j. wear European clothes.

    k. wear a watch.
    l. wear a lot of jewelry.
    m. belong to clubs.
    n. have an expensive wedding.
    o. have an autocratic manner with inferiors.
    p. be conservative—in religion, etc.
    q. be modern—in religion, etc.

    r. ....
    s. ....

90. *In my own opinion*, the 3 or 4 most important factors in prestige are
    a. ....
    b. .. ..

    c. ....
    d. ....

L. AUTHORITY

91. India has traditionally put authority in the *head* of the family, the *head* of the village, etc. I personally respect authority in
    a. my parents.
    b. my religious leaders.
    c. my village's (city's) government.

    d. my nation's government.
    e. myself.
    f. ....

M. TRADITION AND CHANGE IN INDIA

92. India is changing
    a. too rapidly.
    b. too slowly.

    c. in the right ways.
    d. in the wrong ways.

93. I am pleased with the following changes in modern India:
    a. .. ..
    b. .. ..

    c. ....
    d. ....

94. And am worried about these:
    a. .. ..
    b. .. ..

    c. ....
    d. ....

95. I should like to see the following further changes:
    a. .. ..
    b. .. ..

    c. ....
    d. ....

96. The younger generation can "lead" the older generation by
    a. ....
    b. ....

97. My ideas on social change have come from
    a. my parents.
    b. my education.

    c. my friends.
    d. professors.

    e. ....
    f. ....

98. "Traditional" means to me.
    a. the ways things always have   *e.* accepting one's destiny.
        been done.
    b. superstitious ideas.   *f.* ....
    c. the Eastern way of life.   ....
    d. the Hindu way of life.   ....

99. "Modern" means to me
    a. new ways of doing things.   *e.* making one's destiny.
    b. scientific ideas.   *f.* ....
    c. the Western way of life.   ....
    d. secular way of life.   ....

N. PRINCIPLES OF LIFE

100. *In my opinion*, the most important principles of life are

    a. Co-operation.   *n.* Being content with life.
    b. Honesty.   *o.* Respecting people of any age, sex
    c. Sincerity.   religion, class, caste, nation.
    d. Kindness.   *p.* Developing the self.
    e. Good manners.   *q.* Being constructively critical.
    f. Individuality.   *r.* Working for social harmony.
    g. Respect for elders.   *s.* Working for social justice.
    h. Standing up for one's rights.   *t.* Sacrifice of self for others.
    i. Service to others.   *u.* First loyalty to family.
    j. Obedience to authorities.   *v.* First loyalty to cultural group.
    k. Ambition—desire to get ahead *w.* First loyalty to nation.
    l. Doing one's duty.   *x.* First loyalty to all mankind.
    m. Initiative—using new ideas.   *y.* First loyalty to God.
    z. ....
       ....

A famous American poet once said, "The past is a bucket of ashes". I'd appreciate your critical comment.

Some people believe man's essential task is *adjusting to his environment*, others that it is *controlling the environment*. What do you think?

If there is anything else you would like to write about "Changing India" or about your own ideas, kindly use the space below. And thank you very much for your co-operation.

ADDENDUM—FOR WOMEN STUDENTS ONLY

O. PUBERTY

101. I matured when I was the age of   *a.*

102. As regards information and ins-   *a.* I had none.
    truction on menstruation   *b.* I had some but not enough.
       c. I had sufficient information.

103. I learned these matters from   *a.* My Mother.
       b. Auntie.
       c. My sister.
       d. My friends.
       e. Books.
       f. A teacher.
       g. ....

104. The first experience of menstrua-   *a.* Seemed natural to me.
    tion   *b.* Was something of a shock.
       c. Was a very great shock.
       d. .... : ......

105. I was   *a.* Happy to enter womanhood.
       b. Unhappy to enter womanhood.

106. *In my opinion*, girls should be told   *a.* Before it happens to them.
    about menstruation   *b.* After the first time.

107. When I matured I   *a.* Was made to change to saris.
       b. Was more restricted in going out-
    side the house unaccompanied.
       c. Was made to help more in house-
    hold duties.
       d. Began to hear talk of my marriage.
       e. Began to fear marriage.
       f. Began to look forward to marriage.
       g. Felt very lonely.
       h. Experienced no changes.
       i. ....

108. In our home a menstruating girl   *a.* Enter the kitchen and prepare food
    or woman may not   *b.* Eat food with the family.
       c. Enter the prayer room or take part
    in family religious ritual.
       d. Go to the Temple.
       e. Wash clothes for the family.
       f. Take a bath.
       g. Run about or take part in sports.
       h. ....

109. These restrictions are

    a. The same as in the past—in the days of my grandmother.

    b. Less than in the past.

110. When I have daughters I intend to have them

    a. Observe the same restrictions.

    b. Observe fewer restrictions.

    c. ....

111. With respect to menstrual pain

    a. One must accept it—it is part of "being a woman".

    b. One should get medical help, as with any other pain.

112. With respect to the protection of women from sexual advances.

    a. Women cannot protect themselves, and therefore their families and their society must protect them.

    b. Women generally can protect themselves by their own speech and action.

Index

257

Rajagopalachari C., 30
Ramkrishna, Paramhansa, 122
Raman, Latitha Venkata (quoted),
    175
Ramayana, 215
Roy, (Dr.) Punya Sloka, (quoted),
    195, 199
Realism, 168
Recipients, 227
Recreation, enjoyed by respondents,
    65, 66
Regionalism, 15
Religion,
    classification of students by, 50-51
    and ritual, 119-130
    most important aspects of, 123
    and science, 124
    and caste, 126, 128
    and democracy, 126, 128
    place of, 170
Religious & Moral Instruction
    Comments on Report of Committee
    on, 227-28
Renaissance in India, causes of, 12
Revolution of expectations, 18, 19
Reward, for good behaviour, 62, 64
Riesman, David (quoted), 232
Rituals not observed by respondents,
    126, 127
Roy, Ram Mohan, 13, 104, 122, 216

Samsara, 129
Santhanam K., 41
Saraswati, 231, 236
Sardar Patel Vidhyalaya, New Delhi,
    223
Sarkar, Chanchal (ref.), 177, 183, 187
    (quoted), 188, 189, 190, 196,
    197, 199, 209
Sarma, (Prof.) D. S. (quoted), 175, 176
Satyagraha, and students, 191
Schizophrenia, 76
School, role in developing a new
    society, 227
Scottish Church College, Calcutta,
    5, 45
Security, 231

Self-control, definition of, 179
Self-help, 209
Seminar (quoted), 178, 189, 193
Sena, Vinod (quoted), 223
Sex,
    classification of students by, 50-51
    literature on, 84
    and mass media, 100
Sex act, attitude to, 117
Sex-education, 81, 83, 84, 85, 117
Sex-identification, problems of, 76
Sex interest, 209
Sex mores, 209
Sex-role wish, 70, 71
Sex segregation, 100
Sexual advances, protection of women
    against, 101, 116
Shrimali, (Dr.) K. L. (quoted), 174
Social change,
    rapid pace of, 21,
    and social creativity, 26
    sources of ideas on, 157
    as India's main problem, 236
Social consciousness, lack of among
    students, 173
Social dynamism, 217, 218
Social learning, for children, 222, 223
Social responsibility, 173,
    and democracy, 220
Social Welfare Board (Central), 114
Sociality, 220
Society,
    hierarchical, 21, 25
    "closed", 21, 99
    "open", 21, 99, 101
Soviet man, the new, 225, 226
Spinster, 89-90, 91
St. Xavier's College, Calcutta, 5, 45
    186
Standard of living, 16
States, re-organization of in India, 14
Statesman (The), (quoted), 174, 187,
    191, 192, 195, 198
Status
    search for, 20
    of college teachers, 200
    consciousness of, 209
Strains, areas of, 211-12